Aharon Appelfeld's Fiction

Jewish Literature and Culture

Series Editor, Alvin H. Rosenfeld

EMILY MILLER BUDICK

Aharon Appelfeld's Fiction

Acknowledging the Holocaust

INDIANA UNIVERSITY PRESS
Bloomington and Indianapolis

This book is a publication of

Indiana University Press
601 North Morton Street
Bloomington, IN 47404-3797 USA

http://iupress.indiana.edu

Telephone orders 800-842-6796
Fax orders 812-855-7931
Orders by e-mail iuporder@indiana.edu

The paper used in this publication meets the minimum requirements of American National Standard for Information Sciences—Permanence of Paper for Printed Library Materials, ANSI Z39.48-1984.

Manufactured in the United States of America

Library of Congress Cataloging-in-Publication Data

Budick, E. Miller.
Aharon Appelfeld's fiction : acknowledging the Holocaust / Emily Miller Budick.
p. cm. — (Jewish literature and culture)
Includes bibliographical references and index.
ISBN 0-253-34492-1 (cloth : alk. paper)
1. Appelfeld, Aron—Criticism and interpretation. I. Title. II. Series.
PJ5054.A755Z58 2004
892.4′36—dc22

2004021157

1 2 3 4 5 10 09 08 07 06 05

To Sandy

Rachel and Shaul

Ayelet and Yuval

Hananel, Michah, Tzeelah, and Amos

and, as always, in memory of Yochanan

Contents

Acknowledgments

How in a book about acknowledgment to acknowledge all the debts that I have incurred in writing it?

I have acknowledged most of these debts in the usual academic way, in the body of my text. A few special thanks need separate mention, however.

I first began reading Appelfeld's fiction in Hebrew while a visitor at the University of Konstanz. I am grateful for both the time and ambience Konstanz provided me as I ventured into what was for me a new field of academic endeavor. Similarly, I wrote most of the book while on fellowship at the Oxford Centre for Post-Graduate Hebrew and Jewish Studies. The staff at Yarnton Manor and my colleagues at the Centre made this a stimulating and very productive experience. The stunning landscapes of Yarnton made me all that much more aware of the centrality of place in Appelfeld's fiction.

Over the years I have presented portions of this project to audiences in Israel, England, Romania, and the United States: to those audiences (colleagues, students, friends, and others, whom I do not know), I offer my gratitude for questions I could not answer and objections that forced me to think harder about what I was saying. The Hebrew University provided funding at various stages of my venture.

Alfred Ivry was generous enough to correct my transliterations of the Hebrew texts and to put them into proper, professional form.

I am grateful to Meir Appelfeld for permission to use his *Interior II,* ink on paper, on the jacket of this book. The silent speaking in and of shadows, which animates the interior world of objects and people, and which no less than defines the world as we know it, is, I believe, a subject of these drawings, as it is of the fictional texts I have tried to illuminate in this book.

I especially want to thank the person who most inspired this study: Aharon Appelfeld, who took the time to sit and talk with me about matters great and small. In this way, he taught me what is most compelling in his writings: that the way of their wisdom and grace is through the purity of the writer's concern, not with himself, but with the other lives (real and imagined), which his fictions tell. I can't think of a greater privilege than to have been let into his world, fictive and otherwise.

Janet Rabinowitch, Editorial Director of Indiana University Press, has seen this project through from beginning to end. I also want to thank Managing Editor Jane Lyle, project editor Dawn Ollila, and copy editor Joyce Rappaport. Last but not least, I thank Alvin H. Rosenfeld, editor of the series Jewish Literature and Culture. The Press's reader made valuable recommendations for revision, which I have, I hope, taken up to the reader's satisfaction.

* * *

In a book about acknowledgment as a philosophical and literary category, and in relation to no less fraught a subject than the Holocaust, the more personal kind of acknowledging we do in our everyday lives comes to take on special poignancy. In the case of this particular book, the private significance of the project has intimately to do with the way in which it represents my finally landing on Israeli shores in my scholarship as well as in my daily life. There are many debts here to individuals I forbear naming. My greatest debt, however, is to those Israelis who made a foreign country into a home for me and for their father: my daughters, sons-in-law, and grandchildren—Rachel and Shaul Elmakeyes, Ayelet and Yuval Sharon, Hananel, Michah, and Amos Elmakeyes, and Tzeelah Sharon. My husband Sandy has always made our home a home worth coming home to, for all of us.

Acknowledging the Holocaust in the fiction of Aharon Appelfeld has everything to do with an idea of home as that place—here or there, then as now—where we take our being, enact our lives, and experience all the things there are for human beings to experience, from pain and loss to joy and laughter, i.e., life itself. Our son Yochanan died before I began writing this book. He lives on in every one of its pages, as in all of our hearts. I am indebted to Yochanan for sharing the gift of his life with me—for making me see what a gift a life is. Without that knowledge I could not have written this book.

Introduction

In his autobiography *sippur ḥayyim* [*The Story of a Life*], Aharon Appelfeld repeatedly uses a particular word to describe both the dominant register of his own relation to the world and the basic mode of his fictional representations. That word is, in Hebrew, *hitbonenut,* which means *observation, reflection, contemplation,* and *insight.* Related to the kabbalistic concept *binah,* the word is also laden with mystical connotation, suggesting meditation as well. In Appelfeld's fiction, to see is to observe and to observe is to meditate, albeit not necessarily in a ritualistic, religious manner. "I had never been enamored of pathos and big words," writes Appelfeld in his autobiography, distinguishing his own art from that of the mid-century Hebrew literary scene, where he takes up his career. "I continued to like what I had always liked. Contemplation. Conjuring wordless reflections. Evoking the stillness of objects and a landscape that seeps into you without imposing anything" (145). That lack of imposition, the acceptance of the fact that, as he puts it elsewhere, life also happened during the Holocaust (and before and after) is, perhaps, the defining feature of Appelfeld's art.

Nothing could be further, not only from the dominant mode of Hebrew fiction in the early and mid-century, as Appelfeld himself suggests (and as we shall see in great detail later on, when I discuss his autobiography), but from the characteristics of Holocaust writing generally. Appelfeld's Hebrew Holocaust fiction is unique within both these modern traditions of literature.[1] When Appelfeld reached the shores of Palestine in 1946, or, more pertinent perhaps, when he began to study at The Hebrew University in the 1950s, Hebrew literature was just beginning to break away from the subjects, motifs, and ideologies that had defined it in the pre-State period. Like its near relative Yiddish literature, Hebrew literature is distinctive among world literatures for taking its inception and, for over a century, producing a literary tradition outside Jewish national, geographic boundaries. As the international literature of a people aspiring to and finally on the brink of statehood, Hebrew literature in the first half of the twentieth century was as much geared toward helping to produce the reality of a Jewish state as toward describing the real, lived lives of Jews in the diaspora and (increasingly) in the *yishuv* (the Palestinian Jewish community), in *Eretz Yisrael,* the land of Israel. In the Zionist meta-story that began to emerge in these writings, the Old Jew of European descent was replaced (often through fierce intergenerational rebellion and rejection) by the New Hebrew, the sabra or native-born "Israeli," who worked the soil, defended the land, and insured the future of the Jewish people—on wholly new terms—in their new-old homeland.[2]

By the time Appelfeld began publishing his first poems, short stories, and novels in the 1960s and 1970s, writers such as A. B. Yehoshua, Amalia Kahana-Carmon, and Amos Oz were also already beginning to challenge the basic assumptions of the pre-State literary culture. But to the psychological realism and political–ideological protests of these writers, Appelfeld, almost uniquely on the scene of Israeli fiction, added the subject of the refugee-survivor. He wrote about that "old Jew" who not only had come from Europe, but had also survived the Holocaust, and, furthermore, did *not* find in Israel a congenial, welcoming, and comforting new home. These European Jews—intellectuals, peasants, the elderly and the young, males and females, Communists, writers, and rabbis, from the cities and the farms—were represented in Appelfeld's writings, not simply in the new national setting—the newly created State of Israel—but more frequently, and perhaps even more compellingly, in the diaspora itself, in the years preceding and often leading into the war. Although Appelfeld is most widely known as a writer of Holocaust fiction, most of his more than twenty novels and short story collections do not deal with the war years directly. And this is one area in which Appelfeld, as a Holocaust writer, and not only an Israeli writer, achieves distinction among the authors who have dealt with the European catastrophe: the Holocaust is not, for Appelfeld, a subject that either exhausts or displaces the telling of the story of Jews and Jewish history.

As we shall see throughout this study and specifically in relation to *The Story of a Life,* Holocaust fiction in many ways challenges the tradition of writing about the Holocaust. One of the more obvious and widely noted of these ways in which fiction challenges Holocaust writing is by being fiction rather than history, documentary, or memoir—the more generally accepted means of representing the events of the catastrophe, especially for survivors themselves. Although a writer like Elie Wiesel often fictionalizes his autobiography, nonetheless his most important books make clear that they are staying close to his own experience (*Night,* for example; the same is true for Louis Begley in *Wartime Lies*). The autobiographical impulse is even more clearly expressed by memoirists such as Ida Fink (*Scraps of Time*), Shaul Friedländer (*When Memory Comes*), the non-Jewish Charlotte Delbo (*Auschwitz and After*), or for the most important of the first generation of writers on the Holocaust, Primo Levi, who shares with Appelfeld a philosophical bent that is also exceptional in the realm of Holocaust literature.

Nor does Appelfeld's fiction aim at the appearance of factual writing (memoir or documentary). It does not provide extensive detail and contextualization concerning the catastrophe in Europe. Instead, it is highly lyrical, virtually poetic—a kind of prose poem. If Holocaust fiction has been severely scrutinized under the lens of so-called "propriety," Holocaust poetry, as Susan Gubar has recently pointed out, has been the object of even more intense suspicion, since it directly challenges Adorno's endlessly invoked injunction that, after Auschwitz, it is barbaric to write poetry.[3] Appelfeld's prose poems take up a double representational burden.

Related to the spare musicality of his prose, its haunting poetic quality, is its tendency to circle around—hint at, suggest, signal toward—the major sites of suffering and violence rather than represent them directly. This, perhaps more than any other feature of Appelfeld's fiction, differentiates it from other Holocaust narratives. Alan Mintz, writing before the publication of *michreh haqeraḥ* [hereafter, *Ice Mine*], puts it as follows:

> In the case of Appelfeld it is clear that much of his success stems from an extremely fundamental choice about what *not* to represent. Everything having to do with what the French call the concentrationary universe—the transports, the camps, the *Einsatzgruppen,* the fascination with the Nazis and the paraphernalia of evil, that is to say, the entire stock-in-trade of conventional Holocaust literature—all this is left out. Before, after, parallel to—yes; anything but the thing itself. After, especially, as if to say that a catastrophe can be known only through its survivors and its survivals. Like Renaissance perspective paintings, the lines of sight in Appelfeld's fictions all recede to one organizing point [but] the origin here is a point of negative transcendence, a kind of black hole that sucks in representation the closer one approaches. (206–207)

Unlike writers such as Tadeusz Borowski (*This Way for the Gas, Ladies and Gentlemen*) or Jerzy Kosinski (*The Painted Bird*), or even Leslie Epstein (in his grotesque allegorical *King of the Jews,* which does, in its lack of realist conventions, recall Appelfeld's writings), Appelfeld evades the graphic representation of violence.

Nor does he deal primarily with the struggles of the survivor after the war is over, though there are important exceptions to this pattern, especially in his more recent writings.[4] The survivor story is the major mode of American Holocaust fiction, as evidenced by such works as Saul Bellow's *Mr. Sammler's Planet,* for example, or the novels of Cynthia Ozick (*The Messiah of Stockholm, Cannibal Galaxy,* and *The Shawl*), Isaac Bashevis Singer's *Enemies, A Love Story,* Edward Wallant's *The Pawnbroker,* and William Styron's *Sophie's Choice.* These works also often include flashbacks to the scene of violence as well.[5] Most of Appelfeld's Holocaust fiction does not function through such flashbacks, taking place as I have already suggested, paradoxically, *before* the war.

In its deviations from the conventions of realist representation (if we define realism as a certain kind of thick, detailed representation of reality), Appelfeld's fiction, like much of the fiction of others of this generation of Israeli authors, inherits the writer who is probably the foremost Jewish writer of the diaspora, not to mention one of the major figures in twentieth-century modernism: Franz Kafka. Yet, what may be most startling about Appelfeld's relation to Kafka is not the two writers' shared poetics (which are shared as well by other Israeli and Jewish writers, including Appelfeld's other important literary ancestor S. Y. Agnon) but, rather, the way in which Appelfeld's fictions, like those of Kafka, seem everywhere to foreshadow the events of the Holocaust.

In Kafka's case, of course, this foreshadowing comes to exist as a feature of the text only by virtue of the contemporary critic's reading back onto the fiction what Kafka himself could not possibly have known. The case of Appelfeld's writings is quite different. And yet the effect of this foreshadowing, which often takes the form of actual shadows falling over the world of his characters, has, astonishingly, the same uncanny effect as the retrospective act of interpretation, on the part of critics, in relation to Kafka. The imminent catastrophe, which took the lives of six million Jews (and millions of others), appears in Appelfeld's fiction as a palpable presence, an unmistakable feature of the landscape of Jewish history. What this means, exactly, remains to be seen. Yet, we can say already that it is not to be concluded, as some recent critics have done, that Appelfeld's foreshadowings serve to blame the Jews for their victimization. Rather, the shadows of the future that fall in Appelfeld's fiction on the past world of the Jews, along with a series of questions we might assume totally inappropriate to this kind of writing—such as, what is a human being? and, how do I know another human being when I see one?—serve to catapult these texts from the realm of tormented commemorative into the terrain of the deeply theological, philosophical, and ethical.

Appelfeld's fiction, as I have already begun to suggest, is less referential, less inclined to figure forth a familiar, social world in all of its expected everyday interactions, than it is contemplative, meditative, and even worshipful. I will, throughout this book, try to convey something of the flavor of Appelfeld's language, especially the original Hebrew, which translation cannot of course fully capture. But, already to make more concrete what I am claiming about Appelfeld's style, and by way of introducing his writing to those who may not be familiar with his fiction, let me quote briefly from a novel that I will not be discussing extensively, even though it will figure now and again in my discussions of other of his works. The following paragraphs are from the opening of *The Immortal Bartfuss* [*bartfuss ben almavet*], one of Appelfeld's novels that, atypically, does deal with a survivor, and which also (atypically) takes place in Israel:

> Bartfuss is immortal. In the Second World War he was in one of the smaller of those notorious camps. Now he's fifty, married to a woman he used to call Rosa, with two daughters, one married. He has a ground-floor apartment, not very large, with two trees growing at the entrance.
>
> Every day he rises at the same time, a quarter to five. At that hour he still manages to take in the half-light of the morning, the fog, and the quiet before everyone gets up. . . . He drinks a cup of coffee and lights a cigarette right away. The first cigarette makes him feel very good. For a long while he sits next to the window and absorbs the little tremors of the morning: an old man walks to synagogue, a truck unloads a crate of milk. These little sights charm his eyes.
>
> At six he rises, gets to his feet, lights a second cigarette, and, to his surprise, discovers some unpleasant scraps of food in the sink. The old fury rises in him immediately. But he doesn't let the fury take control of him. The muscles tense sharply, in his neck for some reason, and he nips his anger in the bud. He goes straight to his room.
>
> His room is practically bare: just a bed, a chair, and a cupboard. . . . Once Rosa tried to dress up the walls a little. She even brought in a table and chairs. That was years ago, when they still talked. Bartfuss cleared them right out, with his own hands. (3–4)

What most strikes the reader about Appelfeld's prose is its simplicity: it is as "bare" as the scene it describes, as resistant as its major protagonist to dressing up or decorating or cluttering the text with superfluous words and images. And yet one might well feel that the text is also as fiercely restrained as the character it describes, energetically nipping in the bud the old, scarcely contained furies. Furthermore, and for all the pain flickering just beneath the surface, the text is also just as tranquil as the scene it presents. There is verbal pleasure in Appelfeld's prose, a lyricism more evident, perhaps, in the more liquid, more musical Hebrew than in the translation, but apparent in the translation as well: in the delicacy and precision of its images, and in the pleasure they convey: morning half-light, fog and quiet, coffee, a cigarette, and little sights that charm the eye.

Appelfeld's text is spare, minimalistic, and, above all, respectful of its major protagonist, especially of his similar reticence and silence. Whatever Bartfuss has suffered in one of the smaller of those notorious camps, the text will not say. Like Bartfuss, it will not speak of what cannot or should not be spoken about. Nor will it pry indecorously into the workings of Bartfuss's psyche. What Appelfeld gives us is an exterior that expresses more eloquently than any direct foray into the mind the mind's own delicate, untranslatable, interior landscape—the morning tremors, half-light, fog, and quiet, which define this man, this particular human being Bartfuss. This Bartfuss, the text tells us quite directly and without explanation, "is immortal." There are worlds contained in that simple sentence. Within the fictive reality that the text creates, immortality is both Bartfuss's blessing and his curse. It is also, however, what this character, as invented fiction, achieves in the larger-than-life vision he projects of the human potential both for suffering and for survival.

But the text does even more than thus accord Bartfuss his inaccessibility to comprehension and judgment. By issuing as its opening sentence "Bartfuss is immortal," the book also maintains a position of worshipful awe of this man, who, for all his deficiencies, is no mere mortal but a god of sorts. The text represents itself less as creating Bartfuss (which of course it does) than as serving to help convey his dimensions to the reader. I use the word *dimensions* to anticipate the use of that word in the novel that is bound together with *Bartfuss* in the original Hebrew publication: *Tzili: The Story of a Life* [*hakutonet vehapassim*]. There, as we shall see, the word comes to refer as well to the dimensions [*middot*] of God.

The word I want to use to describe this quality of Appelfeld's prose—what I earlier referred to as its contemplative, meditative, worshipful quality—is *acknowledgment*. In my first chapter I will specify my reasons (philosophical, literary, and otherwise) for choosing this particular word, which I take from the writings of philosopher Stanley Cavell. I will also explore there and elsewhere in this study the relevance of Cavell's ideas generally for thinking about the Holocaust. For the moment, however, I invoke the word *acknowledgment* because it already suggests the way in which Appelfeld's fiction is neither ideological nor pedagogical, the way in which it stands aside in respectful attentiveness, and even awe, of the world it conjures. Appelfeld's fiction records a reality (present as much as past) that it neither pretends to comprehend nor imagines it can revise. Even though Appelfeld does not write documentary or history, or witness testimony or memoir per se—to cite again these more prominent forms of Holocaust narrative that his own writing actively resists—he still does produce a form of factual fiction. The novels, novellas, and short stories, however delicately and suggestively, do register with compelling force the sights, sensations, and experiences of European Jewish life preceding, during, and following the Second World War. Appelfeld, furthermore, transcribes these events with such lucidity and simplicity, with such a notable absence of authorial intrusion or commentary, as to give them their own absolute tangibility and authenticity.

This is so despite the fact that Appelfeld writes, as I have been suggesting, a lyrical, suggestive, even somewhat mythical prose, a hyper-realistic fiction, which, in its attention to minute, seemingly insignificant details, and dealing with characters and lives that are anything but familiar to us, often verges on the allegorical. Most of his works take place in the shadowy past, which, in the case of the Holocaust, is made murkier still by virtue of the incomprehensible events that transpired there. The past is always a tenuous realm, evasive of transcription. But Appelfeld heightens this intangibility of a world past by deliberately eschewing a straightforward, mimetic realism. His characters and plots (like those of his masters Kafka and Agnon) twist and wind, always in some slight disrelation or deviation or torque from what we imagine to be the recognizable contours of a recognizable reality. Yet there is a remarkable presentness about Appelfeld's fiction, a haunting familiarity about his strange, often grotesque characters, as if we were even now witnessing these long-gone places, people, and events, which are nothing more than the ordinary, everyday goings on of folks we have somehow known all our lives.

How Appelfeld achieves this distillation from dross to essence, and how he creates the stunning realness of his almost phantasmagoric reality are the objects of this study. Indeed, another reason for my choosing the word *acknowledgment* is that it characterizes my own critical undertaking as well, in two separate, albeit related, ways. If the fiction writer observes the world and contemplates and reflects on it, the literary critic might be said to observe the words through which that observation is transcribed. This makes the critic more of a listener than a perceiver, one who hears the sights that the author sees. In the case of Appelfeld's fiction, this turns out to be a very convenient partnership between the literary critic and the fictional text, since the fictional texts themselves listen as much as they look; they echo as well as tell. And they record the sounds of that world in the music of the text's words. Nonetheless, the differently defined tasks of the writer and critic make the objects of their investigation quite distinct from one another. Though listening to the text's words may help us see what the text itself is looking at, that is not, I think, the primary, or at least not the exclusive, goal of literary scholarship. Rather, criticism seeks to follow the logic of language itself as it unfolds in the text, resonating, hinting, exclaiming, protesting, and, finally, invoking all the many contexts that may or may not be either (ostensibly) in the scene itself or (consciously) on the author's mind. The nuances and insights contained within the linguistic world of the text are the objects of our contemplation, meditation, and acknowledgment as readers. Although I am writing about Appelfeld in English, primarily in relation to translations of his work, I will, whenever possible, bring the original Hebrew into the discussion so as to share with the English-speaking reader something of the aesthetic richness of Appelfeld's prose.

Acknowledgment, then, is, in the first instance, a word that for me conjures the contemplative, listening aspects of both the fictional and literary critical texts, despite their different objects of inquiry. It also, however, identifies for me what both contemplation and listening *do* as activities, which is respectfully to stand aside and consent to and affirm (often with some considerable measure of affection or admiration) the objects of their inquiry. Therefore, acknowledgment is also a moral or spiritual gesture made by one consciousness toward another, one text toward another. This is especially important in relation to a writer like Appelfeld whose subject is almost always the Holocaust, even when the text takes place in the world that the Holocaust destroyed. Acknowledgment preserves the dilemmas and paradoxes of Holocaust representation without surrendering to silence, which the Holocaust sometimes seems to demand as the only way of adequately representing it, but which would finally eradicate the catastrophe from history and memory altogether. It also retrieves from the ruin what there is to be rescued: our sense of the individual human beings in their unique individuality who perished in the catastrophe.

"Literature," writes Appelfeld, "even if it wishes to shout out and shatter the firmament, must first obey a practical imperative: it must deal with the individual, the individual whose father and mother gave him a name, taught him their language, gave him their love, endowed him with their faith. . . . In their explicit wickedness, the murderers reduced the Jew to anonymity, a number, a creature with no face." It is this face that Appelfeld's fiction attempts to restore. "I do not mean to simplify, to attenuate, or to sweeten the horror, but to attempt to make the events speak through the individual and in his language, to rescue the suffering from huge numbers, from dreadful anonymity, and to restore the person's given and family name, to give the tortured person back his human form, which was snatched away from him. . . . The survivor," he goes on, specifically referring to Bartfuss, "has swallowed the Holocaust whole, and he walks about with it in all his limbs. . . . [B]ut he still hasn't lost his human face. That isn't a great deal, but it's something."[6]

Though, as I have said, I take the word *acknowledgment* from the vocabulary of Stanley Cavell, whose philosophical writings inform my own project, nonetheless I would like to conclude this introduction to my study of Appelfeld with a few thoughts from another philosopher, whose writings Appelfeld's words *face* and *form* cannot help but recall. Emmanuel Levinas is pertinent as well because of his direct engagement with Jewish tradition. For Levinas, ethics begin with the face of the other. It is the face according to Levinas that prevents our absorbing the other into the economy of self, even under the guise of identification and sympathy. For all their appeal as ethical concepts, Levinas argues, identification and sympathy can become ways of reducing the other to a reflection of the self. One way of designating the face that preserves otherness, he suggests, might be by way of saying the name of the other. Thus, Levinas introduces the volume entitled *Proper Names* as follows:

> The world wars (and local ones), National Socialism, Stalinism (and even de-Stalinization), the camps, the gas chambers, nuclear weapons, terrorism and unemployment—that is a lot for just one generation, even for those who were but onlookers. . . . [A]t no other time has historical experience weighed so heavily upon ideas; or, at least, never before have the members of one generation been more aware of that weight. . . . The new anxiety, that of language cast adrift, seems to announce . . . the end of the world. Time no longer conveys its meaning in the simultaneity of sentences. Statements no longer succeed in putting things together. "Signifiers" without "signifieds" play a "sign game" with neither sense nor stakes. . . . Perhaps the names of persons whose *saying* signifies a face—proper names, in the middle of all these common names and commonplaces—can resist the dissolution of meaning and help us to speak. Perhaps they will enable us to divine, behind the downfall of discourse, the end of a certain *intelligibility* but the dawning of a new one.[7]

Conveniently enough for our purposes, the first of those proper names in Levinas's alphabetical listing is Agnon. The specificity of Levinas's subject is the Jewish people: the face of the other, the name he speaks, is concretely Jewish.

If Appelfeld's Holocaust fiction accomplishes nothing else, it assigns proper names to the nameless, faceless victims of the Holocaust. In so doing, it acknowledges the suffering of discrete individuals whose painful experiences can never be reduced to our fantasies of them or rendered comprehensible or illustrative or even useful to some moral purpose we might imagine. This, it seems to me, is at the heart of the ethical as well as the aesthetic achievement of Appelfeld's writing, its "faith," which Levinas defines in relation to Kierkegaard (another of his proper names) as "the possibility of attaining truth through the ever-recurrent inner rending of doubt." And Levinas goes on: "Belief is not . . . an imperfect knowledge of a truth that would be perfect and triumphant in itself. . . . [It] is not a small truth, a truth without certainty, a degradation of knowledge. . . . The grandeur of transcendent truth—its very transcendence—is linked to its humility. Transcendent truth manifests itself as if it did not dare to say its name, and thus as always about to leave" (77–78).

There is in Appelfeld's fiction always this humility, this "ever-recurrent rending of doubt," which expresses itself in his faithfulness to the truth, which is no small truth, of human being itself, including his own:

> A writer, if he is a writer, writes from within himself, mostly, in fact, concerning himself. If there is significance to his words it is because he is faithful to himself, to his voice, and to his meter. The themes, the subject—they are the consequence of his art, not its essence. During the war I was a child. That child grew up, and everything that happened to him and in him continued into his adult years: the loss of home and language, the suspiciousness and the fear, the inhibitions concern-

> ing speech, the alienation. Out of those feeling I weave the tale. Only the appropriate words produce a literary text, not its subject.
>
> I don't pretend to be a messenger or a chronicler of the war or an omniscient narrator. I connect myself to places I traversed, and I write about them. I never have the feeling I am writing about the past. On the contrary, the unadulterated past is merely the raw material of the text. Literature takes place in the urgent present, not in some journalistic sense, but as the aspiration to bring the present moment into the ever-pressing continuity of time. (113–14)

Appelfeld has strenuously resisted the label *Holocaust writer.* "There is no label that infuriates me more than that one," he protests in the autobiography (113). By focusing my study of Appelfeld on those of his texts that deal more or less directly with the Holocaust, and by dwelling almost exclusively on the representation of the Holocaust within those texts, I in no way mean to diminish the breadth of Appelfeld's achievement. My book is about acknowledgment, and over the years of my reading and thinking about Appelfeld, I have come to respect the man as much as the writer. Rather, within the differently defined undertaking of the literary critic, I intend only to acknowledge what he himself would argue about literature: that its meaning resides in the specificities of its depictions, in those names and faces it presents. Those specificities in the case of this specific writer have to do very basically with the Holocaust, even when it isn't his ostensible subject.

"My poetics were determined at the beginning of my life," Appelfeld writes in the autobiography, "where by 'beginning' I mean everything I saw and absorbed in my parents' home and during the long years of the war" (97–98). Those long years of war were as a second home to Appelfeld, not a warm and loving, nurturing home such as his parents had provided—quite the opposite, indeed—but nonetheless a home, an idea that is echoed by Imre Kerze in *Fateless,* in which a child-protagonist, much like one of Appelfeld's, insists at the end of the novel on his right to relish and protect his wartime experience. In the forest, village, refugee "home" that Appelfeld knew, the child became who he was to become, to write what he would go on to write.

Therefore, when I acknowledge the Holocaust as at the heart of Appelfeld's enterprise, and when I claim for his own writing its own acknowledgment of that catastrophe, I intend both to affirm the power of his fiction to bring into focus what is otherwise, for most of us, almost literally unthinkable and unimaginable, and, simultaneously, to fall into accord with the fiction's own reverent stepping aside in wonder at the darkness, but also the light, at the heart of the human soul. If *hitbonenut* is one word that circulates throughout Appelfeld's autobiography, *pele*ʾ, meaning *wonder* or *marvel,* is another. Acknowledging the Holocaust, Appelfeld penetrates past the painful devastation to the miracle of human being, which even the Holocaust could not destroy and to which his narratives testify again and again. Indeed, his writing itself is living testimony to that fact, which this study of his writing begins by acknowledging.

Aharon Appelfeld's Fiction

1 Acknowledgment and the Human Condition: Historical, Psychoanalytic, and Philosophical Approaches to Writing on the Holocaust

The following chapters constitute a meditation on the fiction of Aharon Appelfeld. In particular I am interested in the philosophical, psychological, and religious dimensions of Appelfeld's writing as they come to bear upon the subject of the Holocaust and as they enable us to glimpse an attitude or relationship to Holocaust representation, what we might think of as a poetics of Holocaust representation. I choose the word *poetics* carefully, with full consciousness of the potential problems inherent in such a word, and even the offense it might seem to offer to those who suffered the consequences of the catastrophe. Yet, as most scholars who have dealt with Holocaust literature have also pointed out, and as theorists such as Theodor Adorno himself, despite his declarations to the opposite, was fully aware, language and literature might constitute particularly apt vehicles of both apprehending and responding to the catastrophe. Both language and literature were themselves victims and instruments of the Holocaust. Both also offer legitimate, perhaps even inevitable means of our subsequent coping with it.

"Holocaust literature," writes Lawrence Langer in one of the earliest studies of this canon of texts, is not the "transfiguration of empirical reality . . . but its *dis*figuration, the conscious and deliberate alienation of the reader's sensibilities from the world of the usual and familiar, with an accompanying infiltration into the work of the grotesque, the senseless, and the unimaginable, to such a degree that the possibility of aesthetic pleasure . . . is intrinsically eliminated." In Alvin Rosenfeld's words, such fiction affords more than "topical" interest, however significant the historical events in and of themselves. Rather, it is "an attempt to express a new order of consciousness, a recognizable shift in being." Specifically, it is an attempt to wrestle back language from the abyss to which Nazism delivered it and, by so doing, to reclaim the idea of the human. The Holocaust, Rosenfeld suggests, constituted a "double dying" wherein what died, as Rosenfeld quotes Elie Wiesel as saying, was not only "man, but the idea of man."[1]

Holocaust fiction, in other words, is anything but a limited and delimiting literary enterprise. It does nothing less than produce a whole-scale shift in our modes of perception and representation and in our definition of the human. For this reason, even though, as I have already noted, Appelfeld himself has objected strenuously to the label *Holocaust writer,* I pursue my somewhat circumscribed venture into Appelfeld's Holocaust fictions, making no attempt to cover the range of his achievement. Appelfeld is probably the best living chronicler we have of European Jewish life, preceding, during, and even following the catastrophe. As Gershon Shaked puts it so beautifully in his study of Appelfeld, it is as if the angel who, upon our being born into the world, seals our memories of the past reversed the process with Appelfeld, such that he virtually embodies the entire memory of the Jewish people.[2] Insofar as Jews are first and foremost human beings like all others, this is to say as well that Appelfeld is one of our great writers of the human condition.

Yet, as I have already suggested, the Holocaust does weigh heavily on all of his fiction, even where it is not the primary subject. Therefore, what I say concerning a select few of his works will, I hope, illuminate aspects of his larger undertaking as well. By focusing on this single, albeit major theme of his work, I hope to bring into view something of the essence of Appelfeld's craft. This essence has to do with an investment in language as the instrument, not only of the rational and informational communication among human beings, but of their feelings and, ultimately, though obliquely, of their faith as well. Though such faith has everything to do with religion in the ordinary sense of the word, it is for Appelfeld, as we shall discover, also something vaster and more comprehensive than religious faith per se.[3]

Through contemplating Appelfeld's Holocaust fiction, then, I intend to say something about Appelfeld's writing generally, which is to say something about the human condition itself as reflected in his writing. But I also aim at more than the explication of the writings of a single individual, however compelling those writings might be. The Holocaust is not just any subject, most especially for Jewish authors and readers, and even more especially for the Jewish survivors (whether authors or readers) of the catastrophe. Appelfeld is such a survivor, who, additionally, writes the text of his experience in what may well seem to some the language of Jewish national revival. This is the revival that the Holocaust, in convoluted and extraordinarily painful ways (as we shall see), contributed to bringing about. By focusing this study of Appelfeld through the lens of the Holocaust I hope also to recast our thinking about Holocaust narrative in general. I wish to re-examine the questions Holocaust fiction raises and how narrative form and literary language are inseparably a part of the ethical, historical, and philosophical processes whereby we construct, and reconstruct, our understanding of and relationship to the past.

To accomplish my larger purpose of identifying something like a poetics of Holocaust representation, but also to make a point about the intertextuality of culture as the place where both historical and individual experiences occur, I try to read not only the thematic dimensions of Appelfeld's novels, including their psychological, historical, and theological terrain, but also the linguistic texture of his writing. Even though I am writing this study of Appelfeld in English primarily for English-speaking readers, and therefore most frequently quote the English translations of his texts, I have done most of my thinking in relation to Appelfeld through the Hebrew originals (some of the texts I discuss have not yet been translated). Where possible, therefore, I have brought those original texts into the discussion, as a way of amplifying ideas that are to some degree not completely accessible in translation. Translation always involves interpretation. It delivers the text into a new language trail productive of meanings of its own. I have tried where possible to provide the English-speaking audience with something of the original experience and meaning of his work.

This is especially important in the case of a writer like Appelfeld who is not, in any event, writing in his native language. Indeed, language is itself a major, albeit somewhat hidden, theme in many of Appelfeld's writings, the stories he tells necessarily taking place in languages other than the Hebrew in which the text is written (often many different languages in a single text, sometimes even being spoken by a single character). Translation is, then, itself a major subtext of Appelfeld's fiction as of Jewish history—as will emerge more clearly in particular in my readings of *Badenheim 1939* [*badenheim, ᶜir nofesh*] and *The Age of Wonders* [*tor hapelaʾot*]. So is the obliteration of native languages, for Appelfeld himself and for many other Jews, also a part of the story he tells.

Quite surprisingly, then, even though Appelfeld came to the Hebrew language late, and through a cacophony of other languages—some of them his own, some the enemy's, some both—the work his fiction performs is performed largely by the words themselves and not simply by the ideas or insights or dramas (real or imaginary) toward which his language points, as I will be stressing in my next chapter. The language of the text is never in Appelfeld merely a referential, denotative medium by which we are led to some more meaningful realm beyond language, as if words could transparently translate reality into text. As of late, literary criticism has seemed to evade a primary fact of fiction: that in the fictional world created by the text, words are all the world there is. And each one of them, as both Mikhail Bakhtin and Freud remind us, each in his different way, contains within itself other worlds of words and their resonances, which the text thus also calls into play.

To put this differently, despite the apparent simplicity of Appelfeld's language, his wary avoidance of verbosity in general and scholarly or intellectual jargon in particular, there is a surprising, even dazzling, density to his prose. This density might seem, at first, nothing more than a reflection of the suffocating world the text is attempting to figure forth. And to be sure, a sense of rising horror emerges within and through these texts, as the very lifeblood of its characters comes to be choked off. This is a textual feature that I, for one, do not want to dismiss. Yet there is a lyricism to Appelfeld's writing, a musicality, as well as a powerful intertextual allusiveness, that produces out of the thickness of his writing something that one might call tranquility—a feeling of strange and inexplicable beauty and quiet. Since this tranquility in no way reverses or compensates for the tragedy that the texts record, one has to ask what kind of stillness it is, and what purposes it may accomplish within the fiction itself.

The power of Appelfeld's art, I suggest, does not derive from some unbounded faith he possesses either in language or in the world that language would figure forth. In Appelfeld's fiction, faith is always hard won, whether it is the faith represented within the story the fiction tells or the faith that the fiction itself, as art, affirms. Indeed, in Appelfeld's fiction faith emanates from within the very limitations of language (and thought and consciousness), a phenomenon that might be imagined as rendering faith impossible. For Appelfeld, language is never in any way capable of substituting for the world itself, or adequately explaining or representing it. Yet faith there is, in and of Appelfeld's world. And while there is no way for human beings to co-opt supernatural being into the service of a human world, so there is also no realizing the humanness of that world without accepting the existence of a something beyond or outside it, something not bound by human logic and language. For Appelfeld language, which means literature as well, does not register the limitless creative power of the human. Instead, it records its capacity to submit and subordinate itself to a natural and supernatural order that it cannot completely fathom. The modesty of Appelfeld's style produces its worshipfulness, not merely in relation to the other words of other writers, which the text also respects and engages, but to those words that other writers have also tried in vain either to transcend or to transcribe: the words of transcendent being itself.

In my readings of *Badenheim 1939* and *Tzili: The Story of a Life* [*hakutonet vehapassim*], I will specify more precisely what such an idea of transcendent being might mean in Appelfeld's fiction. I will also confront in those readings what, if anything, the Holocaust has to teach us, and how. The lesson of the Holocaust turns out to be, in Appelfeld's fiction, intimately entwined with what emerges as religious tradition or faith—somewhat mystically, kabbalistically conceived. For the moment, let me leave Appelfeld's idea of faith inadequately represented in the form of what Appelfeld's fiction resists: namely, the belief in the totality of rational-humanistic knowledge, the assumption of the completeness of our understanding of the world and other people on the basis of what we can know, factually and evidentially, of that world. As I have already suggested, Holocaust studies are rife with discussions of the representability or non-representability of the events of the Holocaust, and of the decorousness or inappropriateness, even danger, of such attempts at representation. My own focus is on the philosophical, even theological, dimension of the problem of fictional representation. I want to explore how a work of literature might apprehend and express the world in such a way as to acknowledge the incompleteness of human knowledge and understanding, and, through that means, to produce what we might just want to call affirmation or faith or, to pick up the key term in my title: acknowledgment.

Philosophical Skepticism, Ordinary Language, and the Representation of the Holocaust

What is most distinctive about Appelfeld's writing as a form of Holocaust fiction, entrusted with the task of not only making present a long-vanished past but with bringing to bear upon the reader the full impact of the tragic dimensions of that past, is, as I have been arguing, that it eschews the conventions of realism, and not only in relation to its depiction of the Holocaust itself. It is as if the non-representability of the Holocaust has cast its annihilating shadow backwards, over the entirety of Jewish history as well. And yet, Appelfeld's fiction hardly evades historicity or empirical reality. The events it conjures are no phantasms of the mind, either private or collective. They are no mere metaphors figuring forth some terrain other than that of the quotidian world out of which they emerged. Appelfeld's is decidedly a fiction that insists on the epistemologically verifiable eventfulness of the world that it depicts, insisting, further, that we hear and see both the suffering of human beings and the cultural and political, which is to say *human,* forces that produced that suffering.

As a prelude to trying to understand Appelfeld's evasion of realist conventions in his representations of what is always a carefully informed and deeply specified epistemological verification of a real world, I want to set the question of Holocaust representation within a series of different questions. These are questions that Holocaust fiction, more than almost any other kind of fiction, might seem explicitly to foreclose our asking. Nonetheless, they seem to me exactly prompted by the surrealistic, quasi-allegorical mode of Appelfeld's writing. These are the skepticist questions that anti-mimetic modes of representation in general seem to compel, such as whether and how we ever know the world and other people in it; how, indeed, we know other human beings to be human beings, and not creatures of some other sort.[4] My argument concerning the Holocaust fictions of Aharon Appelfeld is that they constitute more than negative representations of the Holocaust (that is, representations that proceed inversely, through the withdrawal from representation) or even abstracted discussions of it. I am also not concerned primarily with what Rosenfeld calls the text's "irreality" (29) or with what Langer describes as their "*dis*figuration" (3)—both of which are important features of his work but which are also, when all is said and done, still mimetic means of representing a grotesque, disfigured but nonetheless epistemologically verifiable real world. Rather, I am interested in the anti-mimetic swerve in Appelfeld's fiction away from realist representation, which calls into question the existence of reality itself—not to deny the existence of the world but to keep alive the question concerning its existence. My subject is the way in which, through this means, the fiction *acknowledges* rather than represents the Holocaust. What does it mean to acknowledge rather than to know and/or to represent reality?

I use the word *acknowledgment* in the sense in which Stanley Cavell develops it, as responding to a claim made upon us by someone else's utterance. Acknowledgment is for Cavell what addresses the doubt of skepticism, which argues that we cannot know the world and other people in it. Rather than dismiss the skeptic's worry as either perverse or as not fully intended (a linguistic game that we can easily dismiss), Cavell proceeds by granting the skeptic's insight that there is a kind of knowledge to which we cannot attain: knowledge as certainty. Granting what we cannot know produces for Cavell the pressure on us to understand what we mean when we say that we do know and to accept responsibility for this kind of knowledge. For, according to Cavell, when we say, for example, that we know another person's pain, we exactly do *not* mean that we know it as a certainty, as a provable or verifiable form of knowledge. Instead, we mean that we understand and respond to a claim made upon us by that individual's expression of that pain. To deny knowledge of this kind, Cavell argues, would be to refuse to acknowledge that pain, and that is not the legitimate expression of one's skepticism, but what Cavell calls "disowning" knowledge.[5]

Let me pursue Cavell's thought a little longer. In the essay in *Must We Mean What We Say?* entitled "Knowing and Acknowledging," Cavell sets out to defend ordinary language philosophy against its philosophical skepticist critics. He does this not, as previous ordinary language philosophers have done, by dismissing skepticism as an exotic, quintessentially unordinary use of language, or by accusing the skeptic of not meaning what he or she says. Rather, Cavell refutes skepticism's refusal of ordinary language philosophy by, in the first instance, defending philosophical skepticism. Cavell takes the skepticist philosopher seriously, as fully intending his or her words as much as ordinary language philosophers intend theirs.

Therefore, Cavell proceeds by demonstrating the accessibility of the philosophical skeptic's claims, their transparency to ordinary thinking. Cavell presses the skeptic's refutation of the possibility of knowing to its ultimate position by placing side-by-side two sentences—the one impossible from the skeptic's point of view, yet meaningful from the view of the ordinary language philosopher; the other possible from the skeptical point of view but not from the view of ordinary language philosophy. These are the sentences: *I know he is in pain; I know I am in pain.* What Cavell then demonstrates is that where the skeptic and the ordinary language philosopher differ in their relation to these two sentences is in their bringing to bear upon these sentences a particular idea of knowledge: knowledge as certainty. What the skeptic means by "I know I am in pain" is not "I am certain I am in pain," which makes no sense, since being in pain is its own verification. Rather he or she means "I acknowledge that I am in pain." Similarly, what the ordinary language philosopher means when he or she says "I know he is in pain" is not, I am certain what his pain is or that her pain is identical to my own. Rather, what is meant is "I acknowledge that he is in pain"—that her expressions of pain call upon me to respond in some way to the pain he or she feels. Both philosophical skeptic, in other words, and ordinary language philosopher converge in meaning knowing as a form of acknowledgment, and not as indicating a certainty, which it makes no sense to claim (254–57).

Cavell puts it this way:

> the head-on effort to defeat skepticism allows us to think we have explanations where in fact we lack them. More important, in fighting the skeptic too close in, as it were, the anti-skeptic takes over—or encourages—the major condition of the skeptic's argument, viz., that the problem of knowledge about other minds is the problem of certainty. At the same time, he neglects the fundamental insight of the skeptic by trying single-mindedly to prove its non-existence—the insight, as I wish to put it, that *certainty is not enough*. . . . [T]here *are* special problems about our knowledge of another; *exactly the problems the skeptic sees.* And these problems can be said to invoke a special concept of knowledge, or region of the concept of knowledge, one that is not a function of certainty. This region has been pointed to in noticing that a first person acknowledgment of pain is not an expression of certainty but an expression of pain, that is, an exhibiting of the object of knowledge. There is an analogue to this shift in the case of third person utterances about pain. (258–59)

Cavell gets to this analogy through introducing what neither the ordinary language philosophers nor the skeptics consider: the case of the second person, "you":

> I said that the reason "I know I am in pain" is not an expression of certainty is that it is an expression of pain—it is an exhibiting of the object about which someone (else) may be certain. I might say here that the reason "I know you are in pain" is not an expression of certainty is that it is a response to this exhibiting; it is an expression of sympathy. . . .
>
> But why is sympathy expressed this way? Because your suffering makes a *claim* upon me. It is not enough that I *know* (am certain) that you suffer—I must do or reveal something. . . . In a word, I must *acknowledge* it, otherwise I do not know what "(your/his) being in pain" means.

And Cavell concludes, "To know you are in pain is to acknowledge it, or to withhold the acknowledgment. —I know your pain the way you do" (263–66). Cavell's defense of ordinary language philosophy hinges on separating out as different kinds of knowledge certainty (about which the skeptic is correct, when she or he says we cannot know, i.e., be certain about, another mind) and what Cavell develops as acknowledgment. What do Cavell's ideas about acknowledgement, especially since they are intimately connected to the matter of doubt, contribute to our understanding of Holocaust fiction?

One question we would think we would want to avoid in a discussion of Holocaust writing, which, we imagine, the literature itself would certainly not choose to raise, is the question that has been obscenely exploited by Holocaust deniers, namely the question, did the Holocaust occur? Or, how do I know it happened, and in this way, to these people? Whatever the relevance of philosophical skepticist thought to the analysis of history, it must be pointed out immediately that Holocaust deniers themselves pitch their denial not on philosophical bases, but on purely historical grounds, the grounds of evidence, which is to say knowledge. They do not deny that events in the world are knowable, nor that an event called the Second World War happened, nor, even that during that war something happened to the Jews. What they reject is that that something is what historians of the period describe as having happened: namely, the premeditated murder, often through gassing, of six million European Jews, who were killed for the simple reason that they were Jews. Some deniers will call the number into question; some the means; some the intention of the Nazis in deporting Jews, and so on and so forth: and they will say in defense of their denial, that there is no definitive evidence of the Holocaust as it has heretofore been described, and that such evidence as exists that something happened has either been forged, or manipulated, or perhaps, merely, misinterpreted.

In her book *Denying the Holocaust,* Deborah Lipstadt makes the important point that there is nothing to be gained, and much to be lost, by legitimizing the deniers' claims through engaging the deniers in rational debate, though ironically Lipstadt herself has had to engage in just such a debate in court.[6] Nonetheless, Lipstadt's point, I think, still holds. Therefore, in what follows I do not mean in the least to lessen the offense of those individuals who put their energies into attempting to diminish the horror of the extermination of the Jews. Nonetheless, there is no way to ignore the vulnerability of historical evidence to disputation, even to disbelief. History drags fictions in its wake, and separating out the one from the other may be perilously difficult. Where the legitimate process of historical revision ends and the illegitimate enterprise of denial begins may not be so easy to define. Even as the Holocaust was happening, when its proof would seem to be no more than a matter of seeing what was before one's very eyes, the Holocaust was, in Lipstadt's words, "beyond belief." Here there is no question, as there is later, of willful or perverse denial, though there may well be evidence of the desire of individuals not to see what is before their eyes (a phenomenon Appelfeld himself deftly, and at great risk, as we shall see, examines in one of his most famous books, *Badenheim, 1939*). Instead there is the simple problem of knowing when someone is telling you the truth or embellishing a story or simply interpreting or misinterpreting for whatever reasons. This problem does not change over time. The question I pose is how this fact concerning historical evidence might further rather than inhibit Holocaust studies.

The commonsense assumption of almost all Holocaust survivors and scholars alike—and this has been a major feature of the critique of Appelfeld's writings, as Appelfeld himself points out in his autobiography—is that factual, evidentiary narration must have precedence over other more aesthetically mediated representations of an event such as this. Indeed, in the opening of Appelfeld's *Tzili: The Story of a Life* we are told expressly (or so it seems) that it is only the concrete, literal and historical, (f)actuality of the text's representations that legitimizes the production of this text against what we are also told, in the original

Hebrew, is an *issur* (a prohibition) against the story's being told at all. This is how *Tzili* opens in the English translation:

> Perhaps it would be better to leave the story of Tzili Kraus's life untold. Her fate was a cruel and inglorious one, and but for the fact that it actually happened we would never have been able to tell her story. We will tell it in all simplicity, and begin right away by saying: Tzili was not an only child; she had older brothers and sisters. The family was large, poor, and harassed, and Tzili grew up neglected among the abandoned objects in the yard. (3)

Rendered more literally, the opening of the book reads as follows:

> The events in the life of Tzili Kraus, it is, perhaps, forbidden to tell. Hers was an ugly fate, without nobility, and were it not for that fact that it occurred, it is doubtful whether we would know to tell it/ know how to tell it. Because it did occur, there is no concealing it any longer. We will tell it directly and say at once. . . .

I provide the more literal translation of the original because the Hebrew embodies more insistently and dramatically than the English the major paradox that controls not only this text but much Holocaust narrative: that the telling of the story represents nothing less than a violation of a prohibition (an *issur*) against its being told. Insofar as permission does exist for telling this story, it derives, "perhaps," from the *fact* that the events *did occur,* i.e., that this story is factual record and not fiction.

What most writers on the Holocaust, however, have realized is that virtually *all* representations of the Holocaust, whether fictional or factual, run the same risk of seeming to mitigate the unmitigatable horror. They also apparently offer catharsis, compensation, and even coherence, where none exist. This tends to produce a Holocaust radically diminished and distorted from the one experienced by the victims. As the use of the word *issur/prohibition* itself suggests, this violation of the incomprehensibility of the event of the Holocaust is no less than the prohibition it recalls—the prohibition against making graven images, which is to say, images of material reality.

Witness testimony, documentary evidence, and historical record are privileged over other more aesthetically mediated forms of representation (literature, painting, drama), because they seem to diminish the risk of aestheticization and, therefore, of pleasure. But as James Young points out (and Lawrence Langer independently confirms), not only is testimony, like all narrative, constructed by the same rules of rhetoric, which threaten the presumed veracity, factuality, of the text that the witness-author would most like to preserve, but the sheer fact of the text's textuality—that we are dealing with narrative constructions and not artifact or even photograph—undermines the author's desire that his or her words serve as irrefutable proof for the facts they cite.

Language, it turns out, can prove nothing but its own existence. As Young puts it:

[F]or the diarist who reported events as they played themselves out before his eyes, the words he inscribed on a page seemed to be living traces of his life at that moment: his eyes, his engraving hand, and the ink on the paper all appeared to be materially linked in the writing act itself. But it is just this perception of words being bodily linked to events that constitutes both the source of these words' evidentiary authority for the writer and the point at which they lose this same authority for the reader. For inasmuch as the diarists and memoirists see themselves as traces of experiences, and their words are extensions of themselves, the line between words and events seems quite literally *self*-evident: that which has touched the writer's hand would now touch the reader. Whether the diarists and memoirists write these events from memory or at the very moment they occur, words and events remain linked by the inscribing hand, a literal part of both the experience and the record of it.

But for the reader with only words on a page, the authority for this link is absent. The words in a translated and reproduced Holocaust diary are no longer traces of the crime, as they were for the writer who inscribed them; what was evidence for the writer at the moment he wrote is now, after it leaves his hand, only a detached and free-floating sign, at the mercy of all who would read and misread it. Evidence of the witness's experiences seems to have been supplanted—not delivered—by his text. Once he withdraws from his words, the writer has in effect also withdrawn the word's evidentiary authority, the only link it ever had to its object in the world. The writer's absence thus becomes the absence of authority for the word itself, making it nothing more than a signifier that gestures back toward the writer and his experiences, but that is now only a gesture, a fugitive report.[7]

If, on first reading, Appelfeld's "perhaps" in the first paragraph of *Tzili* seems to participate in a familiar convention in Holocaust narrative, privileging fact over fiction by drawing our attention to the extratextual fact of the author's own survivor status and the text's fidelity to verifiable real events (whether or not they happened to this particular human being or another), on second reading it may be possible to understand the "perhaps" as serving to question just such privileging. For if the claim of not making up stories concerning the Holocaust is by no means an unfamiliar refrain in Holocaust literature, what makes it unusual here is that *Tzili* is not witness testimony but fiction. Indeed, with its highly crafted language and the fantastic, mythic, and grotesque elements of its plot, it represents a heightened, self-consciously fictive form of fictionality. The text determinately veers away from the very forms of mimetic and realistic representation that it is apparently claiming in justification of its textual existence. If permission to tell this story comes only from its having occurred, then there seems to be absolutely no permission for the telling of this particular story, which is fiction, not fact.

Building on Hayden White's contention that "'poeticizing' is not an activity that hovers over, transcends, or otherwise remains alienated from life or reality, but represents a mode of praxis which serves as the immediate base on all cultural activity," Young provides the following license for fiction: while we cannot "deny the historical facts of the Holocaust outside their narrative framing," he explains, nonetheless it is virtually impossible to "[interpret, express, and act on] these facts outside the ways we frame them."

> [T]he events of the Holocaust are not only shaped *post factum* in their narration, but . . . they were initially determined as they unfolded by the schematic ways in which they were apprehended, expressed, and then acted upon. In this way, what might once have been considered a matter of cultural, religious, or national perspective of the Holocaust assumes the force of agency in these events: world views may have both generated the catastrophe and narrated it afterwards. Thus perceived, history never unfolds independently of the ways that have understood it; and in the case of the Holocaust, the interpretation and structural organization of historical events as they occurred may ultimately have determined the horrific course they eventually took.
>
> This is to move beyond the question of whether or not literary and historical accounts of the Holocaust are "perspective ridden" to understand how various literary forms, cultural and religious traditions, and preceding experiences have indeed shaped the Holocaust. (3–5)

Recognizing the subjectivity that controls Holocaust narrative, whether on the part of historians, survivors, authors, and even diarist eyewitnesses who were recording the events contemporaneously with their occurrence and who in fact perished in the catastrophe, cannot be separated from our thinking about the Holocaust. And yet moving in this direction we clearly threaten to subvert what may be a primary purpose of much Holocaust writing: to establish, beyond a shadow of a doubt, the facticity of this event and to witness the historical moment, whether for oneself or for those who perished and can no longer bring their testimony to bear. Placing Holocaust narrative under the lens of philosophical skepticist thinking can only seem to introduce complexities to the project of Holocaust writing that might be better left out.

Yet, as Young's comments also suggest, accepting the fictionalizing component of perception as inescapably part of the perceptual process, may in fact be necessary for understanding the Holocaust itself as an event produced by a failure to so credit the subjectivity and bias of our sociopolitical and cultural interpretations. Nazism itself wrote a script in which it cast the Jews in a particular role. Mistaking prejudice for truth, it acted on its fantasies. This insight, I think, constitutes a basic feature of one of the Appelfeld novels already alluded to, *Badenheim 1939.* It leads us to the important challenge of Holocaust writing: that it is not enough to expose the atrocities committed during the Final Solution but, rather, we must also avoid repeating the dynamics that produced the event in the first place. In other words, Holocaust writing must not risk the kind of repetition compulsion that might itself have played a major role in the ascent of German Nazism and that has come to seem to certain contemporary scholars an intellectual (albeit *not* a political) feature of some recent Holocaust-inflected theories of philosophy and literature—as we are about to see. Raising the epistemological issue, not to answer the question of knowledge but to keep it present and active, may be a fundamental feature of a skepticist Holocaust writing, which not only informs the reader as to the historical events themselves, but also prevents the occurrence of a deadly repetition compulsion.

Philosophy, Psychoanalysis, and the Problem of Evidence

It is just such a repetition compulsion that seems to Dominick LaCapra a problem in the postmodernist position concerning what has come to be called "after Auschwitz." For an historian and theoretician like LaCapra, as for Young, history never unfolds independently of the ways we understand it, which is to say, historical writing never unfolds separately from the ways we have understood, i.e., interpreted, the already subjectivity-driven events of the past. For this reason, LaCapra would have historians give play to their biases and affective responses rather than aim at something that is, at best, impossible to achieve, and, because it is impossible, perhaps even dangerous to attempt: namely, pure interpretive objectivity. For LaCapra the conceptual framework that must govern our explorations into the past is the one provided by Freudian psychoanalysis. In psychoanalysis the communication between an informant and a listener concerning occurrences in the past now occurs as an interactive process in the present, between two people, one of whom is at least slightly more objective in relation to the narrative unfolding than the other, but who is also influenced by his or her own subjectivities. Psychoanalysis, like historical narrative, involves the enactment in the present in narrative of events that transpired in the past as events. It also involves listening to the voices of the past speaking a pain that has still not been put to rest.

The psychoanalytic approach to Holocaust writing, especially in terms of what has been identified as trauma theory, has been a dominant force on the field of Holocaust studies for the last two decades. It is very much to the point of reading fictional texts like Appelfeld's, which are certainly, among other things, narratives of trauma, in which the protagonist-survivors—Erwin in *The Iron Tracks* [*mesilat barzel*], for example, or the older Bruno in part two of *The Age of Wonders,* or Bartfuss in *The Immortal Bartfuss*—are, many of them, almost text-case neurotics: compulsive, obsessive, haunted, and in many other ways dysfunctional.

Before presenting both the considerable benefits and the equally knotty problems of the psychoanalytic interventions into the field—which tend to duplicate the consequences of asking the question inevitably forced upon us by Holocaust fiction itself, namely: did these events occur? and did they occur in exactly the ways reported to us by these texts and others?—I need to issue the following warning. Whatever the case with other narratives of the Holocaust, Appelfeld's fictions are *not* autobiographical, even where they contain (some of them, at least) fragments of Appelfeld's own experiences; nor do they constitute straightforward, simplistic psychohistories, as if Appelfeld himself were attempting to play analyst to the Jewish people (or, for that matter, to the Nazis). In addition, absolutely no purpose is served, and much is lost, by making the author the object of the critic's psychoanalytic interpretation, as if the texts exist primarily to expose something about their author. The texts cannot be reduced to the contours of whatever psychoanalytic profiles the characters or their author might seem to exhibit. It is, in any event, the case with psychological phenomena that one component of an individual's personality rarely represents one thing rather than another as opposed to two or more things at once. Even more so with literary representations of individuals and events: we are always standing on the ground of a both/and phenomenon, with little possibility of choosing one over the other.

Finally, the goals of fiction (in particular Holocaust fiction) may differ dramatically from those of clinical intervention. The fiction might well not aim at the recovery from trauma, the working-through that will allow the victim or survivor or the people themselves to put the past in the past so as to permit a healthier future to emerge—at least not in a clinical sense. Rather, the objective of the text, especially in non-mimetic or skepticist fiction like Appelfeld's, may be a different positioning of the relationship between trauma and victim, such that a new dynamic of continued working-through can emerge. However the text copes with trauma (and the fact of Appelfeld himself having been abandoned by his father's imprisonment and orphaned by the death of his mother is by no means irrelevant in this context), its intention may be neither an end to the repetition of the experience of trauma it perpetuates, nor its normalization or assimilation into a more healthy present or future. And it may be very much to the case of Holocaust fiction as opposed to private psychoanalytic narrative that the concrete, factual bases of trauma, which often give way in therapy to the more important truth of the patient's subjective perceptions or internal reality, need carefully to be preserved lest the truth value of Holocaust writing (as a documentation of historical events) be sacrificed to other, more aesthetic or emotional, objectives. This last point will return us, at the end of this discussion of psychoanalysis and Holocaust interpretation, to the issue of philosophical skepticism and how, despite the subversions of truth it threatens, it must become a necessary feature of our thinking about the Holocaust and its literary representations.

These cautions in place, there is, as I have already begun to suggest, every reason for placing Holocaust writings under the scrutiny of a psychoanalytic approach. Holocaust fictions are clearly texts begotten of trauma, whether or not the trauma is literally experienced by the author of the text and then dispersed into the fictional form, or is only fabricated by the writer in relation to some character, whose relation to trauma becomes the subject of the text. As such, Holocaust fictions incorporate a fundamental problem of interpretation. What is distinctive, even definitive of trauma, is that trauma is an experience that, on some level at least, bypasses conscious, i.e., verbal, comprehension. The self barely, if at all, registers the event that thereafter continues to inform every thought, every gesture, every aspect of consciousness itself, in coded, often deeply buried and secretive ways. Another way of putting this is that the experience of trauma typically occurs in the absence of words in which to describe it. It happens without narrative structure. Therefore, the telling of the story of trauma, which occurs against and through an eclipse of consciousness, as a story told in the absence of the story's narrative presence in the tale, is often (though by no means always) told non-verbally. This occlusion of words, which is only another way of understanding the eclipse of consciousness that accompanies traumatic experience, is further reinforced by the powerful desire that accompanies such experience: that it *not* be restored to consciousness and to language. The story of trauma, in other words, is typically told in its displacement onto some other enactment, primarily non-verbal, that conceals, and in this concealment expresses, the primary trauma. It is told, when it is told at all, mutely, as a form of silent enactment.

As is, I hope, already clear, certain forms of psychoanalytic criticism can and must immediately be discarded as inappropriate for interpreting fictions of the sort that interest us here. In the heyday of formalist, new criticism (in the 1950s and 1960s), what might more accurately be designated Freudian rather than psychoanalytic readings of texts took as their starting point the same assumptions that informed other kinds of literary-critical readings, namely that there existed a set of textual features—authorial intention, narrative coherence, and an integrated if multifaceted textual meaning—that could be read out (allegorically) in a critical interpretation. Freudian interpretation then applied itself in one of several ways. It might, for example, register the text's own application to Freudian ideas, and in this way interpret the characters, plots, and themes as constructed in order to demonstrate one psychological complex or another. Or one might interpret the text as revealing the writer's own unconscious structuring of the fiction around his or her own unacknowledged complexes. For the most part such early uses of Freud in the realm of literary criticism produced reductive readings, which tended to place the critic in the superior position of interpreter, as against the author's or the characters' blindness. These readings also never quite took the measure of the critic's own psychological inattentiveness or bent in the production of textual meaning.

Largely under the pressure of new reading strategies and linguistic theories, such as deconstruction, new historicism, French feminism, and the like (many of them themselves derivatives or least close relatives of Freudian psychoanalysis), literary criticism had, by the 1970s, largely abandoned such simplistic or reductive forms of Freudian criticism. But it is not clear that even more sophisticated, contemporary literary approaches to psychoanalytic interpretation, such as those formulated by as skilled and subtle a critic as Peter Brooks, completely solve the problem of the suitability of a psychoanalytic approach to Holocaust fiction. Brooks does not imagine psychoanalytic intervention as "curing" the text, rendering it more self-conscious to itself. Rather, by downplaying the actual thematics of Freudian psychology and by developing that aspect of the psychoanalytic relationship, the transference, in which the two participants to the verbal reconstruction might be imagined, momentarily at least, to function more or less as equals in the production of textual meaning, Brooks provides a different model of the relation between psychoanalysis and literature. This model has much in common with the reader response theories of Wolfgang Iser and others, in which, through the relationship between reader and text, another text, generated collaboratively, comes into being.

As Brooks aptly reminds us, there is no story that exists independent of and prior to the act of narration itself. "[The] narrative," Brooks explains, citing the work both of Paul Ricoeur and Freud, "is not simply 'there,' waiting to be uncovered or disclosed. On the contrary, narrative comes into being only through the work of interpretive discourse on story, seen as the raw material . . . which becomes coherent and explanatory only as the narrating orders it in discourse."[8] In other words, narrative is not a conduit by which we travel to a story already constructed, as if the story pre-exists its telling and, like an archeological artifact, needs only to be unearthed. Rather, the telling is all the story there is. Thus, the narrative construction and reconstruction of the story are the same. (In Freud's essay on "Constructions in Analysis," Brooks points out, the word *re-construction*, after an initial usage, falls out of the text.) What validates a story as true or authentic is not probability but conviction. "Parts of the story of the past," explains Brooks following Freud, "may not ever be recalled by the person whose story it is, or was, but may nonetheless be *figured* in a construction of them by the analyst-narratee—a construction which is unsubstantiated, unverifiable, yet carries conviction. . . . Narrative truth, then, seems to be a matter of conviction, derived from the plausibility and well-formedness of the narrative discourse, and also from what we might call its force, its power to create further patterns of connectedness." As Brooks puts it elsewhere in his study, "the only confirmation one can have that the narrative has been correctly constructed and construed lies in the *production of more story*" (59).

For Brooks, narrative fiction is the expression of a story that exists only in its telling. The reader grasps it only through the reader's own production of the story as a narrative of his or her own; hence, the importance for Brooks of the psychoanalytic concept of *transference*. Technically, transference is that process whereby the analysand re-experiences and (often) re-enacts (transfers) old feelings and desires in relation to the analyst, who serves as a surrogate for the original object of those feelings and desires in the past. Since repression itself is a form a transference, in which what cannot be acknowledged from the past (what is resisted) is replayed in coded and usually unsatisfactory and unfulfilling ways (say in obsessive, compulsive behaviors, such as characterize the narrator of Appelfeld's *Iron Tracks*), therapeutic transference, i.e., transference in the clinical situation, enables a protected re-enactment. This can yield to an analysis of and hence a replacement of the symptoms by more self-conscious and hence constructive behaviors and/or narratives. In this process, as psychoanalysis has come more and more to stress, the analyst is not a neutral party. Rather, countertransferring to the patient (though also countering and thereby controlling such countertransferential tendencies), the analyst participates in and helps refashion the direction of the narrative and thereby the patient's life. For psychoanalytic literary critics like Brooks, *story*-meaning, like transferential meaning, is a mutual construction, which does not exist prior to the narrating—renarrating that goes on between the writer and the reader or the teller and the listener.

In relation to the reading of Holocaust fiction, Brooks's approach provides a powerful base of operation, especially as it gives us ways of apprehending what it might mean to acknowledge rather than know or even comprehend a Holocaust narrative. The story told *is* the story told—no more, no less. There is no way to understand anything except by experiencing everything the text says and does and is. In this sense Brooks's ideas very clearly parallel those of James Young, whose own work, unlike Brooks's, deals directly with Holocaust writing. The psychoanalytic approach to narrative also, however, creates problems. The first has to do with an almost inevitable consequence of thinking of stories as being confirmed only in their ability to produce even further stories. This is what Brooks calls the "erotics of form," the "forepleasure" of the text, its clock-tease. "It is my premise," writes Brooks, "that most narratives speak of their transferential condition—of their anxiety concerning their transmissibility, of their need to be heard, of their desire to become the story of the listener as much as of the teller" (44, 29, 34, 50). For Brooks, following Jacques Lacan, the text traces the motions of desire. It evokes the ever unrecoverable because already linguistically mediated moment when desire first (seemed) to come into existence.

Brooks's focus on the production of narrative and its endless and endlessly erotic reproduction in the process of storytelling (his focusing on text as text rather than as the transcription of a pre-existing psychosexual or traumatic experience) may to some large degree get rid of the overdeterminism of earlier Freudian interventions. Nonetheless, in what we might think of as a sort of return of the repressed, it still imports from an earlier Freudianism an idea of sexuality or desire as what governs human experience and, thereby, as what constitutes the basis for thinking of psychic process and textual process as constitutive of each other. Such an idea of an erotics of narration can only serve to reintroduce one of the traditional objections to Holocaust fiction: that it can seem to provide catharsis and aesthetic pleasure where none is appropriate. If, in relation to any fictional text, psychoanalytic criticism runs the risk of reductionism, as if psychoanalytic truth were the grid by which to judge fictional accuracy, in relation to Holocaust fiction it not only threatens to diminish the affective resonance of the text but also, in its more fertile and sophisticated forms (as articulated by a critic like Brooks), to offer satisfaction *on the textual level* quite inappropriate to the intention or *raison d'être* of the text itself.

But there is a further, even more serious objection to Brooks's approach in the realm of Holocaust writing. This has to do with the problematical status of "truth" within psychoanalytic process and theory. In tracing the play between analyst and analysand in the production of textual meaning, Brooks stays very close to Freud's own evasion of whether or not factual bases for any particular trauma actually exist and can be determined or proved. Even more so than for Freud, for the critic of fiction, for whom there literally is no historical or factual condition prior to the text (a feature of fiction powerfully brought into focus at the beginning of *Tzili,* as we have seen), the question of whether the narrative's repetition in the present represents remembering as such (i.e., whether the repetition repeats an actual occurrence) or only a feeling associated with some either real or imagined event, falls away. What is important for the critic and analyst is the repetition itself, whereby the working-through is accomplished and the mutually constructed text, which is the only text there is, is produced. This relationship to truth or fact is extremely problematical in historical or documentary fictions (what have also been called faction or the non-fiction novel) such as Holocaust fictions.[9] It is exactly the point of many of such texts to insist that the motions of narrative construction have real, epistemologically verifiable correlatives in quotidian reality, that the events recalled in the text occurred in the world outside the text, if not to the authors themselves, then to some other real human being who could theoretically be brought in to testify to the occurrence of these events. Indeed, the evasion of epistemology has emerged as problematical for psychoanalytic process itself. In this internal dilemma of psychoanalysis vis-à-vis the truth status of an individual's memories is contained a still further problem for the psychoanalytic reading of Holocaust fiction.

Two recent publications have placed at the center of their concern Freud's inability or unwillingness to remain committed to the factual bases of neurotic behavior. The earlier and more sensationalistic of the two launches an all-out attack on Freudian psychoanalysis. The charge, leveled by Jeffrey Masson, is that, largely for political reasons, Freud abandoned his earlier, more accurate, insight, contemporaneous with the birth of the idea of psychoanalysis itself, that neurotic behavior was grounded in actual childhood assaults. In particular, he dispensed with the idea that his women patients had literally suffered sexual violation by their fathers, uncles, brothers, or other male relatives. Embattled and fighting hard for the survival of psychoanalysis as a field, Freud, the argument goes, yielded ground because he feared that, unwilling to grant the idea of widespread sexual assault of children, his compeers would reject the whole of his theory of psychosexual development. Indeed, Freud's own imagination, in Masson's reading, seems to have rebelled against so repulsive an idea.

Even more unsettling, perhaps, Freud may have suppressed the seduction theory, which he more or less knew to be true, because he saw how it would limit the application of his theories. Reaching for a comprehensive view of psychological development, Freud understood that by displacing trauma from the realm of fact to the realm of imagination, he opened up the possibility of claiming a single, common psychosexual experience of childhood for all human beings. That common experience might, under various different pressures, give rise to just that blurring of the distinction between reality and fantasy that would mislead an individual into imagining his or her disreputable desires as the disreputable deeds of others. This, in turn, might yield to the acting out of the imaginary past in an equally compromised and attenuated present reality characterized by neurotic, obsessive behavior.

The evidence that Masson brings into play suggests that, in fact, Freud's patients most likely *did* experience sexual violation as children; that many psychotic and neurotic individuals probably still endure such traumas; and that by dismissing the real, factual bases of their experience the analyst not only invites the analysand, in the transference, to replay the emotions surrounding the trauma, but, more importantly, and devastatingly, repeats the same denial of the fact that the trauma actually occurred. It is not irrelevant to our present purposes that Masson himself raises the example of Holocaust trauma in order to argue for the necessity of validating the real, literal occurrences of the traumas that haunt the psychoanalytic patient.[10] In this context, also relevant is Nicholas Rand's and Maria Torok's gentler, more respectful interrogation of Freud's evasion of the historical foundations of trauma, which argues that Freud evaded the issue of facticity because he himself was repressing some of the historical bases of his own childhood traumas.[11]

According to several reputable commentators, Masson is likely right about Freud. Nonetheless, it seems to me that Masson rushes in too soon to answer his own questions concerning the historicity of traumatic events. Therefore, he leaves behind too quickly the fundamental unanswerability of the questions they raise. As we shall see in a moment, it may well be the case that leaving questions open to constant reinterrogation is one of the most important properties of trauma fiction in general and Holocaust fiction in particular; for it is in the absence of epistemological truth as something given to empirical proof that other kinds of truths may also emerge. Nonetheless, in Masson's work, as in the more positive evaluation provided by Nicholas Rand and Maria Torok, restoring epistemological responsibility to the psychoanalytic investigation goes some distance toward reclaiming the relevance of psychoanalytic interpretation to analysis of the Holocaust. It does not, however, resolve all the difficulties inherent in the psychoanalytic approach, some of which have exactly to do with the possibility of factuality's intervening in and overwhelming other features of the text.

This is the problem with a second, popular, model of psychoanalytic insight, which takes as its jumping-off point the lived, existentially verifiable, experiences of actual victims of catastrophe. For Shoshana Felman and Dori Laub in their book *Testimony,* the listener/reader/analyst does more than hear, and in hearing enable the survivor's (writer's) reconstruction of his or her experience from the past. Rather the reader witnesses the witness, thus enabling the witness to believe in the historical validity of his or her experience:

> [W]hat precisely made a Holocaust out of the event is the unique way in which, during its historical occurrence, *the event produced no witnesses.* Not only, in effect, did the Nazis try to exterminate the physical witnesses of their crime; but the inherently incomprehensible and deceptive psychological structure of the event precluded its own witnessing, even by its very victims. . . . The historical reality of the Holocaust became, thus, a reality which extinguished philosophically the very possibility of address, the possibility of appealing, or of turning to, another. But when one cannot turn to a "you" one cannot say "thou" even to oneself. The Holocaust created in this way a world in which one *could not bear witness to oneself.* . . .

[T]estimony is, therefore, the process by which the narrator (the survivor) reclaims his position as a witness: reconstitutes the internal "thou," and thus the possibility of a witness or a listener inside himself.[12]

As the passage's own emphases indicate, Laub and Felman ground their theory of witnessing in the actuality or factuality of the events that have occurred. Because these events occurred in the absence of witnesses, however, they may seem to the victims fictions or fantasies. Readers/listeners must do more than lend a sympathetic ear. They must validate for the victim the victim's experience; verifying that it did occur, in the real world, and to the victim himself or herself.

This is all well and good (it is what Masson, for one, is calling for), until one takes into account two things. The first is simply that testimony, as Young and Langer point out, can provide no such verification. In large part, what testimony evidences is the act of testifying itself, not the origins of its claims concerning this or another event. Second, because of the nature of witness testimony, the listener or addressee or reader is not an unimplicated vehicle through which the witness reconstructs the story. Rather, he or she becomes a new, secondary, site of trauma, who may exhibit some of the same symptoms of repression and self-alienation or derealization experienced by the primary victim. This can lead to various problems of representational decorum and efficacy.

As Walter Benn Michaels has taken up the subject in relation to American literature, the Holocaust (like the issue of slavery) can quickly yield to a form of identity politics in which history is falsely, facilely, converted into personal memory. As memory, rather than history, it becomes the basis for an identity linked to a group and based on events one has never actually experienced. The shallowness that this might produce, both in one's understanding of the past and in one's construction of one's self in the present, has been powerfully articulated by Alain Finkielkraut in his study of the "imaginary Jew." The "imaginary Jew" is that individual who claims Jewish identity solely of the basis of a trauma he or she did not personally experience. In such a case, identity is negatively conceived. It is based on a deformation of self originating in someone else's trauma.[13]

Primarily the problem with the construction of "secondary trauma"—the trauma induced through the experiencing second hand of someone else's trauma, as in the survivor–listener relationship described by Felman and Laub—is that it only replicates the problem of trauma. It stands the same risk of bypassing conscious process, making the trauma once again inaccessible to being worked through so that it is, instead, acted out and thereby perpetuated. Felman describes exactly this phenomenon among her students in the essay that opens the Felman–Laub volume, raising important questions concerning the pedagogy of Holocaust studies—especially since one way of understanding the Nazi event is as itself a repressed relation to Jews and Jewish history. If a Holocaust narrative (whether documentary, journalistic, or fictional) inflicts too great a wound, it, too, will be relegated to the unconscious, there to emerge in distorted and destructive new behaviors. If the purpose of the Holocaust narrative is both to engage and inform, such witness testimony, which blocks affect and knowledge both, can only be counterproductive.

It is for this reason that Geoffrey Hartman, in his collection of essays *The Longest Shadow*, expresses reservations concerning a certain kind of Holocaust narrative that gives priority to realistic over imaginative interpretation, truth or fact over the (re)construction constitutive of literary narratives. By linking into the larger psychoanalytically informed perspectives of individuals such as Shaul Friedländer and Dominick LaCapra, and by producing a theory consonant with the insights of James Young and Lawrence Langer concerning the rhetorical strategies of even the most historically grounded Holocaust narratives, Hartman calls into question the efficacy of producing secondary trauma in the reader. Trauma, Geoffrey Hartman reminds us, is

> the result of living through extreme experience without experiencing it—without being able to integrate it emotionally or mentally. The disturbances associated with trauma are, according to Freud, an attempt of the system to prepare retroactively for a shock that has already taken place, to catch up with and master it.[14]

If, for the new, secondary, witness—the witness of the witness—a similar process ensues, the secondary witness may simply discover himself or herself in the same bind of numbness experienced by the primary witness, unable to assimilate, self-witness, and thereby genuinely and self-consciously experience the events.

In ordinary human experience, Hartman explains, "memory, and especially the memory that goes into storytelling," becomes the agency by which primary trauma is overcome without producing secondary trauma in its wake. Memory is

> not simply an afterbirth of experience, a secondary formation: it *enables* experiencing, it allows what we call the real to enter consciousness . . . to be something more than trauma followed by a hygienic, and ultimately, illusory, mental erasure. Memory . . . limits and enables at the same time. . . . [It] is evidence of continuity: that the future will have a past." (158–59)

For Hartman, this potentially mediating and distancing function of memory is what literary language, qua language, achieves. Even while producing the eventfulness in which reader and writer mutually experience the events being depicted by the words, literary language produces estrangement and defamiliarization. It places a barrier between the writer and the reader, which preserves the difference between primary and secondary trauma, between the realness or actuality (in its horribleness) of the one experience and the unrealness and distant, distinctive, fictiveness of the other.

In Hartman's words,

> a massive realism which has no regard for representational restraint, and in which depth of illusion is not balanced by depth of reflection, not only desensitizes but produces the opposite of what is intended: an *unreality effect* that fatally undermines realism's claim to depict reality. . . . [A]rt creates an unreality effect in a way

> that is *not* alienating or desensitizing. . . . [I]t provides something of a safe house for emotion and empathy. The tears we shed . . . are an acknowledgment and not an exploitation of the past. (157)

Hartman's use, here, of the word *acknowledgment* is important to what I want to argue concerning Holocaust fiction like Appelfeld's. Hartman provides a way of appreciating not only the importance of language within the reconstruction of traumatic experience but the special efficacy of poetic or non-mimetic language in such representations as well. But the word-as-wound idea, which informs not only Hartman's writing but also that of Cathy Caruth, reintroduces, on the level of word rather than text, problems similar to those of Brooks and others. Caruth's likeminded formulation of Hartman's thesis concerning distance brings us back to Brooks and exposes what might pose problems in all of these approaches to Holocaust fiction.

"The historical power of the trauma," Caruth writes, "is not just that the experience is repeated after its forgetting, but that it is only in and through its inherent forgetting that it is first experienced at all."[15] And it is this inherent latency of the event that paradoxically explains the peculiar, temporal structure, the belatedness, of the Jews' historical experience. The Jews' historical experience in Caruth emerges as a particular case of trauma that can serve, because of its peculiar, temporal structure, as a *figure* for trauma itself. If Brooks's idea of storytelling as akin to psychoanalytic process threatens to devalue the importance of truth in the construction of historical narrative, to subordinate the events of the world to the eventfulness of the text, and to establish a relationship between reader and writer governed by erotic desire, Caruth's (and Hartman's) word-as-wound, directly responding to Holocaust texts and to their power to overwhelm with truth, risks a similarly problematical attenuation of the text's historical referents.

Witnessing, Acknowledging, Historicity, and Affect

To a surprising degree, literary theory and postmodernist philosophy (especially as recast by French intellectuals such as Jacques Derrida and Jean-François Lyotard) have come to seem no less than defined by Auschwitz, or more precisely by what critics have come to designate as "after Auschwitz"—i.e., the trauma produced by Auschwitz, which is now bracketed or represented along with the designation of time past: "after" in quotation marks. The problem with this focus on "after Auschwitz" as a defining constituent of postmodernism, and the reasons it raises knotty problems in relation to interpreting fiction such as Appelfeld's, is that within such a postmodernism the Jew functions in ways uncannily similar to the ways in which the Jew functioned in pre-modernist and modernist thinking. It is this thinking of the Jew, not as a specific biological, historical entity, but as a "trope" for other, non-specifically-Jewish issues which, according to postmodernism's own account, may well have produced Auschwitz in the first place. Despite its powerful investment in coming to terms with "after Auschwitz," postmodernism, in the views of critics such as LaCapra and Elizabeth Bellamy, seems incapable of properly mourning, and thereby working-through, Auschwitz. As a result the Jew remains repressed, dangerously locked in and as the unconscious of a culture doomed to act-out rather than work-through the centuries-old trauma of the Jew.

"The Holocaust," writes LaCapra, "has often tended to be repressed or encrypted as a specific series of events and to be displaced onto such general questions as language, nomadism, unrepresentability, silence, and so forth." There is a "tendency to trope away from specificity and to reprocess problems in terms of reading technologies that function as discursive 'cuisinarts.' Such reactions inhibit processes of working-through and learning from the past."[16] Or as Bellamy puts it, "From Sartre to Jabès to Finkielkraut, the ongoing process of 'imagining the Jew' in postwar France is a paradoxical process of not just rejecting but also *intro*jecting the anti-Semitic trope of the Jew as the strange and uncanny 'other.' Consequently, the postwar Jewish imaginary in France has become an extended meditation on the themes of *l'altérité, déracinement, l'étrangété*—stereotypes left over from an earlier, modernist anti-Semitism, but which have experienced complex psychic metamorphoses in the post-Holocaust." "Real Jews," she goes on, "have tended to be transformed into tropes or signifiers for the decentered, destabilized post-modern subject in a theoretical system that persists in defining (or "fetishizing") them from without."[17] The phrase *after Auschwitz* serves in Bellamy's text as a shorthand for this troping away of the concrete, material fact of Auschwitz and of the individual Jewish human beings who lost their lives there.

LaCapra redeems a psychoanalytic approach to the Holocaust through the same idea of transference emphasized by critics such as Peter Brooks. But in LaCapra, transference is transformed through its association with history rather than fictional narrative. LaCapra's approach allows us to incorporate both Brooks's and Hartman's insights without running into some of the dangers that their methodologies, not to mention those of analysts such as Felman and Laub, also produce. LaCapra puts his case this way:

> [W]orking-through requires the recognition that we are involved in transferential relations to the past in ways that vary according to the subject-positions we find ourselves in, rework, and invent. It also involves the attempt to counteract projective reprocessing of the past through which we deny certain of its features and act out our own desires for self-confirming or identity-forming meaning. By contrast, working-through is bound up with the role of problematic but significant distinctions, including that between accurate reconstruction of the past and committed exchange with it. These distinctions should be neither reified into binary oppositions and separate spheres nor collapsed into an indiscriminate will to rewrite the past. In addition, working-through relies on a certain use of memory and judgment—a use that involves the critique of ideology, prominently including the critique of the scapegoat "mechanism" that had a historically specific and not simply arbitrary or abstract role in the Nazi treatment of the Jews. What is not confronted critically does not disappear; it tends to return as the repressed. (64–65)

As he puts it in his later book *History and Memory,* "transference is inevitable to the extent that an issue is not dead, provokes an emotional and evaluative response, and entails the meeting of history with memory. When confronting live issues, one becomes affectively implicated."[18]

For LaCapra (and Bellamy, too) a fundamental problem in writing about the Holocaust is the problem that has haunted Holocaust studies from the start: how does one represent an inherently unrepresentable event without distorting or minimizing it, or, even more discomforting, appropriating it for the uses or gains of aesthetic or intellectual pleasure? One response of postmodernism, especially as literary theorists were galvanized into print following the Paul de Man disclosures,[19] has been a privileging of "silence" as the only decorous way of speaking about the unspeakable. But the "after Auschwitz" that is at the center of much postmodernist thinking turns out to be a refusal, not only to say what is unsayable but also to say what is eminently sayable: the word *Auschwitz,* which is to say, as well, the word *Jew.* LaCapra reasserts the importance of confronting something we call the real: the events of a world that, for whatever reasons, and on whatever philosophical grounds, we accept the reality of. As an historian he revisits the same site that Masson, Nicholas Rand, and Maria Torok pull into view as what psychoanalysis may have had to deny in order to establish itself as a certain kind of discipline. Psychoanalysis, its early practitioners determined, would not deal with questions of epistemology. But while psychoanalysis might afford severing its link to epistemology (even though, as we have seen, this is at best a contested issue), Holocaust literature cannot. And this brings me back to Stanley Cavell's idea of acknowledgment.

Above or beyond representing an event that may be inherently unrepresentable and about which any representation can seem to create more doubt that certainty, Holocaust fiction has to *acknowledge* the events of the Holocaust. This means neither dispensing with the question of knowledge nor answering it, even in the affirmative, however tempting such an insistence on epistemological verification might be. And this is where psychoanalytic listening and literary reading may converge: in providing validation, authentication, and affective acknowledgment of someone else's story, someone else's cry of pain, in the absence of some possibility of *proving* beyond the shadow of a doubt that such events occurred, but without, because of such doubt, assuming the absence or irrelevance of the historical, factual bases of the events described. Fundamentally, acknowledgment has to do with witnessing affect, feeling, and subject impressions. But to witness another human being's words requires accepting the possibility that behind the imaginary of an individual's consciousness exists the real of that consciousness's experience of the world. It is incumbent upon us to hear that possibility of the real as well. To listen or read this way is to listen or read through and as a part of one's skepticism, which becomes the foundational condition both of affective sympathy and historical validation.

For Cavell, when Freud declares in *The Interpretation of Dreams* that "the Unconscious is the true psychical reality," he is taking on the skeptical dilemma as passed on to him by philosophy. "[S]een in its relation to, or as a displacement of, philosophy, Freud's assertion declares that for the mind to lose the psychoanalytic intuition of itself as unconscious would be for it to lose the last proof of its own existence." In this, his inheritance of philosophy, Cavell goes on:

> Freud's distinction is to have broken through to a practice in which the Ideal philosophy, the reigning philosophy of German culture, becomes concrete. . . . In Freud's practice, one human being represents to another all that that other has conceived of humanity in his or her life, and moves with that other toward an expression of the conditions which condition that utterly specific life. It is a vision and an achievement quite worthy of the most heroic attributes Freud assigned to himself. But psychoanalysis has not surmounted the obscurities of the philosophical problematic of representation and reality it inherits. Until it stops shrinking from philosophy (from its own past), it will continue to shrink before the derivative question, for example, whether the stories of its patients are fantasy merely or (also?) of reality; it will continue to waver between regarding the question as irrelevant to its work and as the essence of it.
>
> It is hardly enough to appeal here to conviction in reality, because the most untutored enemy of the psychological, as eagerly as the most sophisticated enemy, will inform you that conviction is one thing, reality another. The matter is to express the intuition that fantasy shadows anything we can understand reality to be.[20]

The question that haunts psychoanalysis haunts Holocaust narratives as well: *whether the stories are fantasy merely or (also?) of reality.* When Cavell says that "psychoanalysis has not surmounted the obscurities of the philosophical problematic of representation and reality it inherits," he does not mean for psychoanalysis to settle the question of epistemology. Rather, he requires of it that, as in philosophical skepticism itself, it leave the question open, allowing it to continue to function as a question in the investigation of the fantasies that shadow, which is to say, construct, our realities, and without which our realities as such would not exist. Though one major difference between psychoanalysis and literary criticism is that whereas psychoanalysis proceeds between two human beings, literary criticism is a triangulated relationship. A text speaks through a critic to another person, the reader. Nonetheless, the two processes converge in hearing a story in need of witnessing in the complex philosophical sense Cavell outlines.

I want to claim for Aharon Appelfeld's fiction the bases of philosophical thinking that inform Stanley Cavell's ideas. By probing imponderables, Appelfeld aims to discover whatever there is to discover concerning the human. For Appelfeld, as for Cavell, there is no reality that exists independent of the fantasies that shadow it. This is the case whether those fantasies are individual or private or, as in much of Appelfeld's writing, the larger fantasies of culture (the oppressors' culture as well as the victims'). To say that Appelfeld writes in the shadow of the Holocaust is to put a particular shade to what shadows the reality of his particular characters. It is also, however, to make of their worlds nothing more or less remarkable than any world of any human being. We all live equally from within our subjectivity; we either will or will not entertain the claim made upon us by another's words—including the claim of those words that they speak not only of subjective impressions but of quotidian truths.

For at the same time, and also traveling the same route that Cavell travels, Appelfeld will not sacrifice epistemology to fantasy. Fantasy may shadow our reality; we may never be able to verify reality itself; but to therefore simply dismiss the existence of the world and its events is to miss the point of our skepticism, which is to keep the interrogation into reality, which is to say, into ourselves, alive. To acknowledge is, in the face of doubt and despite it, nonetheless to affirm one's responsibilities and commitments. Acknowledgment, in other words, is no easy or passive acceptance of the world's truth. It is the decision to affirm a truth (whether emotional or historical) that nonetheless we *know* without being able to prove it beyond a shadow of philosophical doubt.

Lionel Trilling once identified as the "secret" of art the idea "that one might live in doubt, that one might live by means of a question."[21] It is this idea of a question that everywhere informs Appelfeld's art. What uniquely drives his fiction forward is the urgency of our mounting a response to this question, of our bringing to bear upon it the range of our affective registers. For Cavell, acknowledgment neither settles the question of doubt, positively or negatively. Nor does it dismiss it as irrelevant or impertinent. Rather, it acknowledges a claim made upon us by another's words. In this way, acknowledgment is like psychoanalysis, which is surely one major source of influence on Cavell's own thinking. But as a concept derived for Cavell from within the epistemological inquiries of philosophy rather than in psychoanalysis's break with and even denial or repression of its link to such questions of knowledge, acknowledgment permits us, indeed requires us, not to lose our sense of the importance of verifying for some other person what happened to him or to her, to his person, to her life. Understood this way, the text becomes the occasion, like psychoanalysis itself, for a joint inquiry, in which reader and writer together discover the conditions that condition the utterly specific life and acknowledge them. There may be no responding to other people's lives and words without our interpreting them. Nonetheless, to respond is not to analyze and we may have to employ limits to our will to interpret.

"The poet," writes Adam Phillips in an essay entitled "Poetry and Psychoanalysis," is "that person who can sustain our belief in the meaningfulness of language. And in this sense the poet could be conceived to be akin to the psychoanalyst; the patient coming to analysis to restore his confidence in words." What the poet has to offer the psychoanalyst, Phillips goes on, is sustaining the place of "not-knowing," the interruption of interpretation.[22] At some point, in relation to texts of trauma like the Holocaust fictions of Aharon Appelfeld, we need to forbear the act of analysis and give ourselves over to the response the text demands of us—the response that forbears knowing and instead acknowledges another person's suffering and pain.

With these preliminary comments concerning Holocaust representation in place, I proceed to read Appelfeld's fiction, beginning with a novel that deals most directly with the problem of knowledge in the context of cultural knowledge, i.e., the ideological underpinnings of our lives in society and culture both: *Badenheim 1939*. Already in this early 1978 novel, Appelfeld struggles with the issue that occupies him throughout the range of his writing: how do we hear the voice of the past? Indeed, how do we hear the voice of other human beings speaking to us their individual and oftentimes incomprehensible and unbelievable pain and sorrow? In other words, how do we acknowledge the cry of pain that comes to us from a world past and gone, to which we have no access other than this almost unbelievable and incomprehensible cry itself? For that matter, how do we hear the cries of others that plead with us in the present? Appelfeld's texts raise these questions, both as stories told within the texts and in what the texts themselves demand by way of response of the readers themselves.

2 Literature, Ideology, and the Measure of Moral Freedom: *Badenheim 1939*

The issue I want to examine in this chapter is what constitutes the ideology of a literary text, and how we might sometimes be called upon by a certain kind of text to acknowledge rather than to know or understand as an epistemological verity something that the text is telling us. For several reasons, I put at the center of my discussion Aharon Appelfeld's 1978 novel *Badenheim 1939.* In terms of its themes and plot, *Badenheim* deals with one of modern civilization's most destructive eruptions of ideology, where such ideology is specifically political, and yet not any less ideological in the contemporary terms that I will, in a moment, specify. This context of the novel's central representation is matched by an equally powerful ideological formation, toward which, as a work of Israeli fiction written in Hebrew, that representation may well seem to point: political Zionism. It is for this reason that *Badenheim,* as we shall see, has occasioned accusations that it is itself ideologically determined. Yet *Badenheim* is an extraordinarily crafted and affecting work of art. Though not primarily political either in its intention or in its construction, it is nonetheless deeply conscious of the problem of ideology for which it is faulted. Indeed, as a work of art within a tradition of such works, it frames and explores this problem of ideology. It both locates and "represents" (in both senses of the word, as itself embodying and as commenting on) one powerful way of recasting the relation between ideology and human moral freedom.

To summarize the novel for those who may not be familiar with it, *Badenheim* is, to quote one critic, a grotesque, Kafkaesque "allegory . . . of European Jewry on the eve of its annihilation."[1] It presents a group of highly assimilated Austro-Jewish vacationers who, on the brink of the Holocaust, flock, as they do every year, to the resort town of Badenheim for an annual music festival. While there, the Nazis (represented by the Sanitation Department) begin the slow process of their incarceration. This culminates in the Jews being deported to what we (and not they) know to be the death camps of Poland. Throughout the story, the vacationers, who represent a motley and eccentric lot at best, respond to their encroaching doom with disbelief and inappropriate, bizarrely heightened gaiety. Till the end they maintain their optimism, believing either that nothing untoward is going to happen or that the imminent deportation to Poland is all for the best.

For most readers, *Badenheim,* like other of Appelfeld's writings, represents a powerful confrontation with the inexplicable pain and horror of the Holocaust. It seems less concerned with analyzing the terrible events that occurred than in figuring forth the victims' incomprehension, a stunned amazement that provides no space for self-reflection or action. If Appelfeld's Jewish characters are self-deceiving, they are no more so than any of us might have been, or might be again, especially if confronted with the kind of phantasmagoric transformation experienced by Europe in the 1930s and 1940s. And if they seem to us grotesque, their oddness serves not to censure them so much as to render visible the ordinarily invisible dimensions of distortion that are both the lot of ordinary humanity and the terrible consequences of the circumstances in which these particular individuals (about to be horrifically murdered) find themselves. In Alan Mintz's words, Appelfeld's "writing works to defuse the norms of judgment . . . and to establish in their place a stance of understanding. Understanding is not forgiveness. . . . To understand means to accept that such is the nature of things, that to survive in a world in which what happened happened means to have done certain things and to be a certain way. Appelfeld's goal is our knowledge of that world."[2] Because the novel, despite its subject, maintains throughout what Geoffrey Hartman has called "respect for reticence, for representational limits," it has seemed exceptional among Holocaust fictions.[3] Both for this reason and because he was among the first Israeli writers to make the Holocaust a subject of Hebrew fiction, Appelfeld has seemed almost unique on the scene of Israeli culture, revalidating for Israelis the disowned and disavowed experience of diaspora Jewry.[4]

Yet in 1994 an American literary critic published a sensitive and intelligent critique of *Badenheim,* which emphatically rejected the dominant reading of the novel. Respectful and appreciative as he is, Michael André Bernstein produces the following indictment of what he sees as the ideological thrust of Appelfeld's book:

> By representing the Jews of Badenheim as irredeemably selfish and petty, he commits the greater offense of leaving unchallenged the monstrous proposition that Europe's Jews were somehow "deserving" of punishment. As Ruth Wisse points out, Appelfeld's allegory can only work by "taking the real terror imposed from without by real human forces and internalizing it, thereby further obscuring its origins and meaning. . . . Fate sits in judgment on all the ugly, assimilated Jews—fate in the form of the Holocaust. The result is a series of pitiless moral fables more damning of the victims than of the crime perpetrated against them." The result described here has nothing to do with Appelfeld's intention, but rather with the logical and rhetorical implications of his formal decisions and with the vision of history correlate with those decisions. (66–67)[5]

This "vision of history," Bernstein goes on to specify, has to do with the nationalistic aspirations of Zionism, with "why and with what consequences it is *primarily* the history of anti-Semitic persecution and the fear of constantly new eruptions of the same disease that are still invoked by the Israeli right to legitimize the actions of the Jewish state rather than the historical values and traditions fundamental to Judaism itself." And Bernstein continues:

> But well before statehood was achieved, Zionist leaders of every political orientation regularly invoked the rights conferred by Jewish victimization in their calculations. . . . So it is scarcely surprising that early in 1992, a senior figure in what was then the Israeli government headed by Yitzhak Shamir said that any territorial negotiations were inherently suicidal because the pre-1967 borders of Israel were nothing but "the borders of Auschwitz." Understanding the extraordinary pressures that this same cast of mind places on Israeli political discourse and self-conception helps to underscore the significance of the September 9, 1993 Israeli decision "to recognize the P.L.O. as the representative of the Palestinian people and commence negotiations with the P.L.O. within the Middle East peace process" (from the letter of Yitzhak Rabin, Prime Minister of Israel, to Yasir Arafat, Chairman of the P.L.O.). The Israeli capacity to negotiate directly with the P.L.O. is part of the general loosening of both the claims and the anxieties of victimhood on the national imagination. (76–77)

Bernstein's reading of *Badenheim* faults it for being narrowly political. Yet the reading itself carries with it a political perspective that extends no less than into Israeli party politics. In fact, it is difficult not to take Bernstein's revisionist reading of Appelfeld as his way of contributing to the national political debate in Israel in the 1980s and 1990s. Only in a footnote to the above passage does Bernstein confess that the sentiments he quotes in relation to the Shamir government only repeat Labor party rhetoric of the late 1960s, thus doubling the ideological problematic of his citation of this material (156).

Before I respond more directly to the problems represented by Bernstein's critique, let me add that it is by no means irrelevant to thinking about the politics of literature and literary criticism that Bernstein's view of Zionism resonates powerfully with a number of other recent statements within academic essays concerning contemporary Israeli issues. These include an aside in an essay on narratology, when a critic feels compelled to note, with no elaboration or contextualization, the way that "Zionism has continued to exclude and marginalize the Palestinians"; a footnote in an article on Chaucer and antisemitism, which makes the point that "Judaic culture" is not "free from violence" and adds that "these days in Palestine [*sic*] . . . children and adults are being beaten and murdered in a struggle for territorial expansion"; the moment, in a reading of the unresolved tensions in the biblical text, when a third critic imports her own ambivalence about modern-day Israel to clinch her argument; and, finally, the announcement in the preface to a book concerning new world exploration and exploitation, that his study is nothing less than a "critique of the Zionism in which [he] was raised."[6] Many of the critics whom Bernstein cites within his own text represent similar political positions within the Jewish political spectrum.

I do not want to mount a defense of *Badenheim* simply by attacking the ideological premises of its critics, especially since I am not unimplicated in this debate. Nor do I want to expose the recurring presuppositions of contemporary literary criticism to make the point, however valid, that as much as literary texts express unexamined ideologies, so do critical readings. Rather, I dwell on this material because it seems to me that *Badenheim* offers one brilliant response to the very problem of ideology and literature that Bernstein and others are raising. The issue Bernstein's methodology inadvertently exposes is how we hear the voice in which a particular text speaks; how, in other words, we disentangle directly political rhetoric from the nuanced, often tormented, structure of a text's engagement with ethics and belief. While, like all human reactions, such ethics and beliefs are themselves political, nonetheless they may, as literary structures, be political in a certain specifiable way.

Foreshadowing, Backshadowing, and the Problem of Ideology

The term *ideology* is slippery at best. For contemporary readers of texts it no longer refers to anything as straightforward as a sociopolitical program or a self-consciously articulated set of convictions. Rather, it has a more philosophical meaning, having to do with the relationship among three basic elements in the cognitive process: subject, object, and representation. For many critics, the revolution in the concept of ideology occurs with Marx. Before Marx, whether subject is preferred over object or vice versa, or whether subject and object seem to enjoy autonomous or mutually constructed existences, the triadic relationship among subject, object, and representation is marked by some measure of transparency. Representation provides a more or less reliable vehicle of referentiality by which a subject might *know* the world. With Marx's concept of "false consciousness," representation wrenched loose of the moorings of mind and world to become the instrument that itself fashions consciousness. Whether such ideology represents false consciousness, as it did for Marx or for Michel Foucault or Terry Eagleton, or whether, as it does for some postmodernists, such as Louis Althusser, Jacques Derrida, or Slavoj Žižek, ideology represents consciousness itself, remains a fundamental issue separating contemporary literary criticisms.[7]

Embedded in the debate concerning the relation of representation to consciousness is the issue of freedom and moral responsibility. The concept of false consciousness keeps open an idea of freedom, since it remains possible to imagine the act by which the mind recognizes the falseness of culture and its own difference from it. But such an idea of the mind's difference from the world it would interpret involves Marxist criticism in a major self-contradiction, since it is not clear, in material culture, how we stand outside culture's ideological constructs. And, indeed, while neo-Marxist critics often assume that texts do not stand outside culture, they seem to imagine, at least in their own practice, that literary critics do. For this reason, a neo-Marxist critic may expose the ideological blindness of a text without necessarily revealing his or her own ideological blindness. Such a critical position also evades one of Marxism's basic concepts: that representation is not transparent. In reading the literary text as an almost unadulterated reflection of the sociopolitical and cultural world in which it is produced, the post-Marxist critic proceeds as if the literary text were indeed transparent. Postmodernism, by insisting that there is no place outside the ideological constructions of our world and by insisting that such consciousness as exists, exists only in its dissemination into the representational field, produces a consistency lacking in Marxist criticism. But in so doing, it may jettison the idea of freedom and responsibility.

Here it must be said that the main theoretical purpose of Bernstein's book is not to indict Appelfeld. Rather, and quite appealingly, it is to highlight the ways in which the standard literary device of textual *foreshadowing,* especially in combination with what Bernstein calls *historical backshadowing,* creates problems for literatures of catastrophe such as Holocaust fiction. For this reason, Bernstein's book is an important contribution to literary and philosophical discussions of the Holocaust and deserves the respect accorded it by the critics who first took up its arguments when the book appeared.[8] Because readers know how the story turns out, historical narratives seem to reach what Bernstein terms "foregone conclusions." They seem to impose teleologies on otherwise unpredictable events. This tends to cast blame on the victims of catastrophe for not seeing what we so clearly see: the direction in which events were heading.

As we have seen, like several other critics Bernstein faults Appelfeld in *Badenheim* for seeming to blame the Jews (and not the Nazis) for their extermination. But Bernstein goes further. Linking textual foreshadowing to another feature of the text, namely its "vision of history," *Badenheim* seems to Bernstein to tend in the direction of an ideological teleology. In the case of a fiction dealing with the Final Solution, in which ideology succeeded in exterminating six million Jews and millions of non-Jews as well, the apparently programmatic ideology of the text is particularly unfortunate. In Bernstein's reading, Appelfeld's text becomes an emotionally manipulative plea for what emerges as Zionism's own solution to the Jewish question.

Bernstein's idea of *sideshadowing* (developed with Gary Saul Morson) intends, admirably, to preserve an idea of cognitive freedom. *Sideshadowing,* explains Morson, "names both an open sense of temporality and a set of devices used to convey that sense."[9] By highlighting "the unfulfilled or unrealized possibilities of the past," it disrupts "the affirmations of a triumphalist, unidirectional view of history" (Bernstein 3). Producing an indeterminate text, *sideshadowing* respects the complexity of the past. Just as importantly, it insists on free will and moral responsibility (Morson 82–113).

Both Bernstein and, more explicitly, Morson set out to amplify a feature of Bakhtinian poetics. The dialogic quality of the word, they suggest, its *double-voiced-ness,* which in Bakhtin's essay "Discourse in the Novel" is termed "heteroglossia"—"a special type of *double-voiced discourse,*" expressing "*another's speech in another's language*"—can, they suggest, in certain kinds of texts, be compromised by other textual features, for example the text's retrospective historical referentiality.[10] Therefore, Bernstein and Morson develop a model in which the author insures heteroglossia by deliberately figuring forth the open, non-contingent nature of the represented world.

Despite the considerable power of Bernstein's and Morson's ideas, *Badenheim* is not in need of the correction afforded by *sideshadowing.* In the first place, and as I have already suggested, it is not the novel's primary purpose to mount a cultural critique, or even to distribute blame on one or both sides of the catastrophe. Rather, the text captures a psychological, emotional moment. This moment belongs as much to the authorial voice, which happens to be, we know, a survivor voice, as to the text itself. This fact of survivor authorship cannot be so easily dismissed, especially in a reading of the novel like Bernstein's, which levels a political criticism against the author. For this reason, one line of response to Bernstein's critique might well follow the guidelines set out by Dominick LaCapra. Not only must the transferential relation between the Holocaust and the Holocaust author or text be taken seriously, in its full complexity and power, but so must the similar relation between the critic of the Holocaust narrative and the texts or events that they are interpreting. As LaCapra puts it, specifically in relation to the problem of teleology that Bernstein is raising, "*Nachträglichkeit* (belatedness) would be utterly misconstrued if it became a pretext for simplistic teleological narratives in which earlier phenomena are portrayed as causing or leading unilaterally to later ones."[11]

Badenheim presents the horror and incomprehension that characterize both then and now. It does this, however, not by collapsing the one into the other or by imagining that the present enables us to understand and thereby free ourselves from the past. Rather, it recognizes the impossibility of even responding to the past without entering into a meaningful, even passionate relation to it. To level the criticism more in Bernstein's own terms, which are also related to the problem of *Nachträglichkeit,* Bernstein's reading of Appelfeld performs a considerable amount of *foreshadowing* and *backshadowing* of its own, in the form of a post-1967 diaspora interpretation of Zionism and its relationship to the Holocaust.[12] In the psychoanalytic categories LaCapra uses, Bernstein (and others) may be as much acting out as working through the Holocaust in their interpretations of Appelfeld's novel.

Badenheim, I want to insist, even if is not *about* ideology in any discursive or philosophical sense, understands exactly what it means that human beings exist within ideologies and the degree to which cultural contextualization collaborates with and helps produce the effects the novel so deftly describes. As a work of allegory, it is deeply invested in the most basic instrument of verbal representation, namely words themselves. Therefore, it preserves at the forefront of its textual consciousness what Bernstein in his reading of the novel perhaps downplays: the multivocality of language that first originates not in textual design, but in the dialogic or multivocal quality of the word itself—in what we just might call *voice.*[13] This multivocalism is not simply the multivalence of the word. Rather, it is the word's historical freight, its accumulated meanings or "contextual residue," through which it speaks another's as well as its own meanings.[14] *Badenheim* does not need to construct contingency structurally or thematically because it realizes such contingency within its very utterances.

For this reason, it is not incidental to Bernstein's and Morson's project that while Morson, in his book, traces the successful *sideshadowing* of certain realist novels, Bernstein takes to task a text that is allegorical rather than mimetic (cf. Morson 5; Young 289–90). In this context, it might be noted that *Badenheim* figures forth its world in a language that is not the language of that world (I will return to this point later), and, further, that it is resident on the scene of Western culture in translation. That is, the book can be read by most of its readers only through an act that breaks its potential for multivocal meaning on the verbal level.

My objective here is not to launch a discussion of literary translation. Nor do I want to exaggerate the inaccessibility of a translated text to interpretation. In the case of *Badenheim,* the English translation is eminently readable, and many of my points can and will be made on the basis of this translation. Nor does reading the text in Hebrew guarantee my particular interpretation. Nonetheless, the fact of the text's existence as a work of translation serves to intensify, perhaps to actualize, the problem of reading as itself an act of translation out of the literal words of the text into one critical vocabulary or language or another, in which the multivocality of the word is necessarily lost. In the case of allegory, especially of Appelfeld's Kafkaesque variety, which Appelfeld also purifies through his linguistic spareness, the non-referential valence of the word and its non-mimetic manner of figuration turn the focus back on the word itself and its historical accretions.

Bakhtin distinguishes between two kinds of words: the "authoritarian" or "'single-voiced' word . . . which does not take into account another speaker's utterance but focuses solely on the object of speech"; and the "double-voiced word," which tends toward heteroglossic discourse (Danow, 24–25). The major representational feature for which Appelfeld's fiction has generally been celebrated, which causes Bernstein to read it as overdetermined, is its minimalism and restraint. This simplicity of language is not, however, as one might at first imagine, "single-voiced." Rather, it is a purification and distillation of language through which the multivocality of the word can only be achieved by traveling the depths of its historical accretions. *Badenheim*'s form of *sideshadowing* is a process of *shadowingforth,* not as a typology or teleology in which present fulfills past, but as an act of recovery. What is rescued is a depth of cultural knowledge that resides within language itself.

The Materiality of Culture

Badenheim, I suggest, does not fail to represent or achieve moral knowledge. Rather, in the first instance, the text establishes the difficulty of just such an achievement. It puts before the reader the non-transcendent place of material culture, in which we are always immersed, which prevents culture from offering itself to our conscious perception as a transparent medium through which we might glimpse some essential truth or law of culture.[15] In this way, the text insists on exactly what Bernstein and others would have the text insist on: the profound inexplicability of this, as of all other, cultural experiences. This is not to say that the novel does not present the Jews' self-willed blindness to the events occurring around them. Like many of us, the Jews of *Badenheim* refuse to see what is too horrifying to admit, what is too threatening to the possibility of carrying on with the ordinary course of their everyday lives. In the case of Jewish history, which is marked century after century by occurrences such as these, how could the Jews of Europe have even begun to comprehend how catastrophic this new wave of antisemitism was going to be? This insight itself constitutes one important element of the novel's understanding both of general human nature and of Jewish history in particular.

Beyond this psychological understanding, however, is the deeper knowledge that Appelfeld shares with Kafka. This is the realization that the depth of material culture is its surface; that there is nothing beyond or behind the surface to give it transcendent meaning or purpose. The one character of the novel, Trude, who repeatedly refers to the world as "transparent" and "diseased" (3, 10) and who, therefore, seems to *see* something, is no prophet but a mad woman. Her madness, furthermore, serves only to infect her husband, who in turn infects several other characters, all of whom seem to see through culture and who therefore go mad (50, 65, 79, 103, 119). Such seeing achieves no purpose. It clarifies nothing. The text provides no prolonged representations of the Nazis themselves, or of their promulgations, or of anything else that might constitute the hidden or latent content of this world. Certainly no one, not Trude, and not the workers in the Sanitation Department, can see what lies beyond the antisemitism of pogroms and deportation to the Final Solution.

Therefore, most of the book's intimation of menace and catastrophe proceeds through its imagery of nature. As a pure authorial device, this imagery puts such knowledge outside the cultural field. It evidences retrospective and extra-cultural knowledge not available to the characters themselves.

This totality of the self-enclosed cultural world is made evident in one of the most prominent features of the text: that it presents the Jews as the Nazis saw them. This is also, the text implies, the way the Jews saw themselves. The degree of the novel's involvement in the antisemitic rhetoric of Nazism is no less than staggering. The book presents its Jewish characters as corrupt, selfish, maimed, disfigured, and degenerate—people who are not quite human, some of them not even quite alive. One character is mistaken, twice, for another character's dead brother (6), while another character dresses up in the clothing of his dead brother (92). There are the twins who are "indistinguishable" from each other and are therefore more half-beings than complete persons (18); a child prodigy who is either prematurely adult or perversely immature: "half-baby half-boy . . . adult lines trembling at the corners of his eyes" (36); a pregnant schoolgirl who similarly blurs the line between child and adult; a mortally ill woman who has escaped from a sanitarium; several certifiably insane individuals; and a half-Jewish waitress, who is referred to in the Hebrew text as *bat hataʿarovet*, the daughter of mixture or blending, the word *taʿarovet* very often referring in common Hebrew usage to a mongrel (Hebrew text 16).

As if this weren't enough a reflection of the Nazis' view of the Jews, the language of the text's descriptions is insistently and self-consciously the language of invasion and infection (1, 4, 5, 11, 13, 18, 20, 23, 26), while the characters are often figured as drunk or drugged (3, 4, 13, 14, 16, 21, 26, 65, 71). The Jews, the text clearly informs us, "had insinuated themselves [into Badenheim] like diseased roots" (4). But so, we are told, had the Nazis, who "stream" (11) and "spread" out (15) just like the Jews, in what becomes more like a natural process than any intention of forethought.

By making the Nazis' view of the Jews significantly indistinguishable from the Jews' view of themselves, *Badenheim* presents the story of the Final Solution in the form of its mutuality as experienced by victims and victimizers, where what separated the two was only (and this was everything) the final solution that one side proposed for the other. Indeed, it is possible to understand this Final Solution as an effort to pierce the impenetrability of German-Jewish mutuality, to distinguish the indistinguishable other from the self. Implicit in Appelfeld's text is condemnation of a certain idea of allegory, which seems to imply the possibility of representational transparency. This has the effect of discovering in Nazism, as in other systems of racist thought, a tendency toward the allegorical perception of human beings, as if people could be reduced to images of one thing or another. It is the fantasy of seeing through our ideological blindness that emerges in this text as producing the call for a Final Solution. *Badenheim* refuses to fall into this deadly fallacy.

The construction of the agency of the Final Solution as unseen, as the natural continuation for Jews and Nazis both, of an ongoing cultural logic, no more to be disputed or opposed than nature itself, comes into vivid focus in the concluding paragraph of the novel. This paragraph serves as a paradigm of the novel as a whole. It also, however, and just as critically, identifies what it is within culture that can release us from its deadly determinism:

> But their amazement was cut short. An engine, an engine coupled to four filthy freight cars, emerged from the hills and stopped at the station. Its appearance was as sudden as if it had risen from a pit in the ground. "Get in!" yelled invisible voices. And the people were sucked in. Even those who were standing with a bottle of lemonade in their hands, a bar of chocolate, the headwaiter with his dog—they were all sucked in as easily as grains of wheat poured into a funnel. Nevertheless Dr. Pappenheim found time to make the following remark: "If the coaches are so dirty it must mean that we have not far to go." (147–48)

Before I suggest what concept of freedom this paragraph constructs, let me suggest how it produces an almost perfect model of the cultural determinism that pervades the text. Action here is not propelled by human will or desire. Rather, it emerges as the consequence of a logic that appears to be embedded in objects and events, in culture, even perhaps in language. "Voices," unidentified and dissociated, order the Jews onto trains, which have appeared as from nowhere, virtually erupting from within the scene as opposed to appearing from outside it, with the consequence that, with little or no reason, "people were sucked in as easily as grains of wheat . . . into a funnel."

Though the quality I am describing exists in the English translation, the agency-less quality of the text is even more pronounced in the Hebrew. The addition, in the English translation, of the words *invisible* and *poured,* for example, tends to imply some agent that, making itself invisible and pouring the Jews into the train, could be discovered. Let me reiterate, it is not my intention to fault this translation or translation in general. My objective is to return the act of reading, and thereby our understanding of ideology, culture, and consciousness, to the self-enclosed space of the representational field. Without accepting the embeddedness of consciousness within representation, which is to say, language, interpretation becomes a meaningless exercise in reading out or decoding, as if representation were, indeed, a transparency leading to a meaning separate from the representation, i.e., to an ideology in the most restrictive and political sense of the word. In the case of *Badenheim,* the language of the text is inseparable from such ideology as the text does, in aesthetic terms, express.

Therefore, let me continue my reading according to the Hebrew original. The text's relocation of agency from human will into language is amplified, in the original, by the text's insistent word play or, more properly, sound play, since some of the words that echo or repeat are not etymologically but only phonetically related. In an almost subterranean manner, the language of the text constructs patterns of images and meanings that emerge not through any independent picture projected by individual words or phrases, but rather through the almost arbitrary logic of the words' sound-sense. Shortly following the emergence of the *voices* (*qolot*), the word *easily* (*beqalut*) appears. Not only do the voices come from nowhere, but the sound of them is, quite without causal connection, everywhere and, therefore, nowhere, as with utter simplicity and naturalness these *voices easily* draw the victims forward to their deaths.

This pattern of word/sound repetition repeats throughout the paragraph. The word *toch* in *mitoch* (*from within*) repeats twice, first in relation to the pit, second (as *el toch*) in connection with the funnel (train). The two words mirror each other across the line of text, establishing a kind of equilibrium or balance between two motions, which comes to seem almost a law of nature, like gravity. This idea is conveyed as well in another twice-repeated word: *standing.* It is as if the language of this paragraph were infected: a notion introduced through the description of the freight cars as *polluted* or *infected* ("filthy" in the English translation). The word *mezuhamim* (*infected*) picks up the series of such images. The logic that controls the train's sudden eruption from within (*mitoch*) may be as much the logic of language as of reality. Language not only mirrors but also produces the infection and pollution of the world. Indeed, as the word *toch* in *mitoch bor* (*within a pit*) points toward its second appearance in the text: *el toch mashpech* (*within a funnel*)—mediated, as it is, by the idea of infection or contagion (*mezuhamim*), which is earlier in the text associated with the Sanitation Department's investigation of the city's sewers—the word *bor* is pulled into relation to the word *mashpech* to suggest (perhaps) another Hebrew word: *bor shofchin,* which means cesspool. It is as if, in this paragraph, words were being sucked into the cesspool of their own contagion, contaminating everything in the range of their signification.

The paragraph avoids development. Everything is implicit in and infected by everything else. Everything stands in its own pollution. The Hebrew root *ᶜayin mem dalet,* meaning *stand,* first appears as the word *ᶜemdah,* used metaphorically in the first sentence to mean something like "their wonder was frozen in its standing" (frozen in position). The word later resurfaces in its more usual sense to describe the Jews as simply *standing* at the scene. The effect of the two words is to emphasize just this quality expressed by each word separately: passivity, stasis, simply *standing,* as opposed to what the word *stand* can also mean, and which is directly implied in the Hebrew *ᶜemdah,* of taking a stand or having a stance. This quality of passive reception is picked up as well in the word play on the root *shin mem ᶜayin* (*hear*): "Nevertheless Dr. Pappenheim found time to make the following remark" (literally: manages or succeeds to make heard (*lehashmiᶜa*), or to imply, the following sentence). The word translated as "it must mean" also derives from the root *to hear.* Its more precise meaning is *to make heard* or *to imply.* Dr. Pappenheim, in other words, manages to say what is implicit in the scene.

As if this tautology were itself not sufficiently frustrating, Pappenheim commits the further sin of announcing his interpretation as law: for the word *mishpat,* or *sentence* (*remark* in the English translation) means both law and trial, as in the Hebrew title of Kafka's *The Trial/Hamishpat,* a text exactly about the authority of the law beyond any truth the law may express and outside our powers to explicate or mediate it. The final line of *Badenheim* exposes as impossible and untrue exactly what Bernstein accuses the text itself of attempting to gain: "the reward of fitting even catastrophic events into a coherent global schema . . . the pleasure of comprehension, the satisfaction of the human urge to make sense out of every occurrence, no matter how terrible" (13). Pappenheim's is satisfaction denied, thrown into doubt (the Hebrew translated as: to have time, *lehaspiq,* containing the letters of the words *sippuq/satisfaction* and *safeq/doubt;* a duplication by eye rather than either sound or etymology; *p* and *f* are the same letter in Hebrew). The source of Pappenheim's error is his desire to see rather than to hear, to announce (*lehashmiᶜa*) rather than to listen (*lishmoᶜa*), to make a remark rather than obey a "law"—such law as, we suddenly come to see (or not, depending on how we read), forms the subterranean structure of this paragraph.

What this text is gesturing toward, not in its ostensible content but *through its language,* is that such production of meaning as this impresario of modern culture engages in is exactly what, within a religious context, is proscribed to human beings. Embedded in the language of the final paragraph, there also not to be seen except through the language itself, and concerning the difference between seeing and hearing, is a particular biblical scene, a scene about the giving of the law, which serves to spring the trap of material culture. This is the scene of *maʿamad sinai* (*standing at Sinai*) in Deuteronomy (*Devarim*) IV.1–V.20, the moment when God gives the Law (*mishpat*) to the Israelites, enjoining their rejection of paganism (i.e., material culture) and granting them their moral freedom. I have rendered in italics those words in the English translation from *Devarim* that utilize the same roots that appear in Appelfeld's final paragraph, where, as in Appelfeld's text, they also repeat themselves:

> And now, O Israel, *hearken* unto the statues and unto the *ordinances,* which I teach you, to do them. . . . [IV, 10–16] "Assemble Me the people, and *I will make them hear* My words . . ." And ye came near and *stood* . . . And the Lord spoke unto you *out of the midst* of the fire; *ye heard the voice* of words, but ye saw no form; only a *voice** . . . And the Lord commanded me at that time to teach you statues and *ordinances* . . . for ye saw no manner of form on the day that the Lord spoke unto you . . . *out of the midst* of the fire lest ye . . . make you a graven image . . . [IV 36] Out of the heaven He *made thee to hear* His *voice* . . . and *thou didst hear* His words *out of the midst* of the fire. [V] And Moses called unto all Israel and said unto them: *Hear* O Israel, the statues and the *ordinances* which I speak in your ears this day . . . The Lord spoke with you face to face in the mount *out of the midst* of the fire [here are given the Ten Commandments] . . . These words the Lord spoke unto all your assembly in the mount *out of the midst* of the fire, of the cloud, and of the thick darkness, with a great *voice,* and it went on no more. [*the addition of the semicolon obscures the confusion in the Hebrew original which leads to the popular midrash that what the Israelites saw on Sinai was not an image but a voice. The passage repeats Exodus 20.15, with its similar blurring of seeing and hearing, when "all the people perceived the thunderings and the lightenings, and the voice of the horn and the mountain smoking."][16]

It is this scene of the giving of the law that, I want to insist, is being parodied and inverted, image by image, by the sudden appearance of the train, multiple voices calling the Jews, who stand and wait, drawing them invisibly and ineluctably to their destruction; its eruption from on low rather than from on high, a materialization insistently and irredeemably material.

What might this scene of the giving of the moral law be doing here on the scene of catastrophe? Equally important, how are we to see or hear it—especially since it is not in the least clear whether we (or perhaps just I, this individual reader of the text) are led to this scene by the conscious intention of the writer or by the inevitable drag of the language backward toward its origins.

I want to suggest that the shadowy presence of the biblical scene within the scene of devastation (whether on the thematic or linguistic level) produces a picture of the paradoxical relationship between the deterministic condition of our lives in material culture and an idea of moral freedom, which opposes ideological coercion, and which is embedded in language. The two conditions exist simultaneously and inseparably intertwined. Each is significantly invisible. But the invisibility of one is not the invisibility of the other. Indeed, one of the scenes, recording the moment when seeing yielded to hearing as the medium of our moral knowledge, reminds us that, contained within the visual forms of material culture, including its words, is the sound or voice of another reality.

This other reality is not circumscribed by culture. It is, however, accessible only through culture. Therefore, the text insists, such freedom as we human beings possess is contingent upon our willingness to place ourselves within, and accept responsibility for, the linguistic and cultural conditions of our lives.

Let me bring this into clearer view.

The final paragraph of the novel is constructed out of three different semantic planes. One of these is the simple plane of reference, signifying the events taking place. This signification is available both to participants and readers, in the original and in translation. Like much else in the novel, it evidences the opacity of culture. The second plane is the linguistic field, which dubiously produces sense as sound, in imitation of the arbitrary logic of culture. This field largely duplicates the first but is accessible only in Hebrew. The insistence on the inextricability of meaning from language has two effects. The first is to reinforce the idea (already present at the level of reference) of the near-imperviousness and invisibility of culture. The second, moving in the opposite direction, is to insist that, insofar as we might interpret culture at all, we must be a part of it. We must be subject to its sound-sense. This sound-sense is what delivers the text the third semantic plane: that of intertextual allusion.

The plane of intertextual allusion releases the text from the determinism of culture by *shadowingforth* another text, also written in Hebrew. The effect of this is double. As allusion or intertext, the passage recognizes the innate archeology of language, its irrepressible power to import meanings from other times and places. But as important as the linguistic work performed by the mere fact of the intertextual allusion is the content of the text thus shadowed forth. The text records a moment between the Israelites' pre- and post-Sinaic sojourns in material culture, when voice was visible and meaning was a virtual object that could be grasped: a moment, in other words, when material surface and transcendent meaning converged. The Hebrew word for this is *davar,* meaning both *thing* and *word;* as we have seen, the book of Deuteronomy is called *devarim* in Hebrew. This moment of seeing voices is never to be repeated, not in material culture. Its single occurrence, however, breaks the authority and determinism of the material world. No lesser voice than the voice of God entered into human language and consciousness from the start, incorporating within the material world a non-material entity.

To put this somewhat differently, the first two levels of the text's referential planes, the one cultural, the other linguistic, reinforce each other, at least in the original Hebrew. In addition, both are distinctly separate from the divine scene, towards which only the linguistic level points us. This has the further consequence that the text constructs two different relationships to cultural determinism. In the first of these, which is figured by the paralleling, each of the others, of the three representational planes, we are rendered capable of clarifying or seeing culture in the sense of producing another, perhaps equally opaque, allegory or picture of it. This seeing illuminates culture, and translates it into somewhat different terms, without in any way lessening its determinism. In the second, however, signaled by the scene of the divine, we are made aware of some space within the cultural field that culture does not occupy. This space permits our exemption from the fatality of material culture. It enables the enactment of our moral freedom. In the comments that follow I will try to specify what it means that the deepest meaning of this text, and the instrument of its moral freedom, is available, not simply to those who speak its language (which is the case of every literary text), but to the particular group of readers whose story this is.

Allegory and Moral Knowledge

One large dimension of Appelfeld's undertaking is to explore, first, the ways in which cultural representations, especially in literature, illuminate or picture culture even if they don't alter its determinism. "It was a moment of transition," *Badenheim* announces on the opening page, and this fact is repeated five times toward the end of the text (139, 143, 146). By materializing language on the page and freezing it (wonder frozen in place), written language does provide a transcript of culture. Such language may be as infected and polluted as culture itself. It may be as apt to deliver us to the death camps of Europe as to the Sinai of Israel. Nonetheless, written language stops the cultural flow. It permits us to see, momentarily at least, what is otherwise not to be seen.

This is, in part, the point of a Kafka story that resonates nicely with *Badenheim,* not only in terms of its larger themes but on the level of imagery as well: for example, the prominence of several dogs on the scene of the action, the trope of the musical festival, and the emphasis on the "investigations" of the Sanitation Department, which are imagined as "show[ing] what reality was" (19). The very fact that *Badenheim* may have this text in mind contributes to its argument concerning literary illumination as residing in its capacity, not to see through culture, but to re-picture it. If, as a text written in Hebrew, *Badenheim* may be thought of as speaking to Jewish readers differently from non-Jewish readers, addressing them in their own language, then as a text concerning and itself produced by European culture, it also insists on speaking, through intertextual allusion to or translation of Kafka, to that culture as well.

In Kafka's "Investigations of a Dog" ("Forschungen eines Hundes"), a canine narrator attempts to penetrate the mystery of the canine world, as represented by its music. He does this first as a kind of proto-Marxist, attempting to understand the conditions of its material production and social organization. Second, he tries, as might a humanist or theologian, to probe the inner essence of caninity—of what it means to be a dog. What the story shows us is that culture is opaque and non-transparent. It reveals nothing but its own laws of internal self-regulation.

This is the point as well of the following statement from *The Trial,* which also, I think, resonates in *Badenheim:* "it is not necessary to accept everything as true, one must only accept it as necessary," to which K responds: "A melancholy conclusion. . . . It turns lying into a universal principle."[17] "Historical necessity" (70; literally: "the requirements of reality," Hebrew text, 52) is the explanation provided by one of *Badenheim*'s characters as to why the Jews are being deported, using the same word *meẓiʾut/reality* used to describe the researches of the Sanitation Department. Material reality may not be true, but it contains the fatal force of truth. In Sacvan Bercovitch's interpretation of "Investigations of a Dog," "Kafka's story is a great parable of interpretation as mystification—facts marshaled endlessly to build up contexts whose effect, if not intent, is to conceal or explain away. It is also a great parable of the limitations of cultural critique—*limitations,* not just illusions, for in fact the story conveys a good deal about the dog's world, in spite of the narrator's inability to transcend it; or rather, as a function of his nontranscending condition."[18] There is something to be gained by our non-transcendent investigations, even if they are nothing more than translations from one script to another, which only reveal the depthless surface of our world.

But "Investigations of a Dog" also offers another idea of freedom, which is even more pertinent to *Badenheim.* At the end of Kafka's story, the narrator discovers himself incapable of succeeding in those scientific researches that would tell him (like *Badenheim*'s Sanitation Department) what reality really is. And what spares him this knowledge and preserves what he realizes is the space of his "freedom" is "instinct."[19] Throughout *Badenheim,* despite the suffocating density of its material world, moments of "hidden fear" (10) or "secret worry" (12) or "hidden melody" (17–18) intrude, the origins of which are outside the scene of the action: "A strange night descended on Badenheim. The cafés were deserted and the people walked the streets silently. There was something unthinking about their movements, as if they were being led. It was as if some alien spirit had descended on the town" (25); cf. "it seemed that some other time, from some other place, had invaded the town and was silently establishing itself" (38). The word translated as *alien spirit* is, in the Hebrew, *ḥofesh/freedom.* The end of the passage, which in the Hebrew makes no reference to the people's being "unthinking," more nearly translates as: "It was as if some other freedom, not of the place, had fallen on the city" (Hebrew text, 23).

This idea of freedom is already oddly alluded to in the original Hebrew title, which is *badenheim ʿir nofesh* [*Badenheim, Resort City*]. The word *nofesh* means more or less the same thing as *ḥofesh* (also *ḥufsha* in modern Hebrew), signifying *vacation* or *freedom.* Material culture may be deterministic, but to enter into its determinism is a choice. In their search for a true home, the Jews embrace what is no more than a bath-house (*badenheim*), a kind of vacation site that vaguely and ironically recalls the *mikveh* (or ritual bath-house) through which Jews might consecrate themselves specifically to their own traditions and meanings. The *nofshim/vacationers* (7) lose their "freedom," and even their "souls" (soul in Hebrew is *nefesh*), when they confuse creation and recreation; when they forget that there is something in culture that interrupts culture and speaks as instinct or melody or voice: as a kind of knowledge not founded in objective, quotidian knowing but in some internal knowing not verifiable as such.

As in Kafka's story, the gain afforded by the accession to innate knowledge entails sacrifice. Such knowing involves a kind of death. In a passage that directly anticipates the opening sentence of the final paragraph, we are told that "the light stood still. There was a frozen kind of attentiveness in the air" (64). More literally this reads: "the light stood apart from its flowing. A frozenness close to [or like] listening" (Hebrew text, 48). The word *haqerovah* (close to) flirts with the word for *sacrifice* (haqravah). As elsewhere in *Badenheim,* this passage demonstrates how, by arresting the invisible circulations of culture, we are momentarily enabled to glimpse them. But the image, linked through the idea of consciousness (attentiveness) to other eruptions of hidden knowledge, takes us further.

Appelfeld's notion that freezing life's flow "produces" consciousness by "sacrificing" it evokes the very experience associated in Kant with the origins of innate moral knowledge: the experience of the sublime. This experience, Kant tells us, is "brought about by the feeling a momentary check to the vital forces followed at once by a discharge all the more powerful," when the mind experiences its supersensibility, its power to "[transcend] every standard of sense." Such a moment, according to Kant, depends on the paradoxical condition of feeling both one's mortal endangerment in nature and one's immunity from peril: "the irresistibility of the might of nature forces upon us the recognition of our physical helplessness as beings of nature, but at the same time reveals a faculty of estimating ourselves as independent of nature, and discovers a pre-eminence above nature that is the foundation of self-preservation of quite another kind from that which may be assailed and brought into danger by external nature."[20] *Badenheim*'s image of the self-interrupting light of consciousness opens chapter 18 of the novel, *yod ḥet* in the Hebrew system that represents numbers by letters. In a popular Hebrew word play, this number signifies *ḥet yod* (*ḥay*): *life.* In the moment of cessation or death, an opening is produced whereby the mind realizes its life independent of the natural and cultural worlds. What the mind is permitted to see in this brief moment is the space that material reality cannot occupy. This space of interruption or pause is the space of its freedom.[21]

For Kant, for whom "there is perhaps no more sublime passage in the Jewish Law than the commandment: Thou shalt not make unto thee any graven image," this experience of the sublime corresponds to an experience of God. It is also, Kant tells us, like the worship of God, uncoerced and free. It is the basis, therefore, of a "moral law" that is "the sufficient and original source of [its own] determination within us" (127, 113–14, and 128). Appelfeld is not a traditionally religious writer. He is, however, as Yigal Schwartz has observed, a writer who continually agonizes over religious issues.[22] *Badenheim* is religious in the sense that it acknowledges a possible other context, outside of human history and culture, by which events in this world might be measured and understood and in which free will can be maintained.

For Kant the experience of the sublime, which is the experience of our moral freedom, requires, within the moment of terror, a sense of safety from the peril that threatens. Even within the straitened circumstances of Badenheim, the dead-end determinism of life in culture is seen to be interrupted by moments of sublimity, which are, for Appelfeld as for Kant, also eruptions of innate moral knowledge. As Yigal Schwartz has demonstrated, a repeating structure of the author's fictional world is the evocation of the always distant, unattainable "other" place (geographical, psychological, spiritual), where the Appelfeldian character does not reside. This place alternately repels and attracts him or her, such that the character remains suspended and paralyzed between spaces, more dead than alive. The ultimate figure for this empty space is the Holocaust itself, which Appelfeld almost never describes (55–139). But there is another set of empty spaces in Appelfeld's fiction, which are intimately, albeit paradoxically, related to these. These other spaces stand for the ideologically uncoerced areas of our moral freedom.

I am not speaking here of what LaCapra and others point to as a negative sublime by which Nazism produced a simulacrum of sublimity out of unmitigated horror and devastation (105–110).[23] Rather, I am suggesting that in Appelfeld's text there is the realization that however much our lives in culture are determined by the invisibility of its laws and the interpenetration of our consciousness into those laws, we do not, as human beings, live by such laws alone. There is something that interrupts the force of culture, something that we human beings *know,* which constitutes our freedom as human beings, and our moral responsibility. In the "cardboard" (145) world of material culture, we are all "marionettes in a play" (11)—to appropriate some of the images of the text.[24] But to imprison ourselves in this prison of language is a choice. This is why the novel produces, from within the cesspool or pit, the nothingness of *sho'ah,* the sublimity of Sinai. What separates the catastrophe of destruction from the immateriality of God is a willingness to accept the moral knowledge that is law and freedom both. Kant calls the experience of the sublime "*astonishment* almost to terror" (120). Appelfeld's word for this, in the first sentence of the final paragraph, is *amazement* or *wonder: hishta'ut,* a word that derives from the root meaning *destruction,* the same root from which *sho'ah,* or Holocaust, is derived.

Sho'ah is there from the paragraph's opening sentence, to be seen and not to be seen, as, in a sense, it is there, and not there, through our retrospective knowledge, from the beginning of the book. This feature of the text, in combination with the biblical scene, may just go to confirm the charge leveled against the book that, knowing where events are leading, the novel blames the victims for their failure to see and act. Failing to obey the Law, substituting a law of culture (a mere sentence or remark) for the Law of God, the Jews bring down the wrath of God upon them. The whole point of God's speaking to the people at Sinai, after all, was to prevent the lapse back into paganism, of which material secular culture is a modern version.

I will, in a moment, reverse the apparent implications of this thought. First, however, let me note one further element lending potential support to such arguments; namely, that the root for *wonder, destruction, waste—sho'ah*—does not appear just any place in the Old Testament. Rather it appears in a particular text having to do with divine punishment. Not incidentally, perhaps, this passage from Isaiah 6.9–12 accompanies Exodus 20.15 as the *Haftorah* in the weekly *Torah* reading in the synagogue:

> "Hear ye indeed, but understand not; / And see ye indeed, but perceive not. / Make the heart of this people fat, / And make their ears heavy, / And shut their eyes, / Lest they, seeing with their eyes, / And hearing with their ears, / And understanding with their heart, / Return, and be healed." / Then said I: "Lord, how long?" And He answered: / "Until cities *be waste* without inhabitant, / And houses without man, / And the land *become utterly waste,* / And the Lord have removed men far away, / And the forsaken places be many in the midst of the land."

I have already suggested that belatedness is not teleology. But I want to suggest further that if indeed an idea of teleology does circulate in this text, such a teleology is exactly not a human teleology (such as the book is being faulted for), but a divine one. Paradoxically, the existence of this other law, be it moral consciousness or divine decree, preserves rather than sacrifices our freedom as human beings. It also entails our moral responsibility. In other words, this other law prevents belatedness from becoming fused or confused with teleology, to which human beings have no access. By lifting the text up off the plane of the material world, *Badenheim* would raise, to leave open, just those questions concerning the relationship between divine omnipotence and human behavior, between God's love and His anger, and between this love and anger, on the one hand, and, on the other, His promises to the people. These are the questions that concern the paradoxical relationship between our embeddedness within material culture and our moral knowledge, which historical and ideological analysis would (to our peril) attempt to resolve.

In the particular case of Isaiah, as Alan Mintz has interpreted it, "the burden of Isaiah's prophecy is to reconstruct the faculty of hearing, to recreate the conditions under which the reality of divine speech regains plausibility" (43). Isaiah, in other words, for all its threat and warning, leads us back to the biblical moment, to which the rabbinic tradition attached it and which *Badenheim* may also be recalling: *maᶜamad sinai* (*standing at Sinai*). This moment captures the paradox of religious belief, in which the giving of the Law obliges obedience to the word in which is granted human freedom. The condition of the people's exodus from slavery to freedom is thus the prohibition against the construction of idols and images. It is the prohibition against self-enslavement to material culture. Sacrificing materiality, the people are able to see in a new way. This new way turns out to be the way of hearing, of language. Such a turn from seeing to hearing conveniently, for our purposes, turns out to bear more than a simple resemblance to the basic structure of Freudian psychoanalysis, as we shall see later. It also places us firmly on the terrain of literature as a form of telling and listening.

Hearing is the dominant mode of knowledge in our post-Sinai world, as in what is the best-known Jewish prayer, *shemaᶜ yisraʾel:* Hear O Israel. This is what God says to the people on Sinai; it is the prayer that observant Jews traditionally recite, when able, at the moment of their deaths (the prayer, as Appelfeld himself notes, that was heard from within the death camps and the crematoria); and it is what they say several times daily, especially in the most important of the prayers, the *ᶜamidah/standing.* The novella *1946,* originally published in the same volume with *Badenheim,* begins with a quotation from this prayer (*shanim veshaᶜot,* 107). Is the final paragraph of *Badenheim* perhaps a prayer?

Voice and Freedom

"Beginning with any text," writes Mikhail Bakhtin, "we always arrive . . . at the human voice, which is to say we come up against the human being" ("Forms of Time," 252–53). For several contemporary critics, a major trajectory of modern Jewish philosophy, extending from Martin Buber and Franz Rosenzweig to Emmanuel Levinas and Stanley Cavell, concerns the importance of voice.[25] This emphasis on voice is not a return to or endorsement of logocentricism or metaphysics. It is not mysticism. Rather, it locates what Cavell, in his own resistance to the deconstruction of consciousness, identifies as what we human beings, given all we cannot prove beyond a shadow of a doubt, *can know.* Such knowledge, as we have already seen, is not for Cavell factual, scientific knowledge of the quotidian world, such as Kafka's dog, Badenheim's sanitation workers, and other materialists pursue. Philosophical skepticism, in Cavell's view, poses questions to which we do not, finally, have answers. But to conclude, as have certain postmodernists, that, because we cannot know some things (like the existence of a chair or the exact nature of another person's pain), we cannot know anything—for example, what another person's words are asking of us—is, in Cavell's term, not a legitimate expression of our skepticism but, rather, our disowning of knowledge. If one postmodernist view of culture is based on the priority of written to oral language, and if, through this genealogy of consciousness, postmodernist thought commits itself to a radical skepticism in which consciousness itself is disseminated into material culture, then, in the view of Cavell and others, the force that resists this deconstruction of consciousness is voice.

For *Badenheim,* voice, which is the instrument of the divine, whose voice now resides in our words, is also the instrument of our human relations, by which we accept the claim made on us by other people's utterances. It is voice, rather than interpretation or explication either of events or of utterances, to which *Badenheim,* finally, gives expression. Indeed, considering how sketchily *Badenheim* presents the social dimensions of its world, it is astounding how many conversations it transcribes. It is one of the more painful aspects of this book that the characters rarely hear and respond to one another's words. This is as true of the Jewish characters in relation to each other as it is of the Nazis. But it is, of course, the Nazis' refusal to hear that produces the horror of the death camps. What did the Nazis have to refuse to hear in order to exterminate millions of people? I do not think that any of us, for a moment, can imagine that a small still voice did not speak within the souls of the murderers and whisper "no." But even if they did not hear a divine voice, or the voice of moral conscience, then surely they heard the purely human voices, which cried out, directly to them, in their purely human agony. Not being able to penetrate the invisibility of culture is not the same as putting people and their pain out of view, in ghettos and concentration camps and ovens.

By seeming to fail to preserve a space of indeterminacy, *Badenheim*, in Bernstein's view, alternately blames the Jews for their deaths *and* interprets their extermination, along with the subsequent establishment of the State of Israel, as inevitable. If the text is, as Bernstein feels, overdetermined, there is, as he implies, no blaming the Nazis. But *Badenheim does*, of course, blame the Nazis. And what it blames them for is both related to and different from that for which it also blames the Jews. From within this difference, which has to do with how both Nazis and Jews might, each within their own traditions, have heard and heeded moral law, is contained Appelfeld's "Zionism" (such as it is) and, more importantly, his faith.

In "Two Concepts of Liberty," Isaiah Berlin differentiates between negative freedom, the freedom from interference in the pursuits of our lives, which freedom society can either promote or hinder; and the (positive) freedom to realize our aspirations (write an opera, be a moral human being), which freedom can never be guaranteed.[26] Throughout his allegory, Appelfeld reminds his readers what it means to so immerse oneself in material culture as to forget the commandments delivered at Sinai. These commandments, as we shall see in greater depth later, cite not the positive freedom to do this or that but the negative freedom cast in the form of a series of "thou shalt nots": thou shalt not covet, thou shalt not murder. The Nazis failed to heed the voices both of their fellow human beings and of conscience, as inscribed in their own Christian culture, in German philosophy and literature (Kant, Kafka) and in the Bible. But by *shadowingforth* the very word of God (in whatever language), Appelfeld retrieves more than a reminder about what we "shall not" do in order to preserve other people's (negative) freedom. He retrieves the origins of our positive freedom in our perhaps innate, perhaps transmitted, knowledge that there is some transcendental, superhuman force (God is one name for this) that places us outside the circumscriptions of material culture.

Rabbi J. B. Soloveitchik puts it this way in one of his few, and perhaps his only, sustained reflections on the Holocaust. "One of the darkest enigmas with which Judaism has struggled from the very dawn of its existence," he begins his essay, "is the problem of suffering in the world."[27] In Judaism, he goes on to say, evil and suffering are to be neither rationalized away (denied or ignored) nor comprehended:

> Judaism, with its realistic approach to man and his place in the world, understood that evil cannot be blurred or camouflaged and that any attempt to downplay the extent of the contradiction and fragmentation to be found in reality will neither endow man with tranquility nor enable him to grasp the existential mystery. Evil is an undeniable fact. There is evil, there is suffering, there are hellish torments in this world. Whoever wishes to delude himself by diverting his attention from the deep fissure in reality, by romanticizing human existence, is naught but a fool

and a fantast. It is impossible to overcome the hideousness of evil through philosophico-speculative thought. (4)

Rather than be glossed over, even by intellectual discourse, evil and suffering are to be confronted and worked through. And it is the willingness to enter into this process of active confrontation, not with the theory of evil and suffering, but with its very real consequences, that provides Soloveitchik with the distinction, corresponding to Berlin's, between what Soloveitchik calls the "'I' of fate" and the "'I' of destiny."

"What is the nature of an existence of fate?" Soloveitchik asks.

> It is an existence of compulsion, . . . a purely factual existence, one link in a mechanical chain, devoid of meaning, direction, purpose, but subject to the forces of the environment into which the individual has been cast by providence, without any prior consultation. The "I" of fate has the image of an object. As an object he appears, as made and not as maker. He is fashioned by his passive encounter with an objective, external environment, as one object vis-à-vis another object. (2)

Opposed to this is "the nature of the existence of destiny," which is

> an active mode of existence, one wherein man confronts the environment into which he was thrown, possessed of an understanding of his uniqueness, of his special worth, of his freedom, and of his ability to struggle with his external circumstances without forfeiting either his independence or his selfhood. The motto of the "I" of destiny is, "Against your will you are born and against your will you die, but you live of your own free will." Man is born like an object, dies like an object, but possesses the ability to live like a subject, like a creator, an innovator, who can impress his own individual seal upon his life and can extricate himself from a mechanical type of existence and enter into a creative, active mode of being. Man's task in the world, according to Judaism, is to transform fate into destiny. (5–6)

It is not irrelevant to reading Appelfeld's novel that Soloveitchik's idea of destiny —in the Hebrew: *ye^{c}ud,* meaning, more precisely, *calling, mission,* or *purpose*— takes in national as well as personal calling. It is also pertinent that Soloveitchik cites as examples of the difference, on the national level, between fate and calling, the Israelites' exodus from Egypt, which was imposed on the people, as opposed to the giving of the law on Sinai, which was preceded by Moses' bringing God's word to the people and their actively consenting to receive it: "We will do and obey" (Exodus 24:7) (55). Indeed, the essay itself was written on the occasion of the eighth anniversary of the State of Israel and deals directly with the relationship between Israel and the Holocaust.

We may never be outside of the fate that often directs our lives, whether on the personal or the communal level. The Jews of Badenheim are not presented as having any choice as to what is about to happen to them: they are Jews being rounded up for extermination. And yet within that ring of fate they choose their words and actions. They choose the way in which they make their fate their own. In *Badenheim,* Appelfeld asserts the possibility of human freedom as, in

Soloveitchik's sense, the active assumption of responsibility for one's pain and suffering, however much that does *not* transform this pain and suffering into something else or deny their existence. At the same time, he also, by writing in Hebrew, retrieves the internal, uncoerced logic of a people choosing to live in and through its language and culture. This, I suggest, with nothing more expressly political in mind, is the expression of Appelfeld's Zionism. Only in our ability to be inside a culture and its language, fully participant both in the construction and interpretation of its words, can we achieve such positive freedom as exists. This condition of linguistic, which is to say moral, competence, might well have been achieved for the Jews in a foreign language, specifically in German, which is the language in which the events of the story presumably take place. This was certainly the hope and expectation of much of European Jewry from the Enlightenment on. But it was not to be.

Likely it is my different relationship to Zionism that, initially at least, prompted my disagreement with a critic like Bernstein. Yet Bernstein and I are fully agreed that an apologetics for the State of Israel, which condemns diaspora Jewry and devalues their experience, would be morally offensive. We also share the wish that Zionism be something more than the consequence of or a response to catastrophe. We would have Zionism express freedom, not fate. My point about Appelfeld's book is that it satisfies exactly these criteria. Through its strategy of *shadowingforth* and, equally important, through the text and language it chooses to employ in this *shadowingforth,* Appelfeld discovers the trace of that positive freedom to live the moral life that exists for all of us and that is contained in our particular cultural vocabularies and textual traditions and ways of thinking: for it is not enough to read this text in Hebrew; it requires as well a willingness to entertain, even if only momentarily, a theological or dialogic as opposed to a purely material idea of culture.

It is a part of our intellectual moment to be deeply skeptical of the objectivity and detachment of any one person's interpretation of anything, especially on the parts of those instruments of cultural expression, like literary texts, which we once assumed to be universal and timeless. None of us doubts that we are all already within the culture we would interpret, as much its product as any of the persons or events or objects we might choose to scrutinize. How, then, do we read literary texts against and over their bias, and our own? *Badenheim* insists that, whatever we can or cannot see in culture, we can listen. For just as *sho'ah* is there, from the beginning of the text as from the beginning of the experiences recorded there, to be seen or not, so it is with the biblical scene of the giving of the law. This scene is concealed within representations that the culture can no longer wholly read, hidden from it in its dissemination into culture. Yet in that dissemination, into language (spoken and written), it is still to be heard in that culture's every word of human exchange, even, or perhaps most especially, in the most everyday utterances of its most ordinary citizens.

Like all texts, *Badenheim* is entangled in the problem of ideology. As a Holocaust narrative, it proceeds against the background of ideologically sanctioned murder. As a Hebrew text, it evidences, even declares, the survival of the Jewish people, even, perhaps, the establishment of a Jewish state. Indeed, insofar as it argues for anything, it argues for the necessity of understanding material culture as a form of ideological engagement from which we can never stand wholly apart. But to read the text as a political or historical treatise and to position oneself accordingly, is not to hear what this text is saying. More importantly, perhaps, it is not to hear how it is saying it. More frighteningly, it is to enter into a repetition compulsion, to repeat just those contours of cultural engagement that the novel is holding up to view. It is precisely *not* to hear, specifically not to hear another's cry of pain. For in the stark minimalism of its representation (which is virtually biblical in quality), in its paring away of the world to reveal the words that conceptualize and give expression to human existence, *Badenheim* emits, even as it records, nothing less than this cry of pain, its own as well as that of its characters. It is this cry of pain that, above all, the text means for the reader to hear. Not to hear it is not to read this text.

3 Fear, Trembling, and the Pathway to God: *The Iron Tracks*

> [The] question is this: What condition must be created so that this or that mute phenomenon may begin to speak, to recount the pain and the accidents of, and the withdrawal into, its inaccessibility—which is to say, our pain at our inability to reach it? The symptom itself—constituted as a symbolic operation, seeking the text of a beyond inscribed within it—alludes to the work that, in the affected man, charts the suffering of its inability to speak.—Nicholas Abraham[1]

Like several other of Appelfeld's most memorable and affecting characters, including Bartfuss in *The Immortal Bartfuss* or the older Bruno in part two of *The Age of Wonders*—whom we shall meet shortly—Erwin Siegelbaum in *The Iron Tracks* is a survivor who has escaped death but not deathliness. His life, therefore, is afflicted by the unceasing torments of loss and what the text calls *ḥaradah,* anxiety and fear. Subject to intermittent bouts of melancholy and depression, Siegelbaum circles Europe by rail (hence the iron tracks of the title), supporting himself by collecting and selling Judaica, and driven forward by his secret mission: to murder the murderer of his parents, one Colonel Nachtigel. The novel traces Erwin's annual route, recording his impressions, memories, and especially his conversations with those individuals who are as much a part of his yearly routine as his journey itself. Some of these individuals are, like him, collecting the remnants of Judaic history in Europe; others are old friends and comrades of his parents; still others the local peasants (Jews, non-Jews, and partial Jews), who run the inns and drive the wagons that constitute his present reality. It is through Erwin's encounters, and the recollections that they inspire, that Appelfeld produces a picture of Eastern European Jewry, before and after the war.

There is no doubt that Erwin Siegelbaum is a textbook obsessive-compulsive: repressive, anxious, and deeply depressed. The iron tracks are internal as well as external. Erwin is, however, also a poet, for whom the world is alternately and sometimes simultaneously a revelation and a nightmare. Were it not for the poetry that pierces his despair with as much illuminating power as his desperation darkens his daily existence, it might be possible to concur with the following grim reading of the story by the writer J. M. Coetzee:

> Despite his ostensible confidence in the healing powers of art (which would make of him a simpler, less self-doubting writer than his master Kafka), the vision of

> the soul of the long-term Holocaust survivor that we get in Appelfeld's fiction remains bleak. Both Bartfuss in *The Immortal Bartfuss* and now Siegelbaum in *The Iron Tracks* are men who have cannily used the confusion of the postwar years to launch themselves to material success; yet in their mature years they find themselves living impoverished, affectless lives, driven by compulsions they do not understand. . . . Killing Nachtigel brings Siegelbaum no closer to release. In this respect, *The Iron Tracks* is a deeply pessimistic and even despairing book, the darkest that Appelfeld has written.[2]

To be sure, the iron tracks take Erwin Siegelbaum repeatedly over well-worn and painful territory, psychologically as well as spiritually: "I know my stations like the palm of my hand. I can reach them with my eyes closed. Years ago a night train skipped one of my stops, and my body stirred at once. I trust my body more than my mind. It detects the error on the spot" (11). "I have learned this route with my body," he tells us; "my route is fixed, more fixed every year. Imprinted on my body, it cannot be shaken" (3, 15). And indeed, his experience of the iron tracks is one of bodily suffering, continuously reinflicted. But the iron tracks are also what convey him from "dread" and "melancholy," which constantly threaten to overtake him (4), into life itself: not only the life of the past, contained in his memories and in the books and artifacts he lovingly recovers, but the life of the present, in the various people and places he encounters. En route he reports: "In marvelous little Herben . . . my regular driver Marcello awaits me on April fifth. When I see him from the train window, happiness rushes through me as if I were returning to my lost hometown. . . . Thus it is every year. And in this repetition lies a strange hopefulness. As if our end were not extinction but a sort of constant renewal." "The trains," Erwin proclaims, "make me free. Without them, what would I be in this world? An insect . . . a kind of human snail. . . . I board the train, and instantly I'm borne aloft on the wings of the wind" (4–5).

In this chapter, I examine *The Iron Tracks* from the twin perspectives of the pain and the poetry it records. Indeed, I will explore the connection between the two, and will conduct that exploration through a particular mode of reading, which, as I already began to indicate in Chapter 1, has recently become important to Holocaust studies, namely psychoanalytic criticism. As the already quoted passages from the book more than amply suggest, Erwin's bodily enactments (his repressive, obsessive behaviors, along the iron tracks) quite readily lend themselves to psychoanalytic interpretation.

Yet we must proceed carefully here. Appelfeld is not a glib, superficial writer who imagines that the extremities of suffering experienced by this or any other of his heroes (or of any human being, for that matter) can be so readily comprehended, or, even more outrageously, bandied into something like either aesthetic or intellectual conceit or pleasure. There are no cures, perhaps not even any satisfactory revelations, for the Holocaust survivor like Erwin. Whatever more comprehensible and familiar neuroses he may share with the rest of us, he clearly suffers as well, perhaps primarily, from a form of trauma quite unlike and in monstrous excess of ordinary human experience, even experiences of trauma. Indeed, as we shall see shortly, Erwin Siegelbaum embodies (quite literally) two different forms of psychological disturbance. These function in widely different ways, both within Erwin's own narrative and experience *and* within Appelfeld's text. A question with which we, as readers, must wrestle is what Appelfeld gains, indeed what he risks or sacrifices, by superimposing, one on the other, these two different layers of neurotic dysfunction. Might not the representation of his survivor protagonist as obsessive neurotic, whose repressions (as we shall see in a moment) have at least as much to do with his pre-Holocaust childhood as with the Holocaust itself, actually compromise the text's representation of the enormity and uniqueness of the Holocaust?

In fact, this question concerning *The Iron Tracks* sweeps back over the range of Appelfeld's fiction to raise similar problems concerning much of his writing. As we have already seen in *Badenheim,* many of Appelfeld's characters more than fit the antisemitic stereotypes assigned to them by the Nazis. As a consequence, some of his critics have leapt to condemn the writer himself for a form of, if not auto-antisemitism, then at least some measure of contempt for the victims of the European catastrophe. How, we might be prompted to ask, do Appelfeld's Jewish grotesques illuminate something about the event of the Holocaust without, simultaneously, suggesting reasons why the nations of Europe might justifiably have wanted to rid themselves of the Jews?

These are the questions I will be addressing in this chapter. Of course, Appelfeld, in describing with excruciating accuracy the experience of a single, particular human being, is likely not intending to offer any large, all-encompassing theory concerning pre- and post-Holocaust trauma and the Jew. He may not even be deliberately launching an interpretation of Jewish history. Yet here and elsewhere in his fiction, such interpretations readily follow from the text. They proceed directly from just that specificity of portraiture that emerges in the psychological dimensions of a character like Erwin, the very exactness of which permits the reader to glimpse and then to attempt to comprehend and sympathize with the familiar, recognizable psychological profiles of a human being in pain. As we shall see, it is of utmost importance in Appelfeld's fiction that individuals be accorded their individuality. This is one of the many things Nazism stole from the Jews, which Appelfeld would help to restore. So, let me say already, by way of preliminary response to the question of what *The Iron Tracks* gains by running certain interpretive risks, that it rehumanizes those who have been dehumanized, not only by the Holocaust but by subsequent interpretations of the Holocaust, which have tended toward large generalizations and sensationalistic descriptions. Simultaneously, it affords the possibility, without indulging in some sort of transcendentalizing negative sublime (such as Dominick LaCapra has described), of discovering what is to be glimpsed and maintained concerning the future of individuals and the collectivity after the catastrophe.

The Iron Tracks, we will discover, travels two different routes, both for the narrator, for whom the iron tracks are alternately deadening and inspirational, and even more so for the reader, who reads the two dimensions of the narrator's experience and is catapulted, as much by the language of the text as by its content, onto another track altogether. Indeed, the bifurcated autobiographical narrative that constitutes Erwin's text is further divided by the twofold nature of his obsessive-compulsive, anxiety-ridden neurosis. In addition to the repression produced by his childhood experiences (of which there are two primary varieties: a rather typical hysterical repression in relation to his father and a more abstracted, more difficult to define anxiety in relation to his mother), there is also the Holocaust trauma itself. This trauma, as if providing no memories to be repressed and re-enacted, is related more to his earlier anxieties in relation to his mother than to his repression concerning his father. It functions more as an objectless and irremediable focus of mourning, a rarified, absolute form of *ḥaradah* or dread, than as either repression or garden-variety anxiety proper. As readers, we travel two sets of doubled and redoubled tracks. One is Erwin's alternately repressed, alternately anxious autobiographical narrative, itself interrupted by the poetry and magic, which, despite himself, he experiences. The other is the fictional text called *The Iron Tracks.* Understanding how we are moved to travel both sets of tracks, and how we get from one to the other, is the task of reading this text.

We will discover that for Appelfeld, literature is veritably defined by the concept of "tracks" or, in the Hebrew, *mesilot.* These tracks, like any set of tracks, lead us some place, including to the other tracks of the other texts, which they (as in the case of *Badenheim*) recall. In this sense, Appelfeld's text, like any fictional work (or like the repressive neurosis of its protagonist), sets itself out to be interpreted by the reader, to be understood and translated into other words. Yet just as Erwin rides the same rails year in and year out to no other place but the origins and repetition of those tracks and their trajectory, so too does the text travel a circuit, which is the return ever unto itself. As in *Badenheim,* there is no arrival at a somewhere else that is either the clarification of inherent meanings or a breakthrough to transcendent ones. In this way, *The Iron Tracks,* again like *Badenheim,* performs its definition of the literary text as the material density of the text itself, with all its evocations and allusions and affects, which we interpret only at the peril of loosening its fabric and destroying it. How to read, not critically, but affectively, acknowledging rather than interpreting the text is the challenge, and the instruction, provided by the novel.

To comprehend this process, and thereby to travel with this text's language to its places of freedom and even faith, we need first to travel the tracks laid out for us by the iron rail of the narrator's repression and his anxiety—the *mesilah* constituted by his psychological *ḥaradah,* which by the end of the text become some other kind of *mesilah* leading to some other kind of *ḥaradah* altogether—the *ḥaradah* of faith that follows a *mesilah* to God. Not incidentally, the first track of the first iron rail, by which we will eventually arrive, through Appelfeld's novel, at freedom and faith, is informed by two other lesser faiths, inadequately comprehended and cruelly inflicted on others, of which Nazism is only the slightly more savage of the two. I begin with the iron track of Erwin's repression of his childhood, pertaining both to his father and his mother, and to the Communist faith the two of them shared.

The Iron Tracks of Repression and Political Faith: The Father's Son in the Father's Language

The son of devoted Communists, Erwin (like many of Appelfeld's child protagonists) lives an orphan's abandonment even before the murder of his parents at the hands of the Nazis. It is difficult, therefore, to determine whether his obsessive behavior, focused on his intended murder of the man who murdered his parents, is motivated entirely by their deaths. It may very well enact a suppressed rage against those very parents whom Nachtigel has killed. In this superimposition of murder on top of a prior Jewish self-hatred and blindness, the book repeats an important ambivalence already embodied in *Badenheim*. Although the Jews are viciously slaughtered by a force beyond anyone's ability to comprehend, let alone foresee and prevent it, nonetheless the orphaned child might well feel himself negligently abandoned to his fate by parents who ought (from the child's perspective) to have been able to protect him.

The criticism of *Badenheim* unfairly exploits the novel's pained protest against the parents' generation in order to accuse the book of being a plank in the author's presumed Zionistic, ideological warfare against European Jewry. But the text's refusal to let go the issue of how the Jews let this happen is nothing less than its honest confrontation with the inheritance of Jewish history by the children who only barely survived the catastrophe. Do children not have the right to this anger against their parents? For a child, the death of a parent—even, or especially, a loving and beloved parent—might well come to seem an act of neglect not outside the parent's control. Certainly Erwin's mother's withdrawal into depression and his father's occasional and casual attentiveness to him throughout his childhood make a case for understanding the hero's responses to his orphanhood as not exclusively to the horror of the camps and the annihilation they entailed.

The father's language of political activism also provides the strong basis for understanding Erwin's actions in the course of the narrative as not solely a response to the murderous politics of fascism but to the prior politics of Communism as well. As in other of his writings, the author does anything but idealize the victims of the Nazi atrocities, who emerge, some of them, as themselves abusive fanatics and self-blinded worshippers of their own extremely faulty truths. At the same time, he also does not withdraw his sympathy from these individuals any more than he does from the bewildered band of vacationers in *Badenheim*. Throughout the story, despite his full awareness of the abuses perpetrated by the Communist movement, Erwin's parents and the other Communists whom Erwin meets on his travels receive the author's full sympathy, sometimes even his admiration. The power of Appelfeld's text is inextricably wrapped up in the power of this sympathy, which coexists, in some degree of palpable torment, with the author's severe judgment on these movements. Here, as in *Badenheim, The Age of Wonders,* and *Tzili,* ideological commitments, however well intentioned, distort and destroy, not least of all the children born into a world of impossible choices.

Whatever our view of Erwin's parents' politics, by any standards this is a dysfunctional family, even though Erwin, more like the child protagonist Bruno in *The Age of Wonders* than Tzili, is a loved child, less well educated than Bruno, yet far more clever than Tzili. In the expanse of his fictional range, Appelfeld rarely duplicates himself. Rather, he produces suggestive overlappings, which construct something like a generalized socio-psycho-history of European Jewish life before the war. In this mapping of Jewish existence, the Siegelbaums epitomize the turn of Jewish intellectuals to the Communist party, which becomes for them a faith far more powerful and commanding than the Judaism they left behind. It also turns out to be far more destructive.

In a sequence that begins with Erwin's uttering a version of the statement that informs a whole range of Appelfeld's text (we'll confront this statement again in *The Age of Wonders* and *Tzili*, where it will move to the center of our discussion)—*man is not an insect*—the power of this faith, and its disastrous consequences, not only for the Jews as a people but for individual Jews like Erwin himself, are clearly delineated, albeit in terms that likely exceed Erwin's grasp. Erwin's comment reverses that of the other texts. "Man is an insect," he insists (153). He is driven to say this by his just having heard a tavern owner utter the name of his parents' murderer. "Whenever I hear Nachtigel's name," Erwin confesses, "my arms go limp, and I am afraid I won't be up to doing the deed. I feel the same weakness in my nightmares" (152). The scene continues as follows:

> The tavern owner widened his eyes. . . .
>
> "Man's a monster, don't you know that?"
>
> That coarse sentence summons up for me, out of nowhere, my father's face. Father used to say, "Conditions corrupt, exploitation corrupts. Remove those obstacles, and man will be revealed to you in all his glory." Even in the labor camp, bent over and reviled, he did not repudiate his faith. Once when he said, "Not even in hell will I deny my faith in man," one of the prisoners, a ruffian, approached him and slapped him in the face to remind him that the Communists had burned down his cement block factory. (153)

Ostensibly it is his suddenly thinking about Nachtigel that causes Erwin to blurt out that man is an insect. His comment seems to reflect his judgment on the Nazis and thus (as in other of Appelfeld's texts) to reverse Nazi rhetoric concerning the Jews as bugs and vermin—a rhetoric that is immediately introduced into the text through the tavern owner's statement that man is a monster. But the tavern owner does not mean by this that the Jews in particular are monsters. Quite the contrary: he is at this moment referring to the local peasants. It is exactly for this reason that his rhetoric exposes the danger of Erwin's own statement. To see human beings as insects and monsters is to expose them to the further danger of being treated as such. Whatever else Erwin's father may be guilty of, he is not guilty of this dehumanization of his fellow human beings.

But Erwin's feeling himself go limp, his experiencing of himself as unable (as it were) to act like a man, exactly does not reverse but, rather, realizes or enacts the overriding assumption of Nazis like Nachtigel that the Jews were somehow less than human. "Without cigarettes I'm not a man," Erwin says at another moment in the text; "if a woman scolds me for smoking in bed, I get rid of her" (24). And even though he remembers in the tavern his father's faith that human beings are *not* monsters, nonetheless his father's face floating into consciousness at just this moment may suggest that Erwin experiences his own father as something of a monster, who produces impotence and limpness in his son. These affects are responses both to the towering model that the father embodies *and* to the failure of that model, since the father, too, proves powerless before the Nazi annihilation. He can save neither himself nor his son and wife. "Bent over and reviled," his father certainly replicates the son's own feelings of inadequacy. At the same time, his insistence on his faith when there is literally no way of acting on it both produces a pressure on the son to make good the father's faith *and* demonstrates to him its hopelessness.

Such an interpretation of the father on the part of the son is not out of keeping with the child's bewilderment at being dragged, before the war, from one place to another and entrusted into the care of individuals who have no concern for him at all. Both incapable of living up to his father's expectations and resentful of his fanaticism, Erwin is in every way his father's son. He is compelled, despite his unacknowledged anger, to carry on, inadequately, his father's mission. Thus he is doomed to the same frustration and failure that his father experienced. The slap on the face that the father receives in the work camp not only validates the truth of human monstrousness but, insofar as the father does not strike back, also places the father in the same position of unmanly vulnerability as the son. (The moment recalls what many commentators have interpreted as a central moment in Freud's own relationship to Judaism and his father: the moment, as narrated to him by his father, when his father refuses to react to and defend himself against his humiliation at the hands of an anti-semite.)

It is no accident, therefore, that at the moment Erwin later approaches the house of the man he is about to murder, he is

> remind[ed] of the days when my parents were alive, and I was shuttled back and forth between them like a defenseless animal. When I was under my father's care, I was entirely his, and even when I wasn't, I wanted to be with him. (167)

And further on in the text:

> In Nachtigel's house no light was lit. I felt that the dread that had oppressed me during the past weeks had subsided inside me. As in the days of my youth, I was prepared to suffer, but I didn't know what the nature of the suffering was to be. For some reason I saw myself running for my life, seeking shelter like my father in the houses of peasants. (170)

Feeling defenseless and weak, and identifying that sense of helplessness both with his father's treatment of him and with his father's own vulnerability, what finally gets Erwin to pull the trigger is Nachtigel's "gesture" of raising his hand to wave goodbye: "[It] reminded me of Nachtigel's comradeship with his young subordinates in the camp, and the warm paternal care he used to shower on them. He treated them like a father, and within a short time he made them as cruel as he was" (179). In the Hebrew text, what is translated as "warm paternal care" is expressed only as "friendship." Nonetheless in the Hebrew, too, Nachtigel is said to treat his soldiers "as a father" ("and an older brother"), thus producing an image of Nachtigel bizarrely linked to the idea of fatherhood and family. Quite deliberately, the story produces the possibility that Erwin's actions are also dictated by the behavior of his own father rather than exclusively by the tragedy that befell them both. Even as a child, Erwin knew no other life than the one of travel he now continues to enact, governed not by a specific destination but by a mission, which ultimately failed, and which the child could in no way understand. For all his claims to the contrary, his father may not have understood his own life on the rails any better than his son.

More oppressive still than Erwin's repetition of his father's and his father's generation's fanaticism is the symmetry between the Communists and the Nazis, which is established by the repetition of the word *faith* (in the Hebrew as well as the English) in relation to both of them. This is so in the passage above concerning Erwin's father. It appears as well in the following description of Comrade Stark:

> On May Day we, the dispersed, gather here, some by train and some on foot, not more than ten. For a moment we bring to life what was and is no more.
>
> Stark has aged. But on May Day he swallows two or three drinks, girds his loins, and goes forth to wrestle with ghosts and melancholy. He used to speak a lot about the future, about change and conquest. Now he speaks of the glories of the past, of the leaders who sacrificed their souls for their faith. (40–41)

In the original Hebrew text, the word for "ten" is *minyan* (25), the quorum of ten men required in Judaism for saying certain group prayers and reading the Torah in the synagogue, thus transforming May Day into something of a secular Jewish holiday. This connection is repeated later, when Erwin tells us that "[i]n the first years after the war, people gather from all over and stay in Stark's cabin. There were about ten of us [a *minyan* in the original, 28]. . . . As always . . . there were those of little faith" (45–46).

But if the actions of the Communists past and present (including Erwin's father) are governed by a faith, so are those of Nachtigel: "faith that the extermination of the Jews would bring relief to the world." "You also believed"? Erwin asks his interlocutor, who served under Nachtigel. "Certainly," he responds. "Without belief, you don't kill" (157). Or as another of the text's Nazis puts it, "We killed Jews. It was dreadful work, but very necessary. Work that brought relief to the soul. True, at first you were repelled by the screams, but little by little you learned that you were doing something important. . . . [It] was an exhausting mission, a dirty mission, but we did our duty to the end" (140).[3] This symmetry between the faith of the Communists and the Nazis that, through devastation and death, they would save civilization is further intensified by the fact that, despite there being many Jewish Communists, the Communists, like the Nazis, also specially targeted the Jews for victimization.

In the final analysis, it is difficult to separate completely Erwin's murder of Nachtigel from the other murders that abound in this story: he shoots him in the back twice, as if he is murdering more than this individual, as if this is more than the single murder of Nachtigel by Erwin but a composite of all the preceding murders that this one repeats. "Extermination of the Jews," we are told, "was a great task, a historical mission" (158); "a great mission" (15), an "exhausting . . . dirty mission" (140). It doesn't help much that Erwin's mission is designated by Stark, one of the Communists who worked with his father, as a "*mitzvah*" [in the Hebrew], a "commandment" rather than a "*mesimah*" (literally the word for mission), which is the word the Hebrew text uses for the Nazi assault against the Jews (the English translates "commandment" as "mission" [44 in the English, 27 in the Hebrew]).

Stark's word *commandment* only restores to the other missions in the text the religious dimension they all assume but to which they do not wholly confess. "Agent Murtschik," Erwin informs us,

> used to talk about the Jews' duty to execute the murderers and to purge the world of its sins. Once he even told me that a religious man was obliged to carry out the sentence—for had the Jews not brought the religion of truth into the world? (170)

It isn't that Erwin doesn't know to be skeptical of this logic:

> Those sayings, which he would repeat in many languages, sounded inflated and unpleasant to me. Besides, I suspected he was trying to flatter me so I would pay him more. (170–71)

Indeed, on one of the few occasions in the text when Erwin overcomes his "muteness," it is to cite the commandment against murder (the English translates *it is forbidden to murder* as "it is forbidden to kill" [157]). "Once he revealed his hidden desire to me," Erwin communicates in relation to another of the many unreformed Nazis he meets on his travels, "I ought to have killed him. There is nothing simpler than killing a man, and yet for some reason, I cannot do it" (15). Erwin would obey the commandment not to murder. Nonetheless, and quite to his own irreparable distress, he is compelled to obey instead the deeper command that violates that commandment: the political faith of the father whom he worships and who holds him prey to his own political passions. "I'm tracking down the murderer Nachtigel," Erwin informs his father's friend Stark, speaking in what he senses to be a "voice not my own" (44). "I spoke with fervor, in words that weren't my own," he records at another moment, when he is defending his parents against the disdain of a couple who were the victims of his parents' political fanaticism (53). And when he "scolds" another acquaintance for becoming addicted to fantasies, Erwin "tremble[s]" at words which "were his father's words, he used to recite them to me" (75).

We will confront the problem of encrypted trauma and its ventriloquism more explicitly later on. Let me say at this point, however, that what is important here is not only the way in which Erwin is completing his father's life through the father's internalized injunctions, but the way in which the trail of murder, borne along the iron track, represents not only his deep repression of his father but his father's repressive behavior as well. "I spent most of the months with my father on trains," says Erwin, "in third class, of course" (57), which is why Erwin insists on going first class. Yet first class or third, the tracks are the same. And these tracks, Erwin already knows, without being able to do anything about it, have caused much suffering, especially to the Jews who had been the special targets of even his father's political activism (57).

Erwin and his mother, if not intentionally neglected, were nonetheless also sacrificed on the altar of the father's beliefs. Erwin himself is "a kind of appendage to his mission" (49). Like the artist fathers in *The Age of Wonders* and in a more recent novel *kol asher ahavti* [hereafter, *All That I Have Loved*], the father in *The Iron Tracks* loves the son. He is, however, simply too preoccupied with his own pain to see the child's. Nor can he fathom that, in enacting his revenge against the world through his politics (as the other fathers do through their art), he is bequeathing to his son just that anger and sense of alienation that is his own doomed and damning obsession.

The final words of the text, therefore, can be understood as delivering a verdict, not only on Erwin's mission, but on all the other missions and faiths that he compulsively, obsessively repeats: "As in all my clear and drawn-out nightmares, I saw the sea of darkness, and I knew that my deeds had neither dedication nor beauty. I had done everything out of compulsion, clumsily, and always too late" (195). What human deed of murder, we are prompted to ask, has dedication or beauty? When is it not committed out of compulsion, clumsily, and too late? We may, at times, have to kill, but killing is not murder. The Communists and Nazis and finally Erwin expect of such acts of justice or revenge something like grace or salvation. This is something that murder, probably even killing, cannot, and ought not, to provide.

Repression and Anxiety: The Mother's Son in the Mother's Tongue

In Erwin's own formulation, he is "a creature of the tracks" (130). And like all creatures, human and animal, his actions are not always choices. Often they are compulsions to which he is driven by forces beyond his conscious control or even perception. "Every time the whip lands on my back," he records, "I board a train and flee. Only a railroad car with its rhythmic vibrations has the power to sooth me and put me to sleep" (30). Significantly, this statement concerning the vehicle that will deliver Erwin into the murder to which he has committed himself appears in the context of a different murder, which he is at the moment fleeing. That is the murder of the Communist Rollman. He repeats this contextualization twice: "Right after Rollman's murder," he tells us, "I boarded a train and fled north" (30). "After Rollman's death my body shrank as during the war. I went from train to train. . . . certain that when I used up the dollars that were sewn in the lining of my coat, my life would end" (36). Even though the trains deliver Erwin into active political life, they also embody an escape. This escape also has origins in the past, specifically in the child's escape from the mother. To add irony to irony, this flight away from the mother into oblivion and sleep also mimics the mother's own withdrawal from political activism, which was also, like Erwin's after Rollman's death, an escape from murder.

As his father's son, Erwin has contempt for his mother's abandonment of her politics. "I was sure that she was wasting her time on nothing," says Erwin, "avenging herself on Father. I was sure that she no longer believed in reforming society. Her silence stifled me. I would flee the house, roam the streets, and take up with the Ruthenian boys. . . . When father came to take me, I didn't kiss her on the forehead but ran to him, as if fleeing an oppressive place" (142–43). Yet his flight from her re-enacts the basic rhythm of her as of his father's life. This repetition of the mother, although it takes the form of hysterical anxiety rather than obsessive-compulsive political activism (as is the case with the father) is also a part of the protagonist's repressed neurotic self-expression.

Yet there is a crucial difference between Erwin's repression of his father and his repression of his mother. On the psychobiographical level, this has to do with the different kinds of materials being repressed. On the textual level, it concerns the difference between the repressions, which characterize the life of this, like every other, individual, and the specific and unique trauma, which is the experience that differentiates his life from that of most other human beings, the experience of the Holocaust. Repression and trauma are two different psychological phenomena. Psychobiographically, they lead to different consequences. Literarily, they point to different textual—historical and cultural—interpretations.

At the juncture between repression and trauma, between the psychobiography of this one individual and the history of the Jews, Appelfeld carefully, cautiously, lovingly places the mother. It is the mother, as we shall see, who ineluctably delivers Erwin and his narrative from the dead and deadening track traveled by his own life story to the more lyrical, poetic, and finally religious, kabbalistic track constructed by the text itself. The mother in *The Iron Tracks*, as in much of Appelfeld's fiction, is related to what seem initially to be two contrary forces: poetry, on the one hand (which includes, as well, other literary and religious texts), and, on the other, the muteness that would seem to be, but is to be utterly differentiated from, the silence of repression and traumatic reenactment.

Here we must recall the distinction between repression and trauma that I presented in Chapter 1. Though at some point repression and trauma shade into each other and are not wholly distinguishable, nonetheless repression is more a form of not-remembering events than the absence of memory altogether. In other words, in repression events that have occurred in the past are, typically, re-enacted, physically, bodily, in the present, with little conscious awareness on the part of the enactor of the why and what of the enactment. Trauma, on the other hand, occurs in the absence of memories to be thus repressed. It represents what one might think of as a limit-case of repression, in which memory must be evoked in its almost literal absence, or in which some other way of apprehending the past, other than memory, has to be employed.

For the most part, Erwin's obsessive-compulsive behavior, which represses and repeats the logic of his father's life with its own repression and repetitions, belongs to the realm of ordinary repressive behavior. As such, it occurs within the registers of the intellectual and verbal life, with its political and social commitments (like Communism and fascism, for example). It is also, presumably, subject to ordinary translation and interpretation from the bodily to the verbal. What Erwin needs to do to understand this dimension of his travels on the train is exactly what we as readers do: dig back into his childhood and recover the relationship to the father that underlies his behavior. And he needs to bring that relationship to consciousness, in words. This is the ordinary psychoanalytic situation with which we are all familiar.

Erwin's repetition of the mother works differently. On the one hand, it requires some of the same self-clarification and rendering conscious of what is not now within the realm of consciousness. Yet as a repetition of withdrawal into silence, characterized by anxiety and dread, his re-enactment of his mother is less susceptible of verbal translation from unconscious into conscious terms. Not for naught is this aspect of Erwin's personality related to his mother, since it belongs, as it were, to an earlier, preverbal stage of psychosexual development, a stage of pure affect or feeling, with the potential for, and rudimentary instruments of, speech, but without speech itself. It is, to appropriate the French feminist/Lacanian vocabulary for this, before Erwin has made himself subject to the law of the Father, before he has acquired symbolic, which is to say verbal, consciousness.

This shift backward to the pre-Oedipal moment is an important move in Appelfeld's text, which links up directly with the larger subject of Holocaust trauma. The most wholly developed figure within the novel for this state of trauma, which simultaneously shifts it to another register altogether and removes it from the provinces of normal psychosexual development, is Wirblbahn. This is where Erwin's yearly route begins and ends. It is the site of his traumatic post-Holocaust entry back into life.

I will discuss this scene shortly. For now, let me say only that it is no more incidental to the story's workings that Appelfeld has Erwin call this the place of his "strange" "rebirth" than the fact that his anxiety in general is linked to the mother (13). In calling his survival a *rebirth,* the text is not being exclusively ironic or perverse, though it is being that as well. Appelfeld knows all too well that the life the Holocaust snuffed out is never to be recovered. Yet, in odd and terrifying and nonetheless strangely inspiring ways, Wirblbahn *is* a place of rebirth. It is therefore linked to the maternal and to what every man and woman must experience as the birth from nothingness into life and language. None of us chooses the terms of our birth, yet born we are. None of us knows how to speak until we move from being speechless to mastering speech. A major informing narrative in Appelfeld's autobiography and other of his writings is how the orphaned child makes an alien and largely uncivilized, natural world a home and how he there acquires a new mother tongue. This new language, as Appelfeld makes clear in his autobiography, is not Hebrew per se but rather the language of fiction.

But I anticipate myself. The Erwin of *The Iron Tracks* isn't yet ready to learn to speak. He first has to recognize himself born. He has to experience his birth as a birth. And we, the witnesses of that birth, have to listen, not in order to clarify and render conscious and in words one repressed behavior or another, but rather to acknowledge affectively and validate a set of feelings, for which (whether they are grounded in fact or not) there literally are no words. How one does this *in* words is part of the challenge the novel sets for itself. How does one say things that almost defy saying—such as the fact that Erwin's experience at Wirblbahn is, for all its pain and horror, a rebirth after all?

From the opening chapter of the novel, we are made aware of the "dread" (4, 25, 83, 110, 125) and "melancholy" (43, 106) that accompany the narrator along his travels, in particular in relation to his planned murder of Nachtigel (125); feelings of dizziness and torment (32), restlessness and dismay (46), which only drink and sleep can alleviate. "When melancholy attacks me . . . I must drug it immediately. Sometimes I have no alternative but to down a whole bottle. I get drunk and crumple like a sack" (85). This terror, as I have suggested, is the mother's disease, which Erwin inherits along with the father's response to it:

> [F]rom time to time, I am oppressed by sudden fear, inexplicable revulsion. These moods, or whatever you want to call them, used to paralyze me. More than once I have locked myself away in a remote hotel because life suddenly seemed dark and without purpose. The winter in these regions is gray and long, and in the morning it is too depressing to get up. Once I spent two weeks in bed because it seemed to me that a new war had begun. A confession: I like to sleep during the day better than at night. The thought that the world is frantically going about its business while I doze in a big bed, wrapped in three soft blankets, is charged with a hint of revenge.
>
> Over the years I've learned to master some of my fears. Today I get up and without hesitation step over to the sink and begin to shave. Shaving, I have learned, is an activity that arouses optimism. Time at the sink restores the desire for travel and the memory of gliding on wheels. The minute I step onto a train, my life opens up, and I walk upon solid ground. (8)

Identifying with the masculine activities of the father, including the father's own cycling of the rails, Erwin's travels do temporarily keep dread at bay. Whirling through space and time, he stands on solid ground. But only temporarily, for, associated as it is both with revenge (which is how Erwin interprets his mother's withdrawal into silence) and with childlike comfort (his mother, he tells us elsewhere, used to wrap him in three soft blankets—49), Erwin's travels are also an escape *to* the mother. Erwin repeats his mother's own anxiety and dread even as, in distancing himself from her through the trains, he opposes and resists them.

For Erwin, the father's political activism is completely comprehensible. Therefore, even though he may not be fully conscious of the degree to which he continues to re-enact it, he is under little confusion as to what it is. Hence his sustained interest in and involvement with his father's cronies in the Communist party. Concerning the mother and what the text repeatedly refers to as her silence or muteness, Erwin is less certain. Thus, he brings to his relationship to his mother's memory not only her anxiety, which manifests itself in her self-destructive withdrawal from the world, but his own anxiety concerning that withdrawal, which is also her withdrawal from him. As in repressive behavior classically defined, he both represses the mother and anxiously tries to keep her in mind.

Therefore, embarking on the father's course of action, Erwin imagines his own fate as not so different from that of his mother, who, he informs us, was "killing herself day by day in her room" (35). He, too, he is convinced, will be killed as a result of the assassination of Nachtigel (181). This makes of his homicidal intention a form of suicidal longing. It brings together in one catastrophic unit both his mother's and his father's life-(or rather, death-) principles. Indeed, returning Erwin to his own childhood responses to his mother's despair, which was to join the father on his missions, Erwin throughout his travels fluctuates between the depths of dread and melancholy and the strength of his political convictions. He shuttles back and forth between these emotions, as once he shuttled back and forth between his mother and father (167), or, for that matter, now shuttles on with the motion of the train. "Afraid" of his mother's "silence" (48), which had so come to dominate her existence that even the conversations between him and her, as between her and her friend Mina, became, we are told, completely "silent" (36), Erwin came to prefer being "handed over to [his] father's custody . . . [dragged] from meeting to meeting and from gathering to gathering" (49; cf. 167). Either way, his journey is escapist and suicidal. No matter which parent he repeats, he betrays the other, and in this betrayal he repeats their betrayal of him and of each other. He also reconstructs the dead end to which the two of them have delivered him, in which neither the withdrawal from the political life nor its active engagement promises anything more than one variety or another of repression, or anxiety, or both. Political activism and the withdrawal into silence promise the same suicidal self-destructiveness.

Yet there is a difference between Erwin's repression of the father and his repression of and anxiety concerning the mother. Potentially at least, this difference might deliver him to a different conclusion, as indeed, if we read the contours of the text this way, it manages to deliver us, the readers. Through his father's political activism, we are told, Erwin learns to speak not only the many languages his father teaches him, including Ruthenian, but also the language of political activism itself. This is why Erwin's primary mission is not to recover European Jewry's Judaic relics (which, as we shall see, are linked to the mother), but to murder Nachtigel. The murder is precisely what prevents him from taking pleasure in his life. It also keeps him from reading the text of his own recovery, which (as we shall also see) is transcribed in the books of Kabbalah and Jewish learning he is so avidly collecting.

Erwin's father is nothing if not vocal. He is constantly reiterating his philosophy, even at moments of extremity, when he is rejected by his compatriots and when he is finally delivered to the camps. But, in this post-Holocaust world, the father's political discourse, which has failed and failed miserably, has nothing to teach Erwin. More to the point, it contains nothing to assuage his pain. It is rather his mother's more tentative and occasional breaking of her silence in the language of poetry that provides a language Erwin might learn. It also identifies the text's own mode of speaking.

"My mother had imparted the German language to me with all its subtleties in poetry and prose," Erwin tells us. "Her loyalty to that language was no less than her loyalty to Communism. At night, before going to sleep, she would read me poems by Heine. I doubt that I understood anything. But the sounds flowed softly into my ears. I would be cut loose from the waking world and slip into deep sleep. Even in difficult times, when she grew morose, swallowing drink after drink, she would pick up a book and read, like someone preparing for better times" (35). On the occasions when his mother would "overcome her silence" she would, with a "surge of affection," "cover [him] with three blue blankets" (49)—the source of those blankets with which Erwin covers himself on the train (8); "my mother spoke little, but the few words that came from her mouth filled my heart" (48).

On the one hand, his mother's silence terrifies him. For this reason, he cannot attach himself to the woman he comes to love immediately after the war, who is from the first associated with the mother's muteness. Bella, he tells us, was "a mute flower adrift in a polluted sea." "Sleep" is her "language," "silence" its mode of expression (18–19). "Afraid of her muteness" and the "madness trapped within her," which her muteness signifies (25), Erwin, in leaving Bella, flees as well the feared silence of the mother and her madness. "It was spring," he explains, in a form of unconscious free association provoked by Bella, "and I was reminded of another spring. The long war years had erased scenes of home from my mind" (20). On the other hand, however, the mother's muteness is the language of her love and care of him and thus a very part of his own erotic desire. Of Bertha, the woman he once wanted to marry, he says that "he learned to love her body and to honor her silences" (69). And of Bella, who is the mother incarnate, he says: "only with Bella did I know true silence. Today I know there is much pretense in talk. Only a quiet person earns my faith" (22).

Faith is exactly the right word for Erwin to use at this moment in the text. Just as he is drawn to and repelled by the mother's silence, so from the beginning Erwin Siegelbaum's crisis has been a crisis of faith—faith in his father and in his mother, as well as in the faiths that defined their own convictions. As the narrative nears its conclusion, these two faiths come to dominate Erwin's consciousness. There is his father's "faith," which was "bound . . . together with his practicality" and which "until his last day he refused to . . . untie"; and his mother's "faith," which is linked to her "despair" and is expressed in her "muteness." Though it is his father's faith that presides over the scene of the murder ("it was as if we had never parted," Erwin tells us, as he approaches the moment of confrontation with Nachtigel), nonetheless, as he nears the end of his mission, Erwin "[feels his] mother's muteness more and more" (167). The path, or in Hebrew *mesilah,* proffered by the mother's faith, the alternative to the *mesilat barzel* of the father's political faith, has more than a little to do with faith in the more ordinary religious sense. It is Erwin's maternal grandfather who is the figure for religious Orthodoxy in this text (54–56). He is also, like Appelfeld's literal maternal grandfather as described in *The Story of a Life,* an embodiment of silence. There is, described in the very books that Erwin has in his possession, but which he can still not fully read (his Aramaic and Hebrew, he tells us, are very rudimentary), the *mesilat elohim*—pathway of God—of faith itself.

To gain this, the other track of Erwin's mental landscape, which leads us, though not him, into the other track that is Appelfeld's text, we need first to pass through the experience that differentiates Erwin's life from that of any other human being growing up the child of parents who are themselves involved in crises and repression: the experience of the Holocaust. It is this trauma that delivers him to a *ḥaradah* of such exaggerated dimensions that it is by no means clear how it might even begin to be contained within the contours of a single psychic life. The central figure for the Holocaust, as well as for the *ḥaradah* that it inspires, is, as I have already noted, the town of Wirblbahn. This is where Erwin begins and ends each year's travels. At the end of the narrative, in a moment of both personal venom and righteous wrath, it is the place he would, in some imitation of the *sho'ah* itself, burn down and utterly annihilate.

Trauma and the Unstoried Past

My omission thus far of the scene of Wirblbahn replicates an important feature of Appelfeld's corpus as a whole: its refusal, until his recently published *Ice Mine,* to depict the experience of the ghettos and the camps directly. This silence or muteness concerning the Holocaust can and has been understood in many ways. What I want to put at the center of my own reading of *The Iron Tracks* is the idea that, for Appelfeld, the Holocaust figures a past that cannot be represented, not because it is so repressed as to be beyond the power of words to retrieve it, or because there are no words commensurate with what transpired in Auschwitz and elsewhere that the events might be described, but rather because the experience itself of catastrophe does not exist in the same way that other experiences of the past exist, on the level of verbalizable memory, to be either consciously recalled or repressed or otherwise reconstructed or reenacted.[4] In this novel of tracks, Wirblbahn—*wirbel* meaning whirlpool in German, *bahn,* track—represents a different kind of track altogether, or more accurately, perhaps, a tracklessness, precluding tracking.

The following is the passage that describes the moment of Erwin's rebirth at Wirblbahn. It is, perhaps, the central passage in the text:

> Every time I leave this place or return, anxiety seizes me. . . . Because of this anxiety, and for other reasons, I have sought to change the starting point of my journey. Until now I've been unable to do so. I will explain: in flat Wirblbahn, which is nothing more than a row of warehouses, a few watchmen's huts, and a wretched inn, in this accursed place, my life ended and I was reborn. The Germans brought our train to this remote station and left us here. For three days we had been bolted inside. On the third day, the train stopped moving. The wings of death had departed, but we didn't know it. We were already captive to visions of death. The next morning someone released the bolt, and a stream of light washed over us. That was our return to life. I still feel the light on my body. As of that morning my strange new life began. Sometimes it seems that everything springs from that morning. Neither death nor rebirth is glorious. That morning the people were not joyful. They remained where they were.
>
> For me Wirblbahn is a mute chapter. A believer makes his lips speak in any situation. But paralysis grips me every time I remember that return to life. . . . Wirblbahn is a wound that won't heal. . . . a wound that lurks in secret and suddenly flares up. I was certain that it was my dormant ulcer, but in recent years I've discovered that the memory of Wirblbahn is what causes this pain in my stomach to grow stronger. . . . Nevertheless, I am compelled to return here every year. (12–14)

As the text makes clear, in some ways Wirblbahn is nothing more than a figure for the text as a whole, which is to say, a figure for the narrator's entire life and story. Wirblbahn is a "wound that won't heal," such that the narrator is "compelled to return" each year in some desperate and perpetually failed attempt, finally, to comprehend and work through his pain. But what is repeated in this return to the moment of his rebirth is not life but the opposite of life. It is the death or paralysis that gripped him and the other survivors at the time, an extinction of consciousness that leaves them suspended between life and death, at the moment of that first return to a life that was no life. "Here my life ended, and I was reborn," he states matter-of-factly. This is the essential truth of his experience. Like Bartfuss, Erwin is Immortal.

Erwin's trauma does not occasion repression in any typical sense, since the object of repression is not a something but a veritable nothing. His response is, rather, the classic response to trauma, which as Cathy Caruth puts it, in a description that could well be about Erwin's experience at Wirblbahn, is

> a kind of double telling, the oscillation between a *crisis of death* and the correlative *crisis of life:* between the story of the unbearable nature of an event and the story of the unbearable nature of its survival. . . . Trauma consists not only in having confronted death but in *having survived, precisely, without knowing it.* What one returns to in the flashback is not the incomprehensibility of one's near death, but the very incomprehensibility of one's own survival. Repetition, in other words, is

not simply the attempt to grasp that one has almost died but, more fundamentally, the very attempt *to claim one's own survival.*[5]

Not incidentally for reading Appelfeld's novel, traumatic memory has essentially to do with anxiety as a general neurotic state. "If repression entails keeping something away from consciousness," Elizabeth Bellamy explains,

> then anxiety, from a Freudian perspective, is the (often uninterpretable) *failure* of repression, a trauma that can be experienced only in displacement. . . . For Freud, an absence of affect does not necessarily mean that the affect has somehow "disappeared." Rather, presuming it does not get repressed, the affect is "transformed into a qualitatively different quota of affect . . . , above all into anxiety." . . . [A]nxiety "*calls the very process of cathexis itself into question.*" Repression, at least, cathects onto a "thing-representation" . . . but anxiety is the neurosis of displacement. . . . Anxiety, in other words, does not always know what it is afraid of.[6]

For the most part, I have been reading *The Iron Tracks* in terms of Erwin's repression of his past life, and his need to prevent memory from erupting in the present and overwhelming him with a sadness with which he can in no way deal. Within this repression, Erwin's anxiety—his *ḥaradah*—simultaneously represses and responds to his mother's own anxiety, vis-à-vis her own life choices. In this way, Erwin unconsciously repeats his mother in the same way that he does his father. But Erwin's anxiety, insofar as it is anxiety, is, like his mother's, also due to the absence of a referent to which the repression can be understood to refer. And it is also, and most dramatically, a product of "traumatic memory," which is essentially no memory at all, but almost pure affect or response to what simply does not exist as conscious experience, verbally encoded, to be recalled.

That this is designated by the text as a "rebirth" links the experience back to the mother in more than one way. What is inaccessible to Erwin is the fact that for all its horridness, this rebirth *is* a rebirth, with all the potentialities of birth (including language) that birth implies. The mother presides over this scene (as in much of Appelfeld's fiction), not simply as a mourned object of loss and pain but also as a guardian angel, who just might lead her son—and if not her son, then perhaps us—back to life.

Erwin's unwillingness to claim this life he is given back can certainly be understood in many ways, as, for example, an expression of survivor pain or guilt or any one of the many other explanations that have been given for the survivor's unwillingness to claim his or her existence or to tell his or her story. But Appelfeld here presents the conditions of Erwin's incapacity to accept his life as his life in the very particular terms of a non-event. The moment to which Erwin is "compelled" endlessly to return is a moment in which nothing in particular occurs. It is a moment of stasis, paralysis, blank. For this reason, Erwin's many attempts to obliterate consciousness, while they certainly function as a block to memory, also more or less replicate the traumatic moment itself. Drunkenness and sleep bodily remember and repeat the absence of consciousness that accompanied his actual rebirth into the world.

Throughout his fiction, and in his autobiography as well, Appelfeld remarks on the body's capacity to remember what the mind has long ago forgotten. This itself can be understood as a fairly conventional figure for general repressive neurosis, in which the denial of memory produces bodily as opposed to mental remembering. But in the particular instance of Erwin, loss of consciousness, brought on by drugs and liquor, is not so much the absence of memory, which then issues in other bodily forms of enactment, as his acknowledgment that there is precisely nothing to *be* remembered. It is, in other words, a highly mimetic form of remembering, for what there is to remember is indeed nothingness itself. Cognac, we are told, "drive[s] away the dismal clouds and the burning dread [*ḥaradah*]. Without cognac," he explains, "the sights of Wirblbahn return to me. Once again I see the horrors of my rebirth, and life no longer has any meaning" (83). With or without cognac, Erwin is delivered into unconsciousness. In the same way, his death wish in relation to murdering Nachtigel also embodies a desire to re-enact the moment of this rebirth, which was, from the start, a being born into death and dying. No matter how he puts it, Erwin is, from his own point of view, already dead.

As a Holocaust survivor, what Erwin must contend with is not only the local traumas of his youth or even the more catastrophic trauma of the murder of his parents and of the entire community of Eastern European Jewry. It is not even the loss of everything in the past, which might, after all, help him come to terms with his present life. Rather, and primarily, the trauma is the raw, decontextualized, non-contingent eruption into a pastless present by which Erwin is delivered into his present life, a life which, for all intents and purposes, has no past and a present that is for all intents and purposes a scene of death. The Holocaust as "rupture" (to use LaCapra's word) is a figure that has circulated in Holocaust studies. It is particularly relevant to Appelfeld's work, especially in relation to its reticence to represent life in the camps and ghettos (in *The Age of Wonders,* as we shall see, the Holocaust is represented in the text by an actual blank page bound into the novel). This idea of the gap makes of silence, not a response to what is too horrid to utter, but a replication of the fact that there is nothing in the reality of the camps and the ghettos to which referential language might usefully refer. And this makes of Erwin's birth into such a reality something of a real birth, by which we are, all of us, delivered pastless into the world to learn that world and its many forms and meanings.

This means that one thing Erwin must learn to do is to speak. And that means he has first to learn to listen, not to his own already verbalized albeit repressed past (associated with father and his childhood), but to the wordless past (linked to his mother) that does not yet for him exist, the past of other people and their repression and obsessions and languages, which he will learn, not through words alone, but through affects and feelings, or, more precisely, through hearing words affectively rather than intellectually or politically. This learning to listen and then speak for the first time also pushes forward the frontiers of psychoanalytic listening for us the readers. What must be heard and then spoken by the listener's reconstructed text as well is what the primary traumatized narrative itself cannot speak of, because it does not exist to be spoken, because there is no event to which its language can adequately refer. There are only the narrator's words adrift, which almost mindlessly and haphazardly come in to fill in the blanks in consciousness and silence (that words themselves can become the objects of repression and thus appear in indecipherable ways we will see in the next chapter). The challenge for us, as for Erwin, is to navigate these words and construct the reality they both obscure and bring into focus without losing sight of the words themselves, which is to say, without missing the affective connotations and not simply the meanings they bring with them. And to do that we have to witness or acknowledge those words rather than interpret and explicate them.

We have to differentiate, in other words, between what has been labeled the pathology of *deficit* as opposed to the pathology of *conflict.* Conflict implies a level of psychosexual development and verbal skill allowing the Oedipal drama to ensue. Deficit signals a far earlier moment preceding the consolidation of mature object relations: "in conflict we are dealing with impulses and affects aimed at internalized representations of former important emotional objects of the person's history"; "deficit transference," on the other hand, "is not charged with specific representational content. It is rather a matter of direct externalization or repetition of undeveloped or distorted structure. . . . [T]he patient in a deficit transference is a person in need of an object able to provide the proper conditions for correction of distorted object representations and for internalization of object functions." What such a patient seeks in therapy, therefore, is not the specific meaning of a particular repressed content, but rather validation or verification of being itself—at least as a precondition for some more intellectual, verbal working through.[7] In the end, we humans are creatures of the intellect who do need to recover, in language, the historical bases of our experience. But we may have to do so all the time respecting the non-verbality of other people's experiences and refraining from interpretive gestures that violate that silence.

As LaCapra so lucidly puts it, in a sentence I have already quoted, even if "there is a sense in which silence may indeed be the only way to confront a traumatic past, . . . this contention does not justify a specific silence concerning something that can be said or with respect to the problem of attempting to say what can be said in the face of the risk that language may break down in a more or less telling manner." Erwin's is nothing if not a hysterical text, breaking down in the telling of an experience for which he has no words. The question we must ask is how we can listen and hear his story in such a way as not to simply replicate his muteness with a muteness of our own (match silence with silence or, as in Geoffrey Hartman's formula as cited in Chapter 1, experience his traumatization as our own).[8] At the same time, we must find a way to substitute for his preverbal incoherence a verbal reconstruction that avoids being inappropriate or inadequate, even hurtful. Erwin's failure to achieve any measure of significant relief in his murder of Nachtigel is the text's own figure for the failure of the ideological and the intellectual to make sense of and thereby put to rest the horrors of the past: for as soon as the murder, which is Erwin's political response and his inheritance of that response from his father at the level of repressed conflictual material, has been completed, Erwin sets upon a venture even more radical and self-destructive—to burn down and annihilate the place of his devastation, which is also the place of his (re)birth: the town of Wirblbahn. Burning down the site of his rebirth into his *ḥaradah* and anxiety, Erwin would try to undo the trauma altogether, make it as if it had never been, as if in murdering the murderer of his parents he would un-murder them and bring them back.

What would burning down Wirblbahn restore to life since there was nothing there to begin with and exactly nothing happened there? To destroy Wirblbahn would be finally and forever to obliterate the nothingness but only by monumentalizing it, simultaneously cutting off any hope of recuperation that his endless repetitive cycling of the rails at least offers to afford. To lead somewhere the tracks need only to provide some sense of being, and being alive, as if to witness in their inarticulate, material (iron) way that this human being does exist and that his life is therefore real.

Mute Chapters, God's Highway, and *Tiqqun ᶜOlam*

The following is surely one of the oddest and most perplexing scenes in the novel. It occurs while Erwin is "sitting and marveling over the annual cycle, which had suddenly reached its end" in more ways than one, since he has now finally accomplished the ostensible purpose of that cycling, his murder of Nachtigel. "A short man dressed in a long coat" approaches him (182). This man is one of Erwin's many rivals (we have met others of them before in the novel). Like Erwin, he travels the rails in pursuit of abandoned Judaica, and as such constitutes a sort of double of Erwin himself (one might pause here to recall that sharing Appelfeld's name, Erwin, like many of Appelfeld's characters, is also a double for the author). "The man's appearance was wretched, and a stench rose from his words as well. But at that moment he was, for some reason, like a brother to me, one whom I had not seen for years. I am your brother, who suddenly appeared and said, don't estrange yourself from me" (183). These words of kinship are especially powerful in the wake of Nachtigel's having just said to him, moments before Erwin kills him, that "today people even forget their fathers and mothers" (177; in the Hebrew text, as noted, Nachtigel is also said to have treated the soldiers under his command as a elder brother). Indeed, in the context of the familial feeling implicit in recovering the Judaica itself, the Hebrew *aḥicha ani—I am your brother* evokes the text of Joseph's reunion with his brothers, who have sold him into slavery and would now be redeemed by his willingness to know them, to recognize them as brothers, and to take them back. (As we shall see later, the Joseph story is an important intertext in another of Appelfeld's novels, *Tzili: The Story of a Life.*)

What happens next is crucial. "You can be proud of what you have done," the rival tells Erwin. "You've discovered all the Jewish antiquities, manuscripts, books. Everything that was buried for years in cellars and attics you've brought out into the daylight. The Jewish people won't forget your contribution," to which Erwin responds, "I sold it all" (the word *sold* also echoing the Joseph story). And as the rival continues to press his case for Erwin's contribution to the "treasury of the Jewish people," "the people of the book who fight for their values," Erwin tells us, "the more he talked, the more his misery was evident. I wanted to shout, Be quiet. Stop making so much noise. Your words sicken me. You're an empty vessel, not a human being" (183–84).

It is not difficult to understand what in his rival's words so infuriates Erwin. Fresh from the murder, Erwin is made suddenly to confront the fact that he may well have chosen to complete the wrong mission. Rather than commit himself to the recovery of his Judaic past and its comprehensive acknowledgment of his brothers past and present, Erwin has, as it were, sold his brothers into slavery. The many books he has collected now form a convent library in the land of the Jews' oppressors. Erwin has committed himself to just that political trajectory of Jewish history that informed his father's life as well, and his death: for, as I have already suggested, in some way it is the father's own faith in the political, which is the faith of Nazism as well, that has conspired to murder him and that would now destroy his son. It is not that *tiqqun ᶜolam* is not an important part of the Judaic tradition, but rather that, as in most things, there is both a creative and a destructive way of bringing about such *repair of the world.* One way carries with it the essence of Jewish tradition, while the other puts tradition itself to an end.

Erwin sees in the mirror of his brother, in particular through the rival mirror's unfounded praise of his recovery of the ruins of Jewish culture, which mission he has forfeited, the "empty vessel" he himself has become in his wrongly conceived pursuit of *tiqqun ᶜolam.* As my own language has begun to suggest, it is not irrelevant to understanding what is going on here that among the books that Erwin collects are many volumes of Kabbalah. "If fortune smiles upon me," Erwin tells us, concerning this other of the two "secret" missions that define his life on the rails,

> I discover treasures wherever I turn. Seven years ago I returned to the station from here with two bulging rucksacks. What didn't I find! Candlesticks, two Hanukkah menorahs, and many wine goblets. Most valuable of all: the books . . .
>
> . . .
>
> The treasure trove contained valuable and rare books, Kabbalistic and homiletic works. When I piled them on his desk, Rabbi Zimmel hugged me and said, "These are treasures. I'll write to Gershom Scholem in Jerusalem, and he will come to visit me."
>
> . . .
>
> It's clear that the treasures grow scarcer from year to year, and it's likely that in a few years there won't be any left. But I'm not worried. What I find not only supports me, but fills me with excitement. . . . When I . . . uncover something, there is no limit to my joy." (83–86; cf. 102–103)
>
> . . .
>
> "Your work is holy," Stark tells him; "You mustn't leave these precious objects in the hands of strangers. Marvelous memories are stored up in them." (81)

Erwin's rescue of the remnants of Eastern European Jewish culture functions as more than an externalized correlative of the internal psychic process he has to undergo in order to recover his past and thereby claim at least some fragment of his present life, even though this is certainly one aspect of this text's primary track within Erwin's hysterical narrative of repetition and revenge. The Holocaust had, as one of its foundational features, the objective of obliterating the Jewish past: both the collective past of the Jews and the private, personal past of the individual Jews through which they, like any of us, might construct a present and a future. The recovery of the artifacts of the past in and of itself prevents this annihilation. Indeed, Appelfeld's own text, recording these events in the ancient language of Hebrew, is a part of the recovery and reassertion of Jewish culture.

But there is more going on here than that. Rabbi Kimmel's reference to Gershom Scholem invokes the proper kabbalistic context for Erwin's acts of recovery. This helps us to travel the second track, both of the narrator's experience, and of the text (Appelfeld's text) itself, the track that leads out of the self-annihilating repetition-compulsion of his behavior and even of his narrative into some more fully realized idea of freedom.

As in *Badenheim,* what distinguishes the reader's experience of the text from that of the protagonists within the text has to do with traveling the circuitry of its language. Unlike the language of the traumatized victim of overly painful and/or obliterating experience, the text's language is the intentional, self-conscious, allusive language of literature. The "secrets" and "treasures" encrypted in Erwin's experience (80, 86, 88, 102, 122), which take their origins from outside of and before his birth, have a textual life as well. Yet despite the fact that his "strange dealings over the years have forced" Erwin to learn "Hebrew and Aramaic," nonetheless his knowledge of these languages is sufficiently "limited" (83) that he cannot make available to himself the knowledge contained within the texts that he himself has collected: the knowledge of *tiqqun* that is contained within the tradition itself. Erwin's illiteracy isn't purely his own. One might say that, for the Jewish people as a whole, learning Hebrew has been forced upon it by its strange post-Holocaust dealings, and that part of the people's recovery is its recovery of the language in which its collective memories have been stored—the language not of Erwin's life and narrative (which occurred in the many languages Erwin speaks: Ruthenian, Yiddish, and German among them)—but of Appelfeld's text, which translates all of these other languages into Hebrew. How we might see in the empty vessel Erwin has become the brother whom we must embrace, and how we might recover and repair a broken world is the *mesilah* to God that Appelfeld's text, not Erwin's, travels. For the *mesilat barzel,* whether understood literally as the railway tracks, or figuratively as the iron-clad routes of the protagonist's tormented psyche (whether repressively or anxiously defined), is not the only *mesilah* (or path or journey) in this novel.

Like the titles *Badenheim 1939* and *Tzili: The Story of a Life,* the translation into English of the Hebrew title obscures the tracks of language that provide the text with its most important intertexts. The word *mesilah* circles back into a set of biblical passages that trace no lesser path than that of divine salvation itself. In this pathway to and of God, the *ḥaradah*—literally, anxiety—which Erwin repeatedly experiences while riding the iron tracks (the word *ḥaradah*, as we have seen, no less than punctuates the entire text), represents, like the *mesilah* itself, more than psychological and spiritual affliction. Recalling such terms as *ḥaradat elohim* or *ḥaradat haqadosh*—the fear of God or of the Holy One—Erwin's *ḥaradah* is intimately connected to the faith that also informs his life and mission. Recalling as well Kierkegaard's "fear and trembling," it discovers what distinguishes the repetitions that enslave from the repetitions that set us free. Kierkegaard, we might recall, had some important things to say about repetition in relation to human freedom and faith—a subject to which I will turn in more detail in my next chapter. The word *mesilah* appears throughout the Bible, but it is especially concentrated in a particular book of prophecy that has already figured in my discussion of Appelfeld's writing: the book of Isaiah, from which is taken, as I have already noted, the *Haftorah* for the *Torah* passages informing the final paragraph of *Badenheim.*

These are the relevant passages (I have rendered in italics the uses of the word *mesilah*):

> The *highways* lie waste, the wayfaring man ceased: he hath broken the covenant, he hath despised the cities, he regardeth no man. (33.8)
>
> Their feet run to evil, and they make haste to shed innocent blood: their thoughts are thoughts of iniquity; wasting and destruction are in their paths. (59.7)
>
> And there shall be an *highway* for the remnant of his people . . . like as was to Israel in the day that he came up out of the land of Egypt. (11.16)
>
> In that day shall there be a *highway* out of Egypt. (19.23)
>
> The voice of him that crieth in the wilderness, Prepare ye the way of the Lord, make straight in the desert a *highway* for our God. (40.3)
>
> And I will make all my mountains a way, and my *highways* shall be exalted. (49.11)
>
> And a *highway* there shall be, and a way, and it shall be called The way of holiness: the unclean shall not pass over it; but it shall be for those: the wayfaring men, though fools, shall not err therein. No lion shall be there, nor *any* ravenous beast shall go up thereon, it shall not be found there; but the redeemed shall walk *there:* And the ransomed of the Lord shall return, and come to Zion with songs and everlasting joy upon their heads: they shall obtain joy and gladness, and sorrow and sighing shall flee away. (35.8–10; cf. 62.10)

Are we meant to understand by this set of intertexts that behind Appelfeld's novel stands a traditionally redemptive meaning? An ethical, political teleology such as we saw just might be lurking in *Badenheim,* and which might serve to blame the victims of atrocity for their own fate?

As in the case of *Badenheim,* it is important, as a first move, to distinguish between human meanings and divine ones: whatever possibilities the biblical texts figure forth, they are not to be understood in straightforward human terms, whether psychologically or historically or morally conceived. But more importantly for our purposes, the texts here cited concerning the divine *mesilah* are not referential texts (as in many ways Appelfeld's texts are not referential but allegorical and impressionistic). They do not explain and instruct and clarify; they are, rather, affirmations of possibilities and directions, which exactly oppose the political rhetoric of murder and revenge.

Like the other faiths represented in the book—Communism and Nazism—and like the words of his rival in the final scene, which send up an off-putting stench of decay, Judaism fails when it commits itself to what it imagines to be the "truth," when it codifies itself into agendas and "sayings." If there is something of value to be found in texts (whether religious or otherwise), it is not, for Appelfeld, ethical instruction as such but rather some way of imagining our relationship to a world beyond that of rational humanism and its institutions. For Appelfeld, Kabbalah exactly resists the political dimensions of Judaism, whether they emerge as halachic or ritual observance or as politics of one variety or another (from Communism to Zionism). As Gershom Scholem himself introduces the concept of Kabbalah:

> "Kabalah" is the traditional and most commonly used term for the esoteric teachings of Judaism and for Jewish mysticism, especially the forms which it assumed in the Middle Ages from the 12th century onward. . . . Kabalah may be considered mysticism insofar as it seeks an apprehension of God and creation whose intrinsic elements are beyond the grasp of the intellect. . . . In essence . . . the Kabalah is far removed from the rational and intellectual approach to religion.[9]

Its "central structural notion," as Harold Bloom takes up the discussion, is

> the *Sefirot* . . . the divine emanations by which all reality is structured. . . . Classical Kabbalah begins with a Neoplatonic vision of God. God is the *Ein-Sof* ("without end"), totally unknowable, and beyond representation. As *Ein-Sof* has no attributes, his first manifestation is necessarily as *ayin* ("nothing"). . . . God, being "ayin," created the world out of "ayin," and thus created the world *out of himself*. . . . The *Sefirot* are complex figurations for God, tropes or turns of language that substitute for God. . . . [They are] complex images for God in His process of creation. . . . [They] are neither *things* nor *acts*, but rather are *relationship events*, and so are persuasive representations of what ordinary people encounter as the inner reality of their lives. . . . *Zimzum*, *shevirah ha-kelim*, and *tikkun* (contraction, the breaking-of-the vessels, restitution) [is the "triple process" whereby, according to Luriatic kabbalism, reality is produced.] . . . *Zimzum* [is] an idea of limitation, of God's . . . contraction [whereby] God clears a space for creation, a non-God. . . . [*Shevriah ha-kelim* produces the creation itself, and finally] *tikkun* [is] the saving process of restoration and restitution, for this is the work of the human. . . . *Tikkun* or restoration of creation must be carried out by the religious acts of individual men, of all Jews struggling in the Exile. . . . The nature of such religious acts of *tikkun* . . . are acts of meditation . . . that lift up and so liberate the fallen sparks of God from their imprisonment.[10]

Later, in my discussion of *Tzili* I will deal with the concept of *ẓimẓum.* For the moment, I focus on *tiqqun ᶜolam,* which is defined kabbalistically as the "restoration" of the "broken vessels" to their original unity. Such meditation, Gershom Scholem emphasizes, is prayer as opposed to the rituals of religious observance as specified in the halacha. And meditation thus defined is intimately connected with language itself, in ways that we have already glimpsed in the not-unrelated theories of Geoffrey Hartman.

Harold Bloom puts it this way:

> As a theory of meaning, Kabbalah tells us that meaning *is* the hurt[,] that meaning itself is hurtful. For Kabbalah tries to restore the primal meaning that God intended when He gave Torah to Moses. But Kabbalah treats Torah as alphabet, as language itself. God gave writing, which was almost primal, except that writing was what we now would call a compulsive sublimation of a more primal instruction. The primal *act* is that God *taught;* the primal *teaching* is *writing. Zimzum* is therefore in the first place Instruction. *Ein-Sof* instructs Himself by concentration and *what* he teaches is then apparent in the *tehiru* (vacated space) as the letter *yod.* God teaches Himself his own Name, and so begins creation." (80)

In every situation, Erwin tells us in the passage concerning Wirblbahn, a believer makes his lips to speak. Not being a believer in the traditional religious sense, and deaf to his own story, Erwin cannot hear his own mute speaking. Before some realities, we fall respectfully silent. This does not mean, however, that we do not speak. Rather, we speak in a certain way. We pray. In Hebrew, the words that conjure the *silence* that this book expresses are *ḥeresh, illem, domem,* and *shetiqah*—words that, much more than their English equivalents, convey a sense of silencing or falling silent rather than just being silent or mute. In Appelfeld's text, silence is not a condition of oblivion or absence of affect or thought. Rather, it is a way of responding to something or someone else. Bella, for example, who (as I have already indicated), conveys the mother's presence into his adult life, is described as "*ḥayyim ḥereshiyim*" (13; a mute presence in the English—17) where the word *ḥereshiyim* derives from the word meaning *deaf,* such that Bella's muteness is a silence that, like deafness, puts an end to hearing. Or in the passage that I have already quoted concerning respect for Bertha's silences, the word used for those silences is the same word that most frequently appears in relation to the mother's own silence, *shetiqah,* which means *becoming* or *making silent* (40; 69 in the English, in relation to Bertha; and in relation to the mother: 22/36; 29/48; 31/51). In perhaps the most telling instance of all, in what is the major passage in this as in other contexts, Wirblbahn, as we have seen, is labeled a *pereq domem* (10), a mute chapter (13). The word *domem* comes from a verb meaning to fall silent. It also carries within it a hint of or a sense of blood (*dam*) and hence associates its silence with the silence of or for the dead. In the presence of the dead one stands *damum* in Hebrew; one falls silent. (There may also be a sense here of the phrase *hatan damim,* referring to the child undergoing circumcision, the *berit milah.*)

Muteness, for Appelfeld, is not silence, but a way of speaking: the mother's way of speaking as opposed to the father's. As such, it also requires a certain kind of listening or hearing on the part of the listener/reader. Erwin himself knows the essential truth of his life, that there is for him "no pleasure . . . like that of discovering an antique" (80). But Erwin cannot enjoy the fruits of his labors, just as he cannot give himself over to the other considerable pleasures of his life riding the rails. Obsessive-compulsive personality that he is, neurotic, anxious, and depressed, Erwin may simply be incapable of enjoying what pleasures remain to him in his life. The text, however, throws this into question as an adequate interpretation of his unhappiness. "I have learned," Erwin tells us, "to appreciate the small things that come my way" (38). "In Gruenfeld they serve me borscht, black bread, and fresh milk and cheese. These miraculously draw me out of the mud. Fresh dairy products, I have learned, are better than medicine" (47). So is coffee served to him with sandwiches on a train; or good music; or cigarettes. Nor does Erwin fail to appreciate the people, like Mrs. Groton, Max, August, the Rabbi, and others who inspire his being.

Erwin is a man who enjoys life, and is as capable of waxing eloquent as of droning on about his troubles. What gets in the way of his pleasure is the act of revenge to which he has committed himself, which is to say his commitment to a political interpretation of and response to his experience. Therefore, he tells us in relation to his pleasure in retrieving Europe's Judaica, that "my heart chides me for that devotion because it can distract me from my main goal: the murderer" (81). Erwin will not permit himself to enjoy the (largely mute or muted) happiness remaining to him.

If we ourselves listen to this text only analytically, then we risk repeating Erwin's own deafness to the story he tells and to the larger Jewish story contained in the artifacts he collects. We may find ourselves bound by the same compulsion as Erwin to act and react and enact politically a scenario of revenge. This is exactly the site that Appelfeld's text, speaking mutely, avoids. I have already suggested that one of the most distinctive features of Appelfeld's writing is that it is not densely realist. It does not fill in all the details of the world it figures forth. Actions, characters, and conversations are more suggestive than three-dimensionally mimetic. Indeed, in many of Appelfeld's writings, words are dramatically, almost grotesquely, severed from the empirical world, to which they now only loosely refer. Though in Holocaust studies it is tempting to end the discussion of this feature of language with the observation that only such grotesquely distorted language can realistically convey the dimensions of so grotesque a reality as the concentrationary world, it is important to resist this temptation. We must come to understand how the evasion of mimesis is a necessary part of the text's attempt to restore, to both our experience of life and of literature, the power of language as language, to speak, not politically or ideologically or even referentially but allusively, evocatively, affectively, silently, as acknowledgment. Erwin is right that in his repeated journeying on the iron tracks lies a strange hopefulness. The trains do somehow set him free (5). What he needs to see in order to experience his own internal knowledge is that the tracks that his life repeats also repeat other communal and textual tracks as well, which are themselves mute chapters of *tiqqun ᶜolam*. These also need to be heard and comprehended in their silent speaking.

As I began to suggest at the beginning of this chapter, we might say that for Appelfeld literature itself is a set of tracks, linguistic and otherwise. They must be traveled, not because they take us to some place of wholly lucid, transcendent meaning to which it is their primary purpose to deliver us, as if the world were coextensive with and therefore to be summed up by its intellectual, political content. Rather, we must travel them because it is only by riding the rails (of psychological, literary, and public experience) that we experience life and its meanings. To travel the tracks is to affectively experience and acknowledge rather than to translate and interpret our lives and the lives of others. It is to claim our lives *as* our lives—exactly what Erwin cannot do.

And yet Appelfeld's fiction is also factual, evidentiary, documentary fiction. There is a real world out there, both past and present, which his fiction intends to figure forth. It matters what happened in that world, both to his protagonist and to the Jewish people as a whole. This also has something to do with claiming a life and making it live. My subject in the next chapter is how we might not forfeit the sense of the realness of the world and of other people in it as we nonetheless strive to put aside judgment and interpretation in order to acknowledge the pain and suffering of other human beings, and perhaps, even, of ourselves. As I have intermittently acknowledged, the voice of Appelfeld's fiction is itself the voice of the orphaned child survivor. If in *The Iron Tracks* Appelfeld gives his own name to his protagonist, in *The Age of Wonders* the hero bears the name of another Jewish writer. This name carries with it a different set of religious and literary texts that we must also come to acknowledge, and in acknowledging commit ourselves once again to travelling the multivarious and multifaceted tracks of Jewish history and tradition.

4 The Conditions That Condition This Utterly Specific People: *The Age of Wonders*

Bruno A. in *The Age of Wonders* is a man very much like Erwin Siegelbaum in *The Iron Tracks.* He too arrives at the place of confrontation with the past (in this case, his place of literal rather than figurative rebirth). He comes by rail—"I came on the train," he says, rather forlornly; "and here I am" (192)—and also to a "warehouse" (182) where he confronts a Jewish traveler. Like many of Erwin's rivals and doubles, this traveler has been riding the rails for twenty years. He is a sort of brother to Bruno in this non-Jewish world. But Bruno cannot acknowledge him. Like Erwin, Bruno journeys back into a past that he cannot fully comprehend and from which he cannot, therefore, release himself. He cannot see his kinship with his own life and the others in it. He thus does not know how to claim that life and make it live.

Structured as a two-part narrative in which the protagonist's past is neatly severed from his childhood by the blank page that stands for the Holocaust itself (it stands for other things as well, as we shall soon see), *The Age of Wonders,* like *The Iron Tracks,* insists on the continuity of the protagonist's experience: this is the life of this individual human being and no other. At the same time, however, providing its protagonist with the name of an important European writer (Bruno Schultz) who was cut down by the Holocaust, as was the protagonist's own father, also a writer, whom Appelfeld nominates in the novel by his own initial A, the book plays out the ways in which access to the past has to do with more than personal experience and psychology. *The Age of Wonders* deals with the continuity (and not only the disruption) of Jewish life and consciousness both before and after the war. The blank page separating Bruno's childhood and his present adulthood represents a communal as well as a personal phenomenon which long precedes the Holocaust. It stands for a feature of Jewish history that, after the Holocaust, has too easily come to seem a break in the Jewish continuity that it actually helps identify and define. How we read the blank pages in Jewish history, and what we choose to write on them, is the task this text sets for us.

As in the case of *The Iron Tracks,* the Holocaust sits on top of what is already the protagonist's troubled childhood. The son of a highly assimilated Austrian writer, the child Bruno observes uncomprehendingly not only the tensions in his parents' pre-War lives—including their unhappy marriage, the conversion of his mother's sister to Catholicism, and the gradual discrediting of his father by the increasingly antisemitic intellectual establishment—but the impending catastrophe as well. But in *The Age of Wonders,* the focus is as much on the community as on the individual family and on the way in which individual psychological dysfunction might be the consequence of traumas having less to do with the individual's actual lived experience (which might then become subject to conventional processes of remembering and working through), than with the various narratives—often not even stories as such, but only individual words or phrases—by which the community constructs its collective identity as an assimilated and integrated Austrian-Jewish community. Similarly, in part two of the novel, which takes place after the war, when Bruno leaves Israel and his own failed marriage to revisit the scenes of his youth and to confront what remains of that world (Jewish and non-Jewish), the critique is as much aimed at the post-Holocaust, intellectual, Israeli Jewish mentality, as at the psyche of this one individual.

To already bring forward the ideas of Nicholas Abraham and Maria Torok, which will in a moment inform my discussion, unremembered bits of the past—whether that past is what precedes European Jewish assimilation or the past that *is* that European Jewish assimilation, which now precedes the state of Israel—are encrypted in *The Age of the Wonders* in words, fragments, and fleeting images rather than in concrete actions or a sustained, continuous interpretation of the past. And they are transmitted from generation to generation as a kind of undecipherable phantom language (a blank page, as it were), the meaning of which cannot be clarified because the individual in whom such phantom words exist has never had the experience of which the phantom speaks but only inherited them unawares and unbidden. Language, then, does not serve to clarify anything for Appelfeld's characters. If in the first instance it is a vehicle of repression, in the second it is the instrument by which that repression is inherited.

In the psychological process Appelfeld is describing, literary texts themselves play an essential role. Understanding the phantom language encoded in the tradition will depend very much on a technology of reading that, as in the case of interpreting Erwin's more bodily expressions of repression, anxiety, and trauma, will be concerned not only with decoding what language cannot say because it does not know that of which it speaks, but also, and primarily perhaps, with experiencing it as coded communication as such. *The Age of Wonders* is about Jewish literary tradition and how it has both succeeded and failed in producing the human freedom toward which the literature itself aspires. It is about how we hear the words we ourselves speak; and how we grant the utter specificity of our own as of other lives as those lives are articulated in words that harbor ghosts and phantoms.

Before I turn to *The Age of Wonders,* I want to stay a while longer with *The Iron Tracks,* and by way of setting the ground for the idea of the specificity of other lives in the words that they and we speak, I want to answer the question that I raised at the beginning of my reading of that novel, the question of why Appelfeld risks diminishing the overwhelming power of the Holocaust trauma by producing in Erwin (as he will produce in Bruno) a rather ordinary sort of neurotic-depressive with many trite and trivial forms of psychological dysfunction.

Repetition, Recollection, and the Conditions That Condition This Utterly Specific Life

The question that shadows Erwin's experience on the purely personal level of an individual life, and that the text forces us to ask is, what enables us to take possession of our lives, to experience our lives as lives worth living? The text's answer is unequivocal. In order to claim our lives, we need to experience them as ours and to experience ourselves in those lives as alive. This is what the text means when it says, at the scene at Wirblbahn, that "the wings of death had departed," but Erwin and the others still "didn't know it" (12). To be reborn, Erwin has to come to "know" that the wings of death have departed. Not to know this is to remain "captive to visions of death" (12), and this is what the text labels anxiety, *ḥaradah,* in which affect is not so much repressed and rerouted as it is distributed without purpose or self-consciousness in the very act of living and breathing—as in a nightmare or vision, terms which punctuate the text from beginning to end. Erwin's condition differs little from that of his beloved Bertha, who decides to return to her hometown. This hometown, Erwin realizes, is now only a cemetery in which the living bury themselves alive (75ff). Erwin also lives his omnipresent death. He lives it in his perpetual reenactment of the moment when he was born not into living but into an endless dying.

The text here is not far from constructing the problem of the cogito in its purest form, as an asking of the question, how do I know that I exist? But rather than answer, as it might, *I think, therefore I am,* which is also, for Descartes, the way back to faith of a specifically religious kind, the text makes recourse to a strategy employed by other writers of allegorical grotesque fiction, such as Edgar Allan Poe and Franz Kafka. This is namely the perversion of the cogito as (in Stanley Cavell's terms) *I think, therefore I am destroyed.* In other words, in the absence of any possibility of affirming my existence in the present, because the present only serves to call into doubt the existence of such consciousness as would declare to me that I exist, I experience myself in my self-destruction, in my having-been. By this means I know that, since to have been destroyed means I must once have existed, I did indeed exist.[1] In this fact, the individual takes a certain modicum of comfort—albeit rather "too late," as the concluding words of *The Iron Tracks* remind us.

We might say that the survivor of the non-event, the eclipse of consciousness, that is the Holocaust (the blank page in *The Age of Wonders*), affirms his or her rebirth in the only way possible, by staging his or her own perpetual self-destruction and loss of consciousness, i.e., staging life as a death, since the coming into existence was, from the start, indistinguishable from a dying out of consciousness, virtually indistinguishable from death itself. And, yet, of course, distinguishable, since Erwin does live, and often beautifully and well. The real tragedy of his present life is that he cannot avail himself of the tremendous bounty of his life on the rails. To do that, Erwin would have had to have come to see his fantasy of being dead is just that. It is a fantasy, albeit one that contains tremendous life-affirming powers. For this fantasy *is* the specific life in which his life consists; it is the condition that conditions that life and makes it his.

As I said earlier, for Appelfeld a primary issue motivating this as many other of his texts is how we speak or write mutely so as simultaneously to respect the impossibility of language to say anything about an experience that itself bypassed language, and yet so as not, at the same time, to forfeit the saying of what can, and indeed must, be said. The text's muteness, I suggested, which is not silence but a particular way of speaking, speaks the conditions that condition an utterly specific life. In this way, the text also commits itself to the concrete factuality of actual events as they happened to real, individual human beings. It does this in two diametrically opposite ways.

First, in rendering the psychological portrait of his protagonist Erwin, Appelfeld would himself say, and have us say, the word that often drops out of the postmodernist celebration of silence, the word *Jew.* Indeed, he would give each and every Jew a name, sometimes (as in the case of this novel, or in *Ice Mine*) his own name, or in *The Age of Wonders,* his initial. In *The Age of Wonders,* as we shall see, the world to which Bruno returns has no word for "Jew" (193). A question that that text raises, to which I shall be returning, is whether Bruno's world ever did.

Thus, before all, including, or perhaps especially, before the uniqueness of the Holocaust experience itself, Appelfeld would establish the ordinary humanness of the survivor, which is to say the uniqueness of each and every survivor as an individual human being *before* he or she became representative of an event that, though itself unique, tends to diminish the uniqueness of the individuals who suffered it. As Appelfeld himself has put it, he has endeavored in his fiction to "remove the Holocaust from its enormous, inhuman dimensions and bring it closer to human beings" not, he emphasizes, "to simplify, to attenuate, or to sweeten the horror, but to attempt to make the events speak through the individual and in his language, to rescue the suffering from huge numbers, from dreadful anonymity, and to restore the person's given and family name, to give the tortured person back his human form, which was snatched away from him."[2] To hear the survivor's story, and to understand it, we must first of all recognize that story as being spoken by a real human being. Indeed, we must hear it as the story of a particular human being, with a life's experience that predates and is outside the dimensions of a catastrophe that seems, in the minds of the observers, to overwhelm and diminish every other feature of this person's personality.

It is part of the uniqueness of human beings, and their humanness, that experience (like Erwin's whip) lands on each of us differently. Appelfeld's troop of grotesque human beings functions, in the first instance, to remind us not only that we are dealing in Jewish history with individuals disfigured by the unnaturalness of Jewish life within the antisemitic nations of Europe, but that each one of these individuals is marked by his own individual, familial, experience of the incomprehensible traumas of childhood, both part and parcel and independent of communal history. In this the text functions as itself a listener (like us) to the stories it recounts, in a process in which (to quote once again Stanley Cavell) "one human being represents to another all that that other has conceived of humanity in his or her life, and moves with that other toward an expression of the conditions which condition that utterly specific life." It is this respect for the conditions which condition an utterly specific life that Appelfeld shares with the project of psychoanalysis and the reason that, in the first instance, psychoanalytic insights, especially in relation to trauma narrative, can fruitfully be brought to bear on Appelfeld's work. There is no underestimating the importance, in Appelfeld's fiction, of the utterly specific life.

Nonetheless, the idea that there are conditions that condition this life opens out onto a paradox that is also fundamental to *Iron Tracks* and others of his novels. This paradox constitutes the second mode of the texts' affirmation of the specificity of the specifically *human* lives they record. Even though human behavior is, for all of us, determined by the experiences (personal and collective) that constitute that individual life, at the same time, the fact that *conditions pertain* pertains to all of us. Experiences both personal and communal (as in *Badenheim*), even transgenerational, *do* condition our lives and determine who we are and how we will react in any given situation. How, then, should any of us (even the murderers like Nachtigel, or, for that matter, Erwin) be responsible for the choices we make, personally or collectively?

Though, as I have already mentioned, I will be dealing with this aspect of Appelfeld's art in more detail later, I want to note now, in the context of this aspect of the discussion of *The Iron Tracks,* the philosophical question that, almost in defiance of our post-Holocaust expectations of such fiction, circulates throughout Appelfeld's fiction: the question of *what is a human being?* Following the Nazis' extermination of Jews, gypsies, and others, and the rhetoric mobilized to facilitate this extermination, such a question would seem to us almost an abomination to ask. Yet, as we have already seen, this is the question behind Erwin's proclaiming, in some significant repetition of Nazi rhetoric, that man is indeed an insect or, in the word of his interlocutor, a monster. For the moment, I want to suggest no more than that by grounding the protagonist's behavior in something like a psychological determinism, Appelfeld acknowledges the constraints that limit the achievement of human freedom and that reduce human beings to something like animals, even insects. At the same time, in clarifying those conditions, or more precisely, in verifying that there are conditions to be clarified, he points the way to our freedom, which is first and foremost the freedom to know who and what we are. Repetition is not the problem in human behavior. Failure to perceive and acknowledge that repetition is. Søren Kierkegaard calls this failure to acknowledge repetition properly "recollection." Recollection is a form of nostalgia, a process of constantly being drawn back into the past, a feature that very much characterizes a figure like Erwin.

This is Kierkegaard:

> Repetition and recollection are the same movement, except in opposite directions, for what is recollected has been, is repeated backward, whereas genuine repetition is recollected forward. Repetition, therefore, if it is possible, makes a person happy, whereas recollection makes him unhappy—assuming, of course, that he gives himself time to live and does not promptly at birth find an excuse to sneak out of life again, for example, that he has forgotten something. . . . It takes youthfulness to hope, youthfulness to recollect, but it takes courage to will repetition. . . . [H]e who wills repetition is a man, and the more emphatically he is able to realize it, the more profound a human being he is. But he who does not grasp that life is a repetition and that this is the beauty of life has pronounced his own verdict and deserves nothing better than what will happen to him anyway—he will perish.[3]

And later in the essay:

> When the Greeks said that all knowing is recollecting, they said that all existence, which is, has been; when one says that life is a repetition, one says: actuality, which has been, now comes into existence. (149)

"My memory is my downfall," Erwin knows, and he elaborates:

> Nothing can deplete it. [It] is a powerful machine that stores and constantly discharges lost years and faces. In the past I believed that travel would blunt my memory; I was wrong. Were it not for my memory, my life would be different—better, I assume. My memory fills me up until I choke on a stream of daydreams. They overflow into my sleep. (9)

This is memory, not, as in Geoffrey Hartman's terms, as that which enables experience by limiting it, but memory as a forgetting of the difference between then and now, producing what Kierkegaard calls repetition backwards as opposed to forwards. Like the return of the repressed, such memory pushes the individual further and further back out of the life moving forward into the present and future, along the "line of locals, trams, taxis, and carriages" that could, but do not, deliver Erwin into his life.

There is, it seems, more life along the iron tracks than at first meets the eye, though one has to not only see it but accept it, with all its painful repetitions. For whatever reasons, Kierkegaard's essay shares with Appelfeld's novel an abundance of trains, carriages, and other conveyances, in addition to a certain protective secrecy concerning the purpose of travel and its revelations. The following passage from "Repetition" produces a scene very familiar to readers of Appelfeld's narrative, with one glaring exception:

> I know a place a few miles from Copenhagen where a young girl lives; I know the big shaded garden with its many trees and bushes. I know a bushy slope a short distance away, from which, concealed by the brush, one can look down into the garden. I have not divulged this to anyone; not even my coachman knows it, for I deceive him by getting out some distance away and walking to the right instead of the left. When my mind is sleepless and the sight of my bed makes me more apprehensive than a torture machine does . . . then I drive all night. . . . When life begins to stir, when the sun opens its eye, when the bird shakes its wings, when the fox steals out of its cave . . . then the young girl also appears. (167–68)

What distinguishes Erwin's journey from the journey charted above is that, whereas for Kierkegaard the object of the journey remains the traveler's precious and carefully maintained secret, in Appelfeld's novel, even though Erwin keeps secret his two missions of rescue and revenge, the true object of the journey, and what motivates it—the unconscious repetition backward of his father and his mother which takes the form of his circling rather than moving on—remains a secret to the traveler himself.

It is the function of the novel not only to decode that secret for us, but to provide us with a model of encryptment as well, as contained in a word, by which we can understand the larger dimensions of linguistic phantoms that haunt, but also inspire, our world. Though as the first-person narrator of the text Erwin himself has access to the word *mesilah,* nonetheless Erwin is primarily a victim of repression, trauma, and anxiety on the personal level. His major recourse to self-understanding has to be to read what his own body and behavior are telling him. The situation for the reader is entirely different. The word *mesilah* hangs there for us both as a temptation to read Erwin's fate as sealed, as a *mesilat barzel* [*iron track* or *rail*], going nowhere, and as a lure to probing the depths of the word, to where it opens up into something not yet completed in the past but about to happen in the present. If we resist the temptation to read Erwin as forever damned to travel this route, and if we read the word itself as encoding both our temptation to fate *and* the possibility of our resistance to it, then we move forward to where Erwin himself cannot move: into the freedom to experience in repetition the actualization of our lives.

We must journey with Erwin on his deadening journey if we are to journey at all. But we must also journey further. To preserve hope, which is to say faith, we must be willing to travel the other highways provided by the text, which lift up out of the life on the iron tracks by burrowing down deep into the other tracks hidden within the very language that those tracks also travel. The absent event of the Holocaust signals what cannot be said, which interrupts Jewish history and throws it into a collective trauma of not-to-be-repressed because barely-if-at-all "experienced" event. This absent event also, however, provides the possibility of our recognizing in the blank page the replication of other blank pages in and of the past, on which written words seemed nothing but rote repetitions, recollections endlessly recycling undecipherable past meanings. These words can, however, be recovered, be made to live again as actualities, if we allow them to happen to us, as linguistic events in the present transpiring between a speaker and a listener. And when this occurs, when we let such language speak its eventfulness, it leads us not only into personal liberation from this or that particular trauma but also into an even broader collective (and in the case of Appelfeld's project, specifically Jewish) human freedom. This is not simply political freedom, the freedom from constraints of one sort or another (Isaiah Berlin's "negative freedom"). Rather, it is the freedom to claim and enact our lives—precisely as repetitions, which is to say, as inheritances of the many lives that preceded ours—including Erwin's, and, as we shall now see, Bruno's in *The Age of Wonders.*

Encrypted Secrets, Blank Pages, and the Inheritance of Trauma

Even though Erwin is not a "believing Jew," nor an "observant one," he is nevertheless "still a Jew" (64, 119). As such, he is the repository of Jewish memory, both his own and that of others, like Mrs. Groton and August, whom he meets along the way and who entrust him with their family heirlooms. Like another of Appelfeld's characters, Bartfuss in *The Immortal Bartfuss,* he is the possessor of hidden treasures that he must lay open to view and interpretation, including the secrets of his own life (205, 238, 241). It is such a treasure, which is hardly only material, that Bartfuss would keep from his family and that obsesses the action of the narrative and organizes his (like Erwin's) repressed, depressive consciousness:

> The treasure consisted of three gold bars, five thousand dollars, two necklaces, a few gold watches, a few pictures of his mother, his father's passport picture, and a small photograph, apparently from school, of his sister. These possessions were very dear to him. He devoted his most pleasant thoughts to them, as if to a beloved woman. The treasure was hidden in a narrow steel box, sealed for some reason with an ornate lock. . . . [I]t made no sense to keep it in a damp cellar, open to the wind and inviting people to dig around in it. He knew that, but he still didn't take it out. (*Bartfuss* 45)

In similar, but even more complex ways, Bruno A. in *The Age of Wonders* is also the inheritor of secrets and treasures that he must excavate and restore to the light of day, if the freedom (both personal and political) that the protagonist desires is to be any kind of freedom at all.

It is not that Appelfeld's novels in the least underestimate the importance of political freedom, the freedom from persecution. It is that they know as well that political freedom is not separable from another sort of freedom, harder to define, more difficult to achieve. Bruno, after all, has achieved that cultural, national freedom his father fought so hard to maintain, and it is a question whether he (as a post-Holocaust, Israeli Jew) is any more free than his father was. The further question that the text raises retrospectively is whether his father was free in anything but a negative way even before the Nazi regime stripped him of his rights of citizenship and stole his life.

Like other of Appelfeld's fictions, such as *Tzili: The Story of a Life* and *Badenheim 1939, The Age of Wonders* binds together two separate narratives, one preceding, the other following the war, the first of which gives its title to the volume as a whole. But unlike these other two books, the two parts of *The Age of Wonders*—"The Age of Wonders" itself and "Many Years Later When Everything Was Over"/"*kechalot hakol vle*ʾ*aḥar shanim rabbot*"—trace the history of a single protagonist, Bruno. The first part of the volume, written in first-person narrative, as if within the consciousness of the child himself, records events in Bruno's life immediately preceding the war: the daily happenings of the already dysfunctional family, largely assimilated and antireligious, who finds itself excommunicated from the only culture it knows, finally to be rounded up in the local synagogue, which most of them have barely ever visited, to be deported to the death camps. The second part of the novel tells the story of Bruno's return to the place of his birth.

Ostensibly Bruno has come to set his father's affairs in order and have him reinstated as part of the Austrian literary tradition. This is a significant action in terms of the book's larger meditation on Jewish European authorship, which finally makes the book something of a reflection on the author's own art. But as Bruno's comments describing his personal life and the break-up of his marriage reveal, he is also clearly on a personal pilgrimage to work out, or work through, his own life crises. Like Erwin and Bartfuss, Bruno is a depressive individual, whose obsessions and compulsions and other forms of hysterical behavior bespeak the deep repressions of his youth. These include but are not limited to the blank page of the Holocaust separating his childhood in Austria from his adulthood in Israel.

Although Bruno claims not to have undertaken his journey home for his own purposes, his reactions once there suggest a different reading of his motives. "A week already gone in this familiar exile," we are told toward the middle of the narrative, "and nothing done" (216); "two weeks here already" (231); "that night in bed he knew that his stay here was coming to an end," his mission not accomplished (252). "Most of the day he spends sitting on a bench measuring the shadows of the church spires; realizing again that nothing has changed here, only him—he is already his father's age" (216). As the text makes clear, Bruno is searching for changes that might reveal to him the passage of time. He is looking, in other words, to verify the difference between then and now and, more poignantly, to warrant that his suffering has made some difference to this world, that it has changed it in some way, as if these changes will evidence his existence and his experience. What Bruno discovers is only the world's changelessness, its indifference.

Or, more precisely, what he discovers is the changelessness of the physical landscape, because what has changed is the population, including himself. And this renders all the more hurtful the indifference of the place to him and to the Jews that used to live there. Geography will validate none of Bruno's desires. "Nothing had changed," he remarks quite early in the narrative (203); the houses "were exactly as he remembered them. The years had come and gone and they had not changed. Only the vividness was new" (208); "there was no change; not a single tree had been uprooted from its place. . . . Except for the light, for the cold reality, it would have been like a vivid dream with all its details painted in carefully and precisely, but the cold reality was clear and decisive: you're here, Bruno, you're here" (200).

But if Bruno is "here" in one sense, ironically and painfully "here" is exactly where he and his community are *not:* "Faces flitted past, but he did not recognize anyone. 'The place hasn't changed but the people evidently have,' he said absent-mindedly as if he were making small talk to himself with ready-made words"

(189–90); "even the Jewish shops," we are told later, "have preserved their outward appearance, like the Lauffers' drapery shop. None of them have survived but their shop is still standing at exactly the same angle as before, perfectly preserved, even the geraniums in their pots. Now a different man is sitting there with a different woman. Strange—they don't look like murderers" (216–17). "Nothing has changed here," he realizes, "only him—he is already his father's age" (216).

The ghostliness of the place, which is picked up as well in Bruno's speaking words not "his own" (270; cf. also 192) is crucial to the experience being recorded here. It is not that the place does not provide the memories that Bruno seeks. Throughout the narrative, what is emphasized is the cold vivid clarity of the place. The "familiar words," we are told, are "like cold water" (183); "how clearly he saw" (185); the "brightness in the air is too much for his eyes to bear. . . . Everything stands in its place, utterly familiar" (206). If at the beginning "Bruno tried to remember, but no memories came" (185), by the end he has acquired more memories than he can cope with: "These little details, which had not come into his mind for years, now broke out of their hiding places. They were no longer forgotten but living, breathing feelings" (207). Yet they come to no avail. The world is just as "clear" when Bruno leaves as when he arrives (269), but by the end Bruno has returned to exactly the state of memory-less oblivion with which he began his journey: Now "not a memory remained with him. It was if they had all been devoured and left not even a trace behind. . . . He stood still for a long time, empty of thought or feeling. His eyes focused vacantly on the blinking railway signal, waiting for the brass plate to fall and the whistle of the engine to pierce the air" (270).

What these passages make very clear is something we have seen in relation to Erwin as well: that, by itself, remembering doesn't necessarily bring psychological relief. It doesn't automatically shift experience from the category of unconscious repetition to that of conscious choice, from the somnambular state of the dreamwalker-dummy, speaking ventriloquized lines, to that of the intentioned narrative performer. It does not even ensure that memories, once remembered, will endure. Indeed, in the case of Bruno, the very vividness of the memories, their clarity, seems to work against their availability as psychological tools. It is as if their "massive realism," to pick up Geoffrey Hartman's phrase, puts them beyond the possibility of their being set into some more accommodating interpretive frame. Retraumatizing Bruno, they lead him not into deeper consciousness but into even deeper oblivion. At the end of the novel, Bruno is still waiting for something sharp and penetrating (like a train whistle) to come and pierce the darkness.

The landscape's excessive clarity and the absence of the people who populated that landscape in Bruno's youth, which is rendered even sharper by that clarity, precisely *reincarnate* (to use the text's own word for this—213) the already moribund, ghostly life of the Jewish community even before the war. Bruno can no more see that now, than he or his community could see it then.

Bruno's is, we are told, a "strange homecoming" (208) to a place of "familiar exile" (216), a site of "familiar strangeness" (219; Erwin, we recall, calls his life his "strange life"). In other words, Bruno comes home to a home that, from the beginning, is a strange place of exile.

"You are my brother. My brother. In this exile," Bruno is told by a Japanese student whom he meets in the bar and for whom the place has absolutely no war-related associations, Christian or Jewish. "God never set foot in this place," the student tells him, "The evil spirits like beer, it seems" (212). To see what is here before his very eyes, Bruno will have to see in the familiarity of the place, or through it, the exilic strangeness that defined the place back then, when to the child Bruno, and to the Jewish community itself, Austria seemed a home and anything but the graveyard of evil spirits that it already was. Ironically, the child Bruno already knows this, albeit not consciously. "Strange," we are told, "When he was a child he would sometimes dream that he had come back to his town and no one knew him. He would wander from place to place, panic-stricken because of the silent, conspiratorial refusal to acknowledge his existence. He had spent a lot of time thinking about these dreams then, and their nightmarish absurdity" (233). Bruno must, in a sense, remember what he has always known but was (like the rest of his community) incapable of crediting as anything but absurd.

Like Erwin in relation to the text called *The Iron Tracks,* Bruno, in order to understand his experience, would have to read part one of *The Age of Wonders.* But he would have to read more than his own words describing the events of his childhood. Those words, tricky as they might be, nonetheless could be rendered the subject of a fairly conventional psychotherapeutic intervention. Rather, he would have to confront the various strange and exotic words floating in the atmosphere of his youth, spoken by others. These words were wholly undecipherable then and now constitute autonomous, incomprehensible, and almost magical compartments of meaning, loosely adrift in the text. Bruno is not the only speaker of ventriloquized words in this text. The text itself speaks such words, as quotations of those words that were spoken in a similarly ventriloquized fashion in the past.

Like *Badenheim,* and unlike part two of *The Age of Wonders,* part one of the novel is written in a choppy, hysterical, chaotic discourse. Not only do the characters' actions seem wildly out of control, but their words also seem grotesquely disconnected both from the characters themselves and from anything a reader might wish to plot as a coherent narrative meaning. The white page separating parts one and two of *The Age of Wonders* stands for more than the interruption produced by the Holocaust. It stands are well for the inaccessibility of the memories in part one to the person in part two who has lived those memories. This is, to some extent, Holocaust related. The shadow the Holocaust casts over the past is less a dimming of that past than, like the intense white light that Bruno meets in his hometown, an excessive brightness. This overwhelming light does not hide and conceal. Rather it dissolves pictures into nothingness. The

Holocaust, as we have seen in *The Iron Tracks*, de-creates the past. It makes it as if it had never been, not by casting shadows that we might nonetheless see through but by overwhelming with brilliant clarity. The challenge is to deflect the glare.

To journey to the past, under the best of circumstances, may constitute less an experience of literally revisiting the geography of one's youth (as Bruno tries to do) than obliquely, through deflection, recalling that youth, putting it down on paper, as it were, and examining its language. After all, and unlike *The Iron Tracks*, this text does not give us any actual Holocaust moment at all, which that blank page might be understood to represent in the way that in Erwin's experience his *ḥaradah* mimics the Holocaust experience at Wirblbahn. Indeed, and this, I think, is where Appelfeld's text so brilliantly takes us, insofar as so much of the past's meaning is contained in words that are themselves the containers of other people's repressed memories and meanings and that therefore cannot be made subject to decoding and conscious comprehension, revisiting the past might constitute nothing more than reading a blank page on which one must transcribe some new, perhaps largely fictive story.

For this reason, Bruno's return to the town of his birth is especially to be differentiated from a dream. "Except for the light, for the cold reality, it would have been like a vivid dream, with all its details painted in carefully and precisely, but the cold reality was clear and decisive: you're here Bruno, you're here" (200). To dream, one must have concrete memories that take the form of objects and places and people to be interpreted. Where there are no memories, there are no dreams, only reality itself. How can one decipher the literal, the real? How does one read a text in a language that is not one's own? How does one read a blank page that is only the world itself?

In his translation of the works of psychoanalysts Nicholas Abraham and Maria Torok, Nicholas Rand describes a form of repression that goes to the heart of Appelfeld's *The Age of Wonders* and the psyche of the pre-Holocaust Jewish world described there and elsewhere in Appelfeld's fiction. Encryptment, in Rand's vocabulary, signals a failure of repression similar to and intimately related to the sort we have already met in Erwin. But encryptment is also the diametrical opposite of the deficit neurosis or traumatic memory that afflicts Erwin. It needs, therefore, to be understood and dealt with somewhat differently.[4]

Essentially, Abraham and Torok distinguish between two kinds of repression. The first, which they label "constitutive" or "dynamic" repression, is the garden variety sort we have already met in relation to Erwin. It can be understood as "hysteria" in which "the desire, born of prohibition, seeks a way out through detours and finds it through symbolic fulfillment"—where symbolic obviously can mean either verbal or behavioral representation (159). The second kind of repression is what they call "preservative repression." For the individual suffering from this kind of repression (whom they designate the "cryptophore") "an already fulfilled desire lies buried—equally incapable of rising or of disintegrating." The past, therefore, "is present in the subject as a *block of reality,*" which becomes a carefully guarded "secret." Indeed, reality itself comes to be defined "as a *secret*" (159).

In his commentary, Rand explains:

> the secret is a trauma whose very occurrence and devastating emotional consequences are entombed and thereby consigned to internal silence, albeit unwittingly, by the sufferers themselves. The secret here is intrapsychic. It designates an internal psychic splitting; as a result two distinct "people" live side by side, one behaving as if s/he were part of the world and the other as if s/he had no contact with it whatsoever. . . . The guiding principle here is introjection, the idea that the psyche is in a constant process of acquisition, involving the active expansion of our potential to open onto our own emerging desires and feelings as well as the external world. (99–100)

Preservative repression inhibits introjection, producing instead what Abraham and Torok identify as incorporation—"the traumatic impossibility of self-fashioning and readjustment," problems located as well in traditional Freudian categories such as "conflict, censorship, and repression" (101) and connected to melancholia.

"The crux of this illness is not the loss of the love-object," writes Rand, "but the secret the loss occasions" (103). Such incorporation, which is to say such preservative repression, does not express desire through its displacement or transference onto some other activity or set of words. Rather, it denies or bypasses desire altogether. It is also, in Abraham and Torok's vocabulary, antimetaphoric. It participates actively in the "destruction of representation," swallowing (as it were) the very words or actions by which desire might be nonetheless, neurotically, expressed (132).

But the secret kept from the self, the encryptment, is not nearly so complex or inaccessible to revelation as another sort of secret that also concerns Abraham and Torok. This other form of encryptment is equally, perhaps even more, relevant to Appelfeld's novel. This is the transgenerational phantom (165), in which the secrets of others enjoy encrypted existence within the self. "What haunts are not the dead," writes Abraham, "but the gaps left within us by the secrets of others," "the tombs of others" (171, 172). "Thus, the phantom cannot even be recognized by the subject" (174), since it is the "formation of the unconscious that has never been conscious—for good reason. It passes . . . from the parent's unconscious into the child's. . . . The phantom's periodic and compulsive return lies beyond the scope of symptom-formation in the sense of a return of the repressed; it works like a ventriloquist, like a stranger within the subject's own mental topography" (173).

Not coincidentally, for our purposes, both Rand in his discussion of Abraham's essay, and Abraham himself make reference to the Holocaust in this context. A question among the others that Appelfeld's texts raise is how we retrieve *encrypted* rather than repressed or obscured memories—memories that do not exist as such because they are not our own. He might as well ask, and, as we have seen, he *does* ask, how we learn to hear words and to speak them. One way of learning to hear and to speak is to learn to read the blank pages in every text as in every psyche. This does not mean filling up the pages with meanings of our own. It means, rather, reading, genuinely reading, the blanks.

Ghostwriting the Past

Though initially Bruno's return to the landscape of his youth seems a rather typical moment of Oedipal re-enactment, especially given its vivid moment of violent revenge when he brutally beats his father's old crony Brum (who, as we shall see in a moment, serves as the surrogate father onto whom Bruno projects his hostilities toward his real, now-deceased father), it contains a far less concrete, less accessible event, without which the Oedipal scene is either simplistic or irrelevant. The fact that Appelfeld dedicates the book to his own recently deceased father is not to be cast aside lightly in this context. Yet it is by no means obvious what we mean when we speak of the love–hate relationship of fathers and sons, either on the personal or the public or even the mythic level.

"Coming back," we are told, "had not been his idea":

> Something stubborn and abiding inside him had sealed off whole sectors of his emotions. In the course of the years he had learned to live without them, as a person learns to live with a paralyzed limb. The two letters suddenly coming from far away had stirred the old scar into a new pain: his father. His father. The disgrace he had not dared to touch, seething silently all these years like pus inside a wound. They said he had died half mad. . . . Almost every year some broken echo had reached him and reopened his hidden wound. His disgrace had many faces: contempt, hatred, deliberate forgetfulness. He gave his father no credit at all. But in recent years, perhaps because he himself was already approaching his father's age, he felt the old, wretched shame swelling inside him in a different way, no longer hatred but a kind of distance and even wonder. (209)

It is no "wonder" then that, "now," having "reached his father's age, perhaps even a few years more," and "[standing] in the place where he had once stood with his father" (209–210), he should suddenly come upon one of his father's old "admirers," Brum (253). In imitation of the mental process at work here, the two passages themselves flow directly from the one to the other: "He had come back to his first place and there was no one left there close to him. So he stood and stared at this strange creature called Brum. In all probability, the old man himself did not remember that his name was Brum, but he, Bruno, remembered that his name was Brum" (210).

Just as the initial by which both Bruno and his father are identified in the text forces us to associate the writer and his son with the author of the text and thus with an idea of Jewish authorship and the literary tradition, so, too, does the similarity of the name Brum to Bruno forge a kind of familial association between the two characters. This is reinforced by the text's deliberate emphasis on the names Bruno ("Bruno A., the son of A"—there is no other name, 215) and Brum, which, we are told, is a name that Bruno and not Brum remembers.

But it is not only the connection between the two names that the text in this way highlights. It is also the prominence and significance of the names as words. The words *Brum* and *Bruno* leap out at us as the only two words that matter here, as if the words themselves carry meaning. This is true as well of a series of almost mystical, incantatory words, which no less than punctuate both parts one and two of this text, often providing the primary linkage between the two parts of the narrative. This is a text haunted not only by secrets and evil spirits, but by words, including the words *secrets* and *evil spirits,* as we shall see, which proliferate throughout the text and define Bruno's inner reality.

As is clear almost immediately, the scars and wounds (181, 209) that come to life in Bruno when he receives the telegram concerning his father may have deeper origins than the "disgrace" of his father's behavior during and after the war, deeper even than his father's disgraceful behavior preceding the deportation, when he strove to sever himself from the Jewish community. Such feelings of shame, part one of the book makes clear, already characterized the father and son—indeed the entire family and community—before the war (53). "His disgrace had many faces," the text says in part two, leaving painfully unclear to whom the word *his,* and thereby the "contempt, hatred, [and] deliberate forgetfulness," refer: Bruno or his father (209). Though this is especially true in the English translation, the Hebrew also permits a blurring of referents here, which receives reinforcement later on, in the Hebrew original rather than in the English translation, when the text says that "in recent years, perhaps because he himself was already approaching his father's age, he felt the old, wretched shame swelling inside him in a different way, no longer hatred but a kind of distance and even wonder": the word *shame* in the Hebrew is the same word that is translated as *disgrace* earlier on: *ḥerpah* (209).

As the first part of *The Age of Wonders* makes clear for us readers, though this knowledge is cut off from Bruno's own consciousness (represented textually by that white page), Bruno the child has already experienced in his father the father's own sense of his life as disgraceful and shameful. This sense of shame was no more comprehensible to the father than it was to the child. It is as if what Bruno inherits, then, from his father, and not in relation to any particular set of events, is a sense of disgracefulness itself, attached somehow to contempt, hatred, and most especially forgetting. Forgetting, too, is something Bruno unwittingly inherits from his father. "Anxiety," says one of the characters in part one, choosing a particularly apt word to describe Father's unconscious self-hatred ("all his rage was turned inward against himself, against the flawed creations of his spirit"—154), is the Jewish "legacy inherited from former generations" (94). Anxiety, which we have seen is Erwin's disease, is also the disease of Bruno and Father. The question that the text raises is how anxiety can become "inheritance"—to pick up another word that we shall see in a moment becomes crucial in the text. How can individuals come to forget what they personally have never experienced to remember, and how might they pass it on, transgenerationally, as a bizarre form of memory-less remembering?

Not for naught does the text describe Bruno's experience in relation to his father as a sort of *wonder*, the word in Hebrew conveying more directly than the English a sense of the magical or miraculous. Every age in the life of the mind, we might say, is an age of wonders. Every age is inexplicable and beyond comprehension, carrying with it the potential for deadly bewitching. And while that age of wonders that was both Bruno's own apparently magical childhood and the presumably equally enchanted life of the Jews in Europe contained marvels to be sure, it harbored ghostly terrors as well. No one, not even the adults of this world, certainly not its child protagonist, was competent to interpret those terrors, which were contained within the words that the characters heard and spoke (including the word *wonder* itself).[5]

Though in part two of the book Bruno does remember certain moments from the past, one of the discomforting aspects of the text is that at no moment (with one partial and telling exception) do we experience Bruno actually recalling any scene that we as readers have been given in part one of the narrative. Therefore, what bridges the two sections as a continuous narrative in the life of a single consciousness, and therefore what is put forward in this text as one model of consciousness, is the language itself. Mystical, magical words are adrift and afloat in both parts of the text, as if searching for their relationship to each other, across a blank page. The one exception that proves the rule is a remembering and misremembering of an episode, or more precisely the juxtaposition of two different episodes from part one that do make their way into part two.

"Are we far from Knospen?" Father is asked close to the end of part one, when he is on his way home from his humiliation at the hands of a supposed old friend (150). "Are we far from Knospen?" the question is echoed in part two, as Bruno is nearing his old hometown (181); and recalled again by him a few pages later: "How far is it from here to Knospen?—quarter of an hour, no more. When he was a boy, there had once been a heavy snowfall in the spring. The family had returned from Vienna and the carriage that should have been waiting for them at the station had failed to arrive. And his father, in a fur coat and a strange mood, had flung his arm out toward the avenue and said, 'How far is it from here to Knospen?—quarter of an hour, no more.' It wasn't a real voice, only a kind of question in the air" (186). The text itself leaves the question hanging in the air, leaving unclear as well whether the question that now lies hanging there refers to the same scene we are given in part one or whether, in its second occurrence in part two, it refers only to its earlier utterance in part two. Hanging there in the text, three times, the question achieves a status quite independent of what the words in the sentence literally mean or refer to. It becomes something like voice itself, a strange voice hanging in the air of the text, like so many other magical words that the text employs.

What haunts pre-war Europe, we come to realize, is not the about-to-come event of the Holocaust. This is the event that seems in both parts of the book to be what those phantasmagoric words like *evil spirits, disgrace,* and *secrets* allude to. It could seem as if those words now represent fulfillments of prophecies already afloat in part one. The text might then be open to the interpretation (levied by some in relation to *Badenheim*) that it is condemning those who were incapable of seeing into the future. But the words in part two do not refer to anything concrete that could have been deciphered. They do nothing more than repeat or, to pick up once again the text's own word for this, *reincarnate,* what were already ghostly words in the past, when they were no more susceptible to interpretation than now. The evil spirits of pre-war Austria, furthermore, do not come from outside this world. They are a part of it, within its resident Jews themselves, who, like all of us, can in no way see themselves as the vehicles of their own ghostly self-haunting.

The concept of reincarnation is introduced into the text by the same Japanese student, from outside the world of European Jewry and the Holocaust, who identifies Austria as a godless place of exile and evil spirits (212–13). When asked if he believes in reincarnation, Bruno responds: "I know someone. His name was Brum. A tall thin man who hardly opened his mouth, and he was suddenly changed into somebody else. Now he doesn't answer to his name. I call him and he doesn't answer to his name." "Of course," answers the student; "He's been changed into someone else. He can't answer. He doesn't remember" (213). What is significant here is that Brum's "reincarnation" "into somebody else" is not a recent affair. Rather it preceded the war:

> In the bitter days of the last year, before the deportation—in the terrible confusion when people were exchanging their religion, selling their shops, abandoning beloved wives, taking drugs like alcohol—in those bitter days, Brum had married his housemaid. Within a few weeks the miracle had taken place: Brum the thin, Brum the ascetic, was metamorphosed into a different kind of Brum. He grew taller, his shoulders filled out, and a luxuriant moustache appeared on his face. . . . Bruno's father said, "Would you believe it?" . . . Who would have imagined that he of all people, this man of delicate and morbid sensibilities, this bachelor of so many years' standing, would achieve the impossible? Would be reincarnated in his own lifetime into the likeness of an Austrian cattle farmer, completely erasing all the soft, delicate lines of his former self. . . . Everyone, it seemed, understood that the old Brum was dead. The new one wasn't Brum any more. (201–202)

Although in the present moment of the text (in part two), Brum reincarnates for Bruno Bruno's father, whom Bruno also himself reincarnates—thus linking reincarnation with a fairly familiar idea of the return of the repressed and even the uncanny—Brum also reincarnates himself. What this means in the context of this novel is that ghosts do not necessarily come from without (from another place and another time). They may dwell within, such that oneself in one's own being is the crypt of secrets and treasures.

What haunts Appelfeld's text, as what haunted Europe both preceding and following the catastrophe, is not so much evil spirits per se as the words *evil spirits,* which appear in both parts of the text as a kind of mantra, no fewer than ten times in these very words (24, twice 25, 26, 39, 75, 140, 267), and in others closely verging on these (83, 93, 150, for example). "It's not right for you to come here and stir up evil spirits," Brum says to Bruno, in what surely imports into the novel a typical representation (like Bruno's father himself) of the auto-antisemitism of European Jewry. "Don't arouse the evil spirits, don't stir them up again," he continues. "Nothing in your character has changed, I see. The same old Jewish impudence" (267).

At first Bruno's response seems the appropriate post-war Jewish, even Israeli, response: "When Bruno grasped these words in all their nakedness he rushed at Brum, seized hold of his coat, and said in a voice full of power, 'Anti-Semitism from you is something I won't permit. From you I expect a little remorse'" (268). But set as this response is within a clearly Oedipal frame, and leading directly into Bruno's departure back into the life of dysfunctional forgetting that has set him upon his enterprise to begin with, the text raises the question of whether Bruno can even begin to fathom the ghostly and still-haunting depths of the auto-antisemitism Brum's words express, which not only characterized Brum's double, his own father, but which continue to characterize his father's other double in the present moment, Bruno himself. The evil spirits Brum would banish in banishing Bruno do indeed inhabit Bruno in ways of which he himself is quite unaware and that are not in the least to be dispelled by Bruno's militaristic ("Israeli") response to what he sees as the self-hatred of the father's generation of European Jews.

It is clear, and many critics have remarked it, that *The Age of Wonders* deals intensively with a subject that informs much of Appelfeld's fiction: the subject of auto-antisemitism.[6] But what such auto-antisemitism actually is, Appelfeld's novel makes us see, is not to be assumed a priori. It is certainly not a disease for which the state of Israel is the cure. Despite all his bravado, Bruno, too, is seen to be a self-hating Jew. He carries on a tradition of such self-hatred, reincarnated generation after generation, both in the *galut* (diaspora) and in Israel, by *evil spirits* that virtually defy definition, even comprehension. As Appelfeld puts it more directly in one of his essays, "Jewish self-accusation" is "passed on . . . like a curse" ("Beyond Despair," 12).

What Bruno cannot see is the tradition that he unconsciously but nonetheless emphatically inherits: a tradition of evil spirits that he himself, if he had children (which he does not—the text makes a point of this) might well pass on. This tradition takes place in the disowning of those ghosts (their denial) and the displacing of them onto others—in particular, and in imitation of the non-Jewish world surrounding them, onto other Jews. Therefore, just as in part two of *The Age of Wonders* Brum (in imitation of the Austrian non-Jewish society that he has joined) imagines these evil spirits to be Jews themselves like Bruno, while Bruno himself imagines them to be the self-hating Jews like Brum, so too in part one Bruno's father and his contemporaries projected those evil spirits onto someone else—namely the *Ostjuden.* These are the Jews of Eastern European flowing into Austria and presumably compromising the gains the Austrian Jews have won for themselves there. "When Mother told him about the strange night train that had stopped to have its Jewish passengers registered, [Father] denounced the bureaucracy at first, but immediately added that ever since the *Ostjuden* had arrived things had gone haywire. They must have brought evil spirits with them" (24).

What the text then describes is a situation far more complicated and fraught than the child's simply imbibing some cultural prejudice that he then unconsciously re-enacts either by repeating it verbatim or by displacing it onto some other object. For the "evil spirits" that take their inception in the mind of the child are quite unrelated to and distinct from the "evil spirits" to which his father is referring. "I was apprehensive," says the child narrator Bruno almost immediately after his father's comments concerning the *Ostjuden,* "maybe because of Louise, and maybe because of the evil spirits haunting the house. The evil spirits were many—many because intangible, appearing only in my fantasies. But sometimes they appeared in the real world too—lately in the form of the fleshly maids who had come to clean the house" (25). And a few sentences later he continues: "The nights seemed empty; only the evil spirits left behind by the maids remained. Everything was ready was for an incomprehensible freedom. An obscure terror seized my heart" (26).

In the swerve from the first usage of the term *evil spirits* in the text, referring to the *Ostjuden,* to the second, which catches on to that meaning only to attach it, with increasing insistence, to evil spirits of a very different sort (the young maids), is contained nothing less than a paradigm of the process whereby cultural prejudice takes root in the individual psyche.

To the child Bruno, as later to his adult self, it seems that evil spirits are afoot. For the older Bruno these evil spirits are, as his father also imagined, real-life Jews of one variety or another, though in a process typical of a son's rebellion against his father, the Jews who were evil spirits for the father are not the Jews who are evil spirits for the son. For the child Bruno, however, the evil spirits are nothing other than a word or figure for the child's own unabidable thoughts (in this case, his budding sexual desire). These desires get projected onto others as *their* corruption—not his—*and* they take an inappropriate, irrelevant name from the incomprehensible adult vocabulary surrounding him. The passage, in other words, exposes how words that are afloat in the air get attached to the child's own individual psychosexual development—giving false names to what is completely otherwise: for these are no demons that the child is experiencing, but his own quite natural, internal psychosexual desires. At the same time, these words, because they are severed from their meanings, put out of reach any clarification of what those terms conceal, either in their primary or secondary usages. Father, too, does not see what the words *evil spirits* hide. This is not only his own self-hatred but the psychosexual origins of that self-hatred as well.

This is what the son's misuse of the term ironically and unselfconsciously recovers. Later, Father will use the words *evil spirits* to refer to the Nazis: "To leave at a time like this with evil spirits raging meant admitting that reason had lost out, that literature was to no avail" (140). Once more he will locate to his own satisfaction the origins of suffering and human evil in particular persons. But he will do so in such a way as to have clarified nothing at all. Indeed, his comments mystify what is not in the least mysterious, for the Nazis are real life people, not evil spirits. They will have to be physically rooted out, not exorcised in words, the power of which are in any event neutralized by their having becoming so commonplace as to be beyond interpretation.

What these passages reveal is the deep psychosexual structure of incomprehension and denial that produces the need, first, to identify *evil spirits* and give them names, only, then, to further conceal the realities to which words might refer and render those realities mysterious. Like the son's demons, so, too, are the father's a cover for something else. This represents not only the father's more reasoned, intellectual auto-antisemitism, or, finally, his disappointment at not having achieved the literary fame he desired. Rather, as the child's unwitting witnessing makes very clear to us, the father also experiences "inappropriate" or at least worrying sexual feelings for those very same maids that so tempt the child (he does as well for a young Jewish woman who comes to live with them later on and whom Mother forces him finally to evict—one more family "shame," the text tells us—98). Bruno the adult has not only to deal with his father's apparently disgraceful behavior during the war and with what he has also come to view retrospectively as the father's disgraceful behavior as an auto-antisemitic Austrian Jewish writer even before, but he has to cope with the father's own sense of his behavior as disgraceful, not because it is auto-antisemitic, but because it reflects erotic passions and longings that, as an intellectual and writer, he believes he should not feel.

Throughout the text, Father's life is shadowed by one "disgrace" or "shame" after another, some associated with his ailing stepmother (49), some with Mother's depressive sister Theresa (57), some with his own behavior toward women (98), and also, of course, in relation to his Jewishness (62). The writer A's auto-antisemitism goes very deep indeed, past what defines him as a Jew to what defines him as a man, though when he has to find an object or a word for this self-disdain, he discovers it in Jewishness, or rather, in his Jewishness projected onto other Jews as their Jewishness, and not his own. The book parades before us many of the classic stereotypes, in relation to Father and Bruno both, concerning the Jew's lack of physical prowess. "Here's a little Jew for you," Dr. Mirzel says of the child Bruno, adding, "Boys should be toughened up when they're young" (40; cf. the character of Helga in *The Healer* [*be*ᶜ*et uve*ᶜ*onah aḥat;* literally: At One and the Same Time], who, according to her brother Felix, has been turned by schoolwork and piano lessons into a "Jewish weakling" [17]). As we shall see in a moment, circumcision as the mark of male Jewishness brings forward this sense of Father's that Jewish manhood is a sign of physical inadequacy and ill health (37, 120–21).

Bruno, then, is confronted with no less a challenge than *not only* to decipher his own relation to the non-Jewish world of his childhood and what that world did to him and his family, *and also* to decode his anger and resentment and judgment of his parents (in particular, his father), both in relation to himself and those same childhood events, *but also* having to discover in his relation to both these aspects of his experience his incorporation of his father's own repressions and denials in relation to these things, as those repressions and denials were contained in words that have now seemed to have achieved, over time and through lack of conscious attentiveness to them, an independence and autonomy of their own. One more word that gathers up these separate threads of *disgrace* and *shame* is a word we have already met, both in this text as in *The Iron Tracks:* the word *anxiety.* This is a word that, like auto-antisemitism, is also all too easily misunderstood and misdefined. What we mean by Jewish *anxiety* is no more obvious than what we mean by the term *auto-antisemitism.*

The Anxiety of Language

As we have already seen, anxiety is one name for the conventional, diagnosable neurosis from which Bruno and his father, like Erwin, suffer. As such, it has nothing whatsoever to do specifically with Jews and Jewish history. To pull into play once again Elizabeth Bellamy's definition, anxiety is fear that does not know what it is afraid of. It is a general, enduring human condition. But just as Erwin's anxiety (which he, like Bruno, also inherits from a parent, though in his case from his mother) is also intimately related to a specific event neither so general nor pervasive in the population, the event of the Holocaust, so the anxiety Bruno embodies is related to another psychological phenomenon that is also not so common in the general population. This is what Abraham and Torok define as encryptment. In *The Age of Wonders,* the already excruciating complexity of anxiety is given one more agonizing turn of the screw. Not only is anxiety a psychological state in which, for one reason or another, the relation to the formative event has been severed, but it is an inheritance of such similar severings, passed on in words, that become the vehicles of transmitted repression.

As an educated and enlightened intellectual, Bruno's father has no problem detecting and defining Jewish anxiety in others. The most simply defined case of anxiety in the novel, and also an influence on Bruno's own later neuroses (though not, obviously, the major one), is exhibited in Bruno's violin teacher, Mr. Danzig. But Father's anxiety, and later Bruno's, cannot be adequately explained by Father's definitions or what father presents as the "classic case of Jewish anxiety" embodied in Mr. Danzig. His "extreme" "pedantry," Father suggests, "could only be explained by the desire to punish himself—in which he undoubtedly succeeded" (29). It is this self-loathing and self-flagellation that Father also so perfectly represents. But Father represents more.

Not accidentally, the scene when Mr. Danzig comes to take his leave of Bruno and his family, and in which his anxiety is most fully displayed for the reader, is set within another scene of anxious crisis concerning Father himself: "[Danzig] was about to sail for Australia, but before leaving Europe he wanted to come and apologize to us. It was all his fault. Some hidden flaw, some defect he was incapable of locating, was ruining his playing" (52); "little flaws," Bruno realizes, that "could not be rooted out [and] had turned into open wounds" that he transferred to his pupils (53). Immediately preceding this description in the text is the more complicated case of Father:

> [A's] literary successes had begun to sour. One of his publishers had demanded cuts and complained that the manuscript was wearisome and too long. Father, I remember, was very upset; but in the end, as usual, he found that the man was right. There was a flaw in the structure—to be precise, many flaws. . . . He wrote a long, apologetic letter and asked for the manuscript back.
>
> Just about that time, the ugly old business of the inheritance came up again, and he decided to go to the provincial capital and get that affair, at least, out of the way. Perhaps a successful campaign in the courts would make his humiliation at the hands of his publishers easier to bear. (50–51; concerning the flaws in Father's writing, see also 154, 158)

"Be so good as to tell me," Father asks one of his friends later in the book, "what, precisely, is Jewish about my writing?" to which he is answered in words I have already quoted: "The anxiety. Isn't that a legacy inherited from former generations?" (93–94). "The violin teacher had not come yet," Bruno says earlier in the narrative, "but I felt his anxiety in the fingers of my left hand" (27).

Flaws. Wounds. Anxiety. Inheritance. These, in their accelerating progression, are what doom not only Father's work but also Father himself, and, later, Bruno. It isn't that in presenting a critical, even damning view of Father, Appelfeld is by any means ignoring the actual antisemitism that sentences not only Father's writing but, more terrifyingly, Father himself to what is anything but a cultural or figural death. "One of Father's unknown enemies began publishing a series of articles denouncing his work" (71). This process, which increases its momentum as the story proceeds, merges in the end with the rounding up and deportation of the community itself. Still, what emerges as far more important to Appelfeld's reading of Jewish history, in particular the Jewish literary tradition of Kafka, whose name punctuates the text along with those of Wasserman, Zweig, Schnitzler (108, 151), and we might add Schultz (who, not part of the vocabulary of German-Jewish writing of this period, is obliquely remembered by the text through Bruno's name), is the Jewish intellectual's willingness to consent to this verdict about himself and his art. "Kafka," said Appelfeld, in an interview with Philip Roth, "spoke to me not only in my mother tongue, but also in another language which I knew intimately, the language of the absurd. . . . To my regret, I came to Bruno Schultz's work years too late, after my literary approach was rather well formed. I felt and still feel a great affinity with his writing" ("Beyond Despair," 63–65).

What people call you and how they treat you may determine your political liberties. These factors may determine as well whether you live or die. These are no small matters, to be sure. What you call yourself, however, may determine a freedom that is equally vital and far more difficult to define. On a simple, practical level, the Jews' willingness to consent to their exclusion from the European literary community involved a considerable amount of "forgetting" about or denying the conditions of antisemitism that had produced both Jewish anxiety and auto-antisemitism. More complexly, it had to do as well with a reluctance or an inability to read the Jew's own literary text, and the tradition of texts, including Jewish texts, in which it participated. For what Father's unknown enemy faults him for and what he finally accepts as the fatal flaw in his art is paradoxically just that depiction of the Jew that Father does indeed produce in his fiction. This depiction is not only its most distinctive literary feature—its "beauty" (72) in the critic's own word—but its legacy from the figure whom Father considers the most brilliant writer of his generation and the "prophet of truth" in the modern world, Franz Kafka (82).

It is this disavowal of his art that most intensely concerns Appelfeld. "Who are the author's heroes?" Father's critic asks contemptuously of his fiction; "neither urban Austrians nor rural Austrians, but Jews, who had lost all semblance of humanity and were now useless, corrupt, perverted; parasites living off the healthy Austrian tradition, not their own marrow but the marrow of others. It could not be denied that this parasitism possessed a certain beauty, but it was a parasitic beauty" (72). "The Jewish parasite," the critic concludes, referring now to the writer himself, "must be rooted out" (75). Appelfeld puts before us that all-too-familiar moment when rhetoric makes that fatal swerve from the metaphorical to the literal. This moment is repeated later, as well, when a fellow passenger on the train suggests that the Jewish merchants (whom Father also despises) be "exterminated" (138). Language carries a force and a momentum of its own. Appelfeld would have us see this truth about the danger of words throughout his writing. But this is not the most important element in the battle between Father and his critic.

The more important, specifically literary truth, here, is that, ironically, the critic is in many ways right about Father's art, and about Father himself. He *does* write about the Jewish parasite, whom he despises. And while Father might have every right to be a part of Austrian culture, he is not; therefore, he *is* in a sense living off the marrow of a culture not his own. This is the hard truth in Appelfeld's opinion, concerning Jews in Europe before the Holocaust. And their "parasitism"—in the fullness of its truth—is a story to be told, indeed a story that European culture needs to read. In his failure to read his own text, Father agrees with the condemnation of himself but for the wrong reasons. He fails to see the Jewish, which is to say as well the *human,* truth encoded in his own writing.

It is the failure of culture to read itself that Appelfeld holds up to view in *The Age of Wonders.* As we saw as well in *Badenheim,* the terms of culture are shared terms, and this is part of Father's problem. Father's views significantly converge with those of his enemy. There is nothing exceptional or unnatural about this. Therefore, like his enemies, Father bears contempt for the "hornet's nest of petit-bourgeois Jews" (45) as he does as well for the "droves" (61) of *Ostjuden* "infesting Austria like rats, infesting the whole world, to tell the truth" (133). "Father cursed the little Jews who could think of nothing but money" (54) and who are contending with him for his rightful cultural inheritance. He "denounced the Jewish petite bourgeoisie, for whom the world consisted of nothing but money, hotels, and holiday resorts, and a stupid superficial religion" (83; cf. 135). Therefore, it is no wonder he concurs with the critic's assessment both of his texts and of the Jewish world represented there: "Can't you see," he says to

Mother in the critic's defense, "that he bases everything on the texts themselves" (76).

Exactly. What the critic reads out of Father's writing is indeed what that fiction says. But by the same token, everything that Father needs both to defend his art and himself is contained in those very same words his critic will use to damn him. Father is no better reader of his text than his critic is. He can see neither his own defection to a culture not his own nor the Jewish-European textual tradition that his significantly repeats. Father's fictional heroes, and his vocabulary, are not different from those of the writer who is for him (not to mention for Appelfeld) the progenitor of modern literature (Jewish and non-Jewish alike), the writer whose works Father knows by "heart" (44).

Father, we are told, "was a sworn devotee of Franz Kafka," whose "few published works had converted him completely" (44). Only Kafka, he later tells Bruno, had discovered "the hidden nucleus that every artist seeks" (158). Mightn't one say, in the words of Father's critic, that this "nucleus" in Kafka's works (and Appelfeld's for that matter)—in works such as "The Metamorphosis," for example, or *Badenheim*—is that "parasitic beauty" that Father's own writing, like his life, figures forth? And that this parasitic beauty is a form of "beauty" in a literary sense because it identifies a truth about Jews, which in its specificity, in its realization of the conditions that condition an utterly specific life and people, says something about human beings generally as well?

Father is as blind to the meaning of the texts he values as he is of the texts he writes, including the text that is his life, which is now the text we are reading, Appelfeld's text. For Father's fictional protagonists are not so different from those of Appelfeld himself, not least of all in the very book we are reading. Father is the hero of a book Father himself could well have written, but not have read, any more than he (like other of Appelfeld's characters) can interpret his life's experience. "The arguments about Kafka would sometimes go on until late at night," Bruno reports; "It was then that a word struck my ears for the first time: decadence. But these arguments, to tell the truth, belonged to my sleeping rather than my waking hours" (44). Exactly.

The Age of Wonders, like much of Appelfeld's fiction, is about rendering conscious what is not conscious. For this reason, the text is careful to distinguish the critic's comments from the rank antisemitism that they also, clearly, embody. Because the critic is himself Jewish, "we couldn't even argue that the articles were written by an anti-Semite" (73). This, we realize, is nonsense: we may call Jewish antisemitism by another name, but it is antisemitism all the same. Nonetheless, there is something to what the text is claiming here, especially since in the end Father comes to accept the critic's condemnation of him. Indeed, he comes to celebrate it, making the problem less the critic's judgment of Father than Father's judgment of himself. If Father, in his own view of himself, undergoes a metamorphosis from man to parasite (a man to a beetle), the critic who has thus condemned Father (Michael Taucher by name) is made to experience the reverse process. He is made into a god: "The obscure critic was transformed. No longer the scoundrel, but Taucher, Michael Taucher in full. And Taucher, moreover, the perceptive, Taucher the discriminating . . . thus Taucher settled down and took up residence amongst us as an adopted member of the family" (76). Or, more properly he takes up residence as one more ghost in a family haunted by ghosts: for by this time young Michael Taucher the critic has died.

There are several fairly straightforward points being made here, which I wish to touch on briefly. As is most likely the case with every writer, Father sees himself as flawed, especially when he is compared with a genius like Kafka. In the same vein, it is clear that what begins as ordinary, normal self-doubt become exaggerated and monumentalized into a fatality because it is given a name to which to attach itself (in this case, the name *Jewish*). This is much like the process whereby the child's early sexual desires come to seem evil spirits because that is the word out there for him or her to apply to some feeling for which he or she does not yet have a suitable name. What interests me more is that what we are being made to observe here is something about the Jewish literary tradition itself: the way in which it is inhabited by ghosts of self-loathing.

This self- and communal-haunting isn't simply antisemitism or auto-antisemitism in the political sense. Rather, it is the very textuality of Jewish existence, in which what is being in/visibly expressed/repressed is the whole history of Jewish experience in Western culture in a place of "familiar exile" and "strange familiarity." To read themselves and their own tradition, Jews have to read this text of their history, as written, for example, by a writer like Kafka, who did not necessarily seem to a writer like Father to be a Jewish writer, even though, as much contemporary criticism has shown us, he quite definitely is. Father, in other words, like his son later and like Erwin in *The Iron Tracks,* has to accept the specificities of his life and his text as *his,* despite, or perhaps because of the strangeness itself—though that strangeness might have to be interrogated and analyzed—as a blank page to be read.[7]

The text forces us to see that Father's writing, like his sense of himself generally, is haunted from within, by the Michael Tauchers both living and dead, who would condemn the author's work for exactly what distinguishes it as art—its faithful representation of the world it figures forth. They would call that authenticity by another name: the alien, the parasitic, the Jewish, in order to disclaim what they themselves understand about it: that it is truth of a certain kind. In so doing, they close down the possibility, for the Jewish writer and reader as well, of understanding what that truth is. This hauntedness of the Jew, which is internalized long before Taucher comes upon the scene and dies (to become an adopted member of Father's family of ghostly voices), does somehow manifest itself as a form of parasitism sucking the marrow of society. This is the case, not because the Jews are not worthy of inclusion within the cultures of Europe, but because the fact of the matter is that they have been excluded. And rather than blame European society for that, they blame themselves. In this way, they become self-alienated from their own culture. They become inauthentic, culturally neither here nor there, and in their hunger, nonetheless, for the European cultural goods that are being denied them, they do become "parasitic."

The self-alienation of auto-antisemitism turned "parasitism" concerns Appelfeld because it prohibits Jews from achieving that human freedom that is not purely political (and negative) but creative (and positive) as well. It is only through accepting the specificity of the utterly specific history and tradition of the people themselves—both its experience of European culture *and* its knowledge of its own different and despised non-European culture—that, in Appelfeld's view, the people can achieve independence and artistic freedom. Art is about the specific and immanent, not the general and transcendent. It says the word *human,* or the word *Jew,* and means it.

Human Freedom and the Jewish Literary Text

At two crucial junctures in the story, Father betrays even his love of Kafka and the other German Jewish writers to put forward as a model of literary perfection the French tradition with its "quiet, unemotional detachment." In both moments, the context is the same: the decision of his half-Jewish friend Kurt Stark to undergo ritual circumcision and live a more traditional Jewish life. That the passages repeat suggests their centrality to the novel. This is the first, which begins with Father's articulating his judgment to Stark and quickly passes on to the literary subject:

> "Why take this trouble on yourself at a time like this? . . . It passes my understanding." . . . As for Father . . . during the past year the literary journals had stopped counting him among the writers of Austria. Once they would allude to his Jewishness indirectly. Now they spoke openly about the alien elements, the germs of decadence, sown in all his sentences. Healthy people should keep away from his works. Father used to declare: "Freedom of expression above all. Without freedom of expression there is no room for thought." . . . Now Father ground his teeth and blamed himself, his writing, which had never amounted to anything because he had failed to learn from the French. Only they knew the right frame of mind, the quiet, unemotional detachment without which all writing was moralistic or fantastical, or rootless. And he was thus ready to admit that neither he nor Wasserman nor Zweig nor even Schnitzler had attained any real standing in art. (107–108)

And this is the second passage. It incorporates the key concept that informs *Badenheim* and *The Iron Tracks* as well and that I want now to develop in relation to art and the Jewish tradition, the concept of freedom:

> The silence among us lasted a long time. In the end Father's sorrow burst out and he spoke of his incurable literary defects. The French again. Only the dispassionate French artists, Stendhal and Flaubert, only they were true artists. . . . "Why take this trouble on yourself, Kurt? You're a free man. Even your posture speaks of freedom. Your artistic heritage is one of freedom. Your father, an Austrian by birth, left you land, health, hands fit to carve stone, and you want to exchange this health, this freedom, for an old, sick faith. Take pity on your freedom, take pity on your body, which never had to suffer a senseless mutilation. Banish these evil thoughts from your mind. Believe me. You are dearer to me than a brother." (120)

What is "freedom" that Father should see in Judaism an old sick faith and bodily mutilation, which for him represent the opposite of freedom, while Kurt is propelled by a "obscure passion to return to the crucible of his origins, the origins of the mother he adored; it was her faith, or rather the faith of her forefathers, that he wanted to embrace" (103)?

It is no accident that the adjective that Father uses to describe Stark's thoughts is the same word that coupled with the word *spirits* drifts throughout the text: *evil.* Or that the word *freedom,* which is crucial in both the above passages (and elsewhere in the book) first appears earlier in relation to the child Bruno's thoughts of evil spirits (the young maids): "Everything was ready for an incomprehensible freedom. An obscure terror seized my heart" (26). To embrace freedom is a terror, on the other side of which passion is something other than mere freedom from persecution.

In another scene, also associated with Stark, Appelfeld supplies the more political definition of negative freedom that lies behind Father's rhetoric, which is what neither Stark nor Bruno is referring to. Visiting Stark, who is recovering from the circumcision, Father encounters a resident in the same Jewish hospital, which serves as a microcosm of the Jewish world as it is and also as it is seen through Father's eyes: "Jewish atmosphere . . . in abundance: dirt [and] the corruption of businessmen." In relation to this Jewish world, the patient exclaims: "I have been deprived of my freedom. My son does not want to give me back my freedom. And ever since he deprived me of my freedom, I am not at liberty to leave" (125).

The liberty to leave Judaism is certainly not a freedom to be denied. But it does make of the words *freedom* and *liberty* negative rather than positive concepts, freedom from and liberty not to. What Stark, on the other hand, gravitates toward is something the text calls "passion" and "origins," both of which are, like Bruno's "evil spirits" and the "incomprehensible" and therefore terrifying freedom they represent, linked with the maternal, the female, the sexual. Father attributes Stark's artistic capacity (his hands) and his "freedom" to his Austrian father. Stark himself, like Erwin in *The Iron Tracks,* understands himself as the mother's son—a psychological feature that picks up the fact that in Jewish law Judaism is transmitted through the mother not the father. For this reason, perhaps, the mother (even when she is not herself religious) is associated throughout Appelfeld's writing, including his autobiography, with the religious tradition. She is also, as we have seen, associated with the silent speaking, the mute chapter, of literature itself.

It is Stark, the half-Jew, about-to-be-(re)converted to Judaism, who would say with dignity and pride the word that Father and even Mother can barely say at all, the word that Appelfeld would especially have his texts say loudly and clearly, which is also the "secret name" of the characters Kaufmann and Hofmann in part two of the novel (238, 241), the word *Jew:* "you must be, how shall I put it . . . ," says the half-Jewish Regina in part two, "Quite simply," says Bruno, "a Jew" (193). What is this lack or absence of the word *Jew*? "Who are those people?" Mother's sister Theresa twice asks her: "Mother bent down and whispered, 'Jews,' as if she were explaining an incomprehensible word picked up on the streets" (61). Stark's uttering of the word in the context of an antisemitic moment provides a clue as to why this word is so difficult to pronounce, for Jews and non-Jews alike: "Don't say Jews," says Stark, the one character in this book who can say the word *Jew* with pride; "say people" (112).

In order to establish the equality of the Jews, history has required (as in the above scene) the not saying of the word *Jew*, the negating of it in the word *people*. First and foremost, Jews are people, human beings like everybody else. But what is a *human being*, *The Age of Wonders* forces us to ask, if not a specific human being, *this* human being and not another, a *Jew* and not a Christian, for example? Jewish history has made the word *Jew* one more of those secret words that drift through culture, like *evil spirits*. These are words that repress sorrow and fear and guilt and many other forms of "incomprehensible" terror. They also repress, however, an equally *incomprehensible freedom*: for our freedom as human beings, our positive rather than our negative freedom, is no more comprehensible than the ghosts that inhabit it. And it is no easier to achieve than the ghosts are to banish. Indeed, it comes out of the acceptance of those mistakenly designated *evil spirits*, which are only, we must come to realize, words by which we speak those phantoms we do not understand, including our repression and displacement and inheritance of those very passions and desires that define us as human beings.

In the view of this book, Jews will remain "parasites" living off the marrow of other cultures until they are able to call themselves by their proper name: *Jew*. *Jew* does not mean non-European. It does not mean religious Jew, or, in the contemporary world, Israeli. It means a specific individual with his or her particular affiliations and history. Other peoples may, in the past, have determined the Jews' political (negative) freedom. The blank page in Jewish history is there to stay. But the Jews themselves determine what they will do with that blank page, how they will write the text of their lives and their human definition. For Appelfeld, the asking of the question *What is a Jew* is inextricably linked to the asking of the question *What is a human being?* a question not in the least susceptible of any easy answer, as we shall now see. Indeed, to be a human being one may have to accept, rather than deny, one's relationship to what seems outside the realm of human being—including the insects and animals and parasites that human beings are not. It is to that definition of the human, and its evolution within the context of Jewish tradition, to which I now turn.

5 Religious Faith and the "Question of the Human": *Tzili: The Story of a Life*

A question that circulates throughout Appelfeld's fiction, virtually in defiance of what we would imagine as a decorous or legitimate inquiry for Holocaust fiction to make, is, as I have begun suggesting, just that question that Nazism itself asked—and answered—about the Jews: how do I know that another human being is in fact a human being, to be treated by me one way and not another? We might at first be inclined to respond that Appelfeld's texts raise this question of the human to ask it in relation to the Nazis, or, perhaps, in asking the question vis-à-vis the Jews, to reverse Nazi rhetoric and answer with a resounding affirmation of the humanness of all human beings (including or especially the Jews). But this is not, I think, the case.

Not that there is any doubt throughout Appelfeld's fiction that human beings (Nazis, Jews, others) *are* human beings and not creatures of another sort. Indeed, that affirmation of the human, severed from some sort of logical, rationalistic proof that might constitute an answer to the question of how I *know* another human being is a human being, is one of the hard-won achievements of Appelfeld's writing. In Appelfeld's fiction, we *know* other human beings to be human beings by some means other than scientific knowledge per se. Accordingly, we must acknowledge them to be human.

This is not to say that we necessarily know how to treat other human beings as human beings. Morality may not be instinctual, though like much human behavior it may originate in or at least be perpetuated by something like instinct. Nonetheless, knowing other humans to be human is a part of our internal wiring. Since the Nazi program of extermination was based as much as on anything else on the claim that the Jews were *not* humans, retrieving the fact of this inborn knowledge is one basic rebuttal of Nazism itself. "The Jews are undoubtedly a race," Art Spiegelman quotes Adolf Hitler in the opening volume of *Maus*, which is his own exploration of the limits of human definition, "but they are not human." Is there any way at all that even Adolf Hitler could have meant this?

The Question of the Human and Rational Humanism

In order to set aside some of the things that Appelfeld's questioning of the human might have meant but does not, I need to cite several features of his writing. One such feature of Appelfeld's fiction, which calls into doubt whether it intends to raise issues concerning the humanness of the Nazis, is that there is little depiction of them in his fiction. At the same time, and more perplexing perhaps, his fiction very frequently presents its Jewish characters through just those stereotypes that were used by the Nazis to raise questions about the Jews' humanness. This aspect of the text may reflect Jewish self-understanding (like the auto-antisemitism of the fathers in *The Age of Wonders* and *The Healer*). It may also have something to do with representing the considerable ideological component of culture such that (as we saw in *Badenheim*) we all participate in its essential assumptions, even when they are mortally self-destructive. But there is more than this going on here, especially given the equally noteworthy fact of the antimimetic style of Appelfeld's writing, which makes it possible to ask the other presumably unaskable question: how do we know that this catastrophe happened, and happened this way, as reported by survivors and witnesses?

There is to Appelfeld's fiction a decidedly Kafkaesque, allegorical, and surrealistic quality. Even if his fiction, as I have been arguing, is anything but a decentered, deconstructed postmodernist text, nonetheless the bearing of contemporary thought on Appelfeld's writing is, I think, quite considerable. A return to former modes of Holocaust representation, which centered on making real—morally, historically, descriptively—the world of the catastrophe, will not illuminate the deepest levels of Appelfeld's enterprise. Appelfeld's fiction resists what such modes of writing can threaten, which is to reproduce an ideological form of thinking that, however right or accurate the texts' ideologies might seem to us, verges on replicating a central feature of fascism: its "faith," to use Appelfeld's word in *The Iron Tracks,* which it shares with Communism and with certain institutional forms of Judaism and Christianity as well, that it *knows* a truth, which it therefore has the right to implement.

Such ideological thinking, Appelfeld's fiction implicitly argues, cannot provide an adequate response to the experience of the Holocaust. Indeed, it repeats a fundamental problem of ideology, which may well have contributed to producing the Holocaust to begin with. If postmodernism suffers from a return of the repressed, as LaCapra and Bellamy and others have argued, the pre-postmodernist position suffered from a kind of mirroring of the same. By simply inverting or reversing certain assumptions about the Jews, this position did not necessarily transform the mode of thinking that produced such systems as fascism and totalitarianism in the first place. It might well have left intact the same problematical dynamics of accusation and scapegoating: if for antisemitic Europe the Jews were the enemy whom they needed to eradicate, now, instead of the Jews, it is the fascists and the Communists who occupy the enemy position.

The problem with simply protesting European antisemitism and presenting the Jews in a more favorable, more human light, would be in suggesting, inadequately, that because the Jews were *not* as the Germans and others perceived them, they did not deserve their horrific fate. The more agonizing question would be: *what if* they had been as the Germans perceived them? Would their annihilation then have been justified? I do not for a moment intend to imply that in Appelfeld's view the Jews *were* as they were judged to be. Nonetheless, at least some Germans acted out of a deep if grotesquely distorted sincerity. They believed their perceptions and beliefs to be true and acted accordingly. How do any of us ever stand outside our cultural convictions so as to evade the tyranny of cultural prejudice? Is the recognition of other human beings as human beings something we learn from culture, and is humanness therefore to be adjudicated culturally?

Similarly, to present the Germans as themselves depraved—they, and not the Jews, the degenerate beasts—might (especially given the known historical consequences of such thinking) only serve to evidence our ill-considered, often unthinking submission to the dictates of our own culture. Tzvetan Todorov puts this very well when he points out that whereas in nineteenth-century America to be an abolitionist opposing slavery was to take a significant moral stand, to be antiracist now represents little more than social conformity.[1] The question Appelfeld's fiction raises is how we maintain a position of non-conformity in the Emersonian sense, such that we preserve the possibilities of moral action despite our biases and convictions.

One response to the abuses of culture, which Appelfeld shares with other writers (some of them Jewish writers highly conscious of Jewish history, such as Franz Kafka and Isaac Babel), is to raise questions rather than to make statements or even to propose answers to the questions the texts raise. Literature for these writers serves an interrogatory function. When such writers ask *what is a human being?* they do not ask in order to say what a human being *is,* but, rather, to bring into focus the unanswerability of the question itself. One consequence of this kind of asking of the question of the human, in order *not* to answer it, might be—and this is the case in Appelfeld's fiction—to insist that, even if we cannot define what a human being is or prove one person or another to be a human being, we *know* another human being to be a human being when we encounter one. As Anne Michaels has pointed out in *Fugitive Pieces,* the very attempt to humiliate the Jews before exterminating them undid its own underlying claim that the Jews were less than human: animals do not suffer humiliation, human beings do.[2] What the Nazis tried to do, against their knowledge to the contrary, was to prove, beyond a shadow of a doubt, that the Jews were *not* human beings. Is this any more to be proven than its opposite? The Final Solution did not seek only to exterminate the Jewish vermin, but to prove that they were vermin to be exterminated. How does one disprove another human being's humanness? And if such humanness cannot be proven any more than disproven, how does one conduct one's behavior in relation to what we know (however we know this) are other human beings?

It is one of the most often cited lessons of the Holocaust that words unleash deadly force. Thus, all formulations of human beings as parasites, insects, vermin, and animals constitute a danger not to be taken lightly. "What is a man?" Bruno is asked by the Jewish traveler he meets immediately upon his return to Austria. This gentleman continues: "No better than an insect. He'll sell himself body and soul for a tasteless mess of pottage. . . . A man is nothing" (179–80). "Man is an insect," says Erwin, whose words, as we have seen, are echoed back to him by the local tavern owner who says, not concerning the Jews but the local peasants, "Man's a monster, don't you know that?" "The trains," Erwin proclaims, "make me free. Without them, what would I be in this world? An insect . . . a kind of human snail. . . . I board the train, and instantly I'm borne aloft on the wings of the wind" (4–5). "Cursing" the "hordes" of Eastern "Jews infesting Austria like rats, infesting the whole world" (133), Father in *The Age of Wonders,* like Erwin and others (Jews and non-Jews alike), participates in the slander of human beings that in Nazi Germany eventuated in the annihilation of European Jewry.

Whatever else is going on here in these citations concerning human beings as insects or animals or snails or monsters or creatures of another sort altogether, one consequence of this oft-repeated motif in Appelfeld's fiction is that it does recall the problem of forgetting the difference between human beings and other forms of organic life. This issues in two very important and different, albeit intimately related, ethical injunctions. Both are very much to the point of Holocaust fiction, though neither is, for me, the rich moral lode mined by Appelfeld's writing.

In the first place, Appelfeld's manipulation of Nazi rhetoric suggests how easy it is to dehumanize other human beings. While there may be every difference between, on the one hand, the Nazis' condemnation and hatred of the Jews (or, for that matter, the Jews' condemnation and hatred of themselves and other Jews), and, on the other hand, the Jews' and others' condemnation and hatred of the Nazis, nonetheless to call the enemy an insect may pose similar and very comparable perils. *The Iron Tracks,* after all, is a story of revenge, in which the protagonist's murder of his parents' murderer does not in the least yield him any peace and respite from his sufferings. Whatever else it is, murder is not a noble human response. It is certainly no way for the individual to achieve mental and ethical salvation.

Just as important, and this is, perhaps, what explains the lack of fulfillment Erwin experiences in the act of murder itself, to see other human beings as insects or monsters, as much as it may facilitate our exterminating them as such, simultaneously invalidates our reasons for exterminating them at all—at least in terms of any concept of justice. The problem exceeds Primo Levi's eloquent expression of the fact that, to revive Hannah Arendt's considerable insights into the matter, evil is a very human affair. "Monsters," says Primo Levi, "exist, but they are too few in number to be truly dangerous. More dangerous are the common men."[3] Even more serious than this, the problem with imaging human beings as monsters is that it puts them outside our moral right or capacity to judge them. As Stanley Cavell puts it, "to understand Nazism, whatever that will mean, will be to understand it as a human possibility; monstrous, unforgivable, but not therefore the conduct of monsters. Monsters are not unforgivable, and not forgivable. We do not bear the right internal relation to them for forgiveness to apply."[4]

To call human beings insects and animals is to subject people to being treated as such, either in terms of a denial of their human rights or in the impossibility it produces of placing individuals within the law of human morality. In and of itself, then, this debate, conducted by Appelfeld's characters on the issue of whether or not men and women are insects, produces the necessity for us to recognize the grounds on which we stake our claim, not only for including other human beings within the category of our humanness and thereby protecting them from our treatment of them as something other than human, but, finally, for judging them altogether as worthy of either our condemnation or our love. For this reason, the sentence that circulates throughout Appelfeld's writing, which ostensibly reverses Nazi rhetoric, is the statement that *man is not an insect.*

Yet what improvement is offered by Father's reversal of rhetoric, for example, as when he insists in *The Age of Wonders* that "man is not a dog" (148; "man is not an animal," says Mother [207])? Father's statement culminates in his condemnation only of those who, in his view, go "willingly into that den of animals" (133). "Are we animals?" he asks (94); and the implied answer is, no. And yet, in Father's view, some of us are. This isn't so far from what the Nazis were saying about Jews, gypsies, and homosexuals.

At very least, to say that man is *not* an animal reproduces the problematical assumption that we *know* what a human being is. This is *not* the same as saying that we *know* another human being to be a human being when we see one: this, as I have already suggested, Appelfeld affirms over and over again in his fiction. However distorted, grotesque, and downright peculiar his characters are, they are exquisitely human—precisely, perhaps, for their being so odd. What is being held up for condemnation in Appelfeld's fiction is the idea that we can *define* human being and therefore decide who does and does not fit our definition. For this reason, in addition to the varieties of assertion made by the novels' various characters that man is and is not an insect, there is the texts' own primary ascriptions of animal-like qualities to many of their characters.

In *The Age of Wonders,* for example, at moments in the text that do not particularly reflect the consciousness of the characters or their antisemitism (auto- or otherwise), the face of one character is described as having assumed "the terrible features of a wounded animal" (217), while the "upper lip" of another "tremble[s] like a frightened animal" (230). "The people looked strange next to the coaches," we are told early in the novel by the innocent child narrator of the novel, long before the text has made explicit the subject of the Holocaust, "like little insects wrinkling the straw with their feet" (9). What if human beings are like animals or insects or even parasites after all?

The Elemental Right of Being

Like *The Age of Wonders, Tzili: The Story of a Life* is virtually obsessed with the question, *What is a human being?* Yet *Tzili* provides a way of preserving this query such that it not only affirms the humanness of human beings but also links it to something equally important: the transcendence of a realm beyond the human by which the human might be recognized and judged without determining exactly what and who a human being *is. Tzili* tells the story of a young girl abandoned by her family when the Nazis invade. Tzili is the very opposite of the Jewish genius by which European Jewry had staked its claim to participation in enlightened Western culture. Simple, innocent, and "feeble-minded" (7), she can barely learn her primary school lessons. The novel follows Tzili's experiences, much like Appelfeld's own as recorded in his autobiography, after her abandonment, as she travels the countryside seeking protection from the devastation. In particular, the book focuses on her relationship with an escapee from the camps, Mark, with whom she takes up residence in the forest, and by whom she becomes pregnant, only to have Mark abandon her as well, and to lose her pregnancy. By the end of the book she has become part of the wave of refugees making their way to Israel.

The statement "a man, after all, is not an insect" or "a man is not a mole" becomes in *Tzili* a virtual mantra, recurring in the text no fewer than five times. (In one version it appears as "a woman is not an insect" [139], which is picked up by Tzili's response to a peasant woman who "beat her as if she were a rebellious animal": "No, you won't. I'm not an animal. I'm a woman" [116].) Despite these assertions, however, we are throughout the story reminded of the ways in which human beings are indeed like insects and moles.

Already in the opening chapter, we are told, quite offhandedly and apparently without any particular significance, that the father in the family "would grind his teeth" in anguish over his daughter's lack of intellectual achievement (3). Related to the word for *insect* (the fathers in *The Age of Wonders* and *The Healer* are also described as grinding their teeth), this moment links up with the text's more direct assertions that people are like ants (4), animals (41), reptiles (60), and, in defiance of what the text seems elsewhere to be insisting, insects (119). One couple, we are told, communicates in "grunts" (50), and we are told by the camp survivor Mark, in a remark that recalls not only Erwin in *The Iron Tracks* but also Bartfuss in *The Immortal Bartfuss:* "without cigarettes I'm an insect, less than an insect, I'm nothing" (77).

Nor are all these moments intended as condemnations of the characters thus described as animals. Tzili herself is described on the opening page of the novel as being like a squirrel (1), while one kindly old refugee, later in the story, is said to "sit by her side as dumb as an animal" (167). Throughout Appelfeld's fiction, and, in particular, in his autobiography, animals are associated with a muteness designating a knowledge that transcends and abhors words. Moreover, the behavior of the "dull-witted" (2) Tzili is, on more than one occasion, animal-like. Though the characterization of Tzili in relation to the peasant who attempts to rape her and who, therefore, "trie[s] to quiet her as if she were a restless animal" is obviously to be rejected, the fact that she escapes by "wriggl[ing] out from under [his] weight" and "crawl[ing] on all fours into the field" (19) is in no way the text's incorporation of the peasant's view of her. It is the text's own description of the animal vitality that throughout the story proves Tzili's salvation.

Similarly, when she flees an old peasant woman who beats her and we are told that "she was content, like a lost animal whose neck has been freed from its yoke at last" (57), we are meant to experience the positive power of her animal prowess.

In forging the analogy between human beings on the one hand, and, on the other, animals and insects, the text is to some degree perhaps making a straightforward point about the commonality of human experience. The refugees, we are told late in the novel, "against the vast whiteness . . . looked like swarms of insects. Tzili was drawn toward them as if she realized that her fate was no different from theirs" (119; the same image appears in *The Age of Wonders,* as we have just seen). Even more powerfully, the text suggests the elementality of the human, the life force it shares with even the most minimal and marginal of God's creatures. Set as it is within the context of the family's and community's suspicions concerning the "feeble-minded" (7) Tzili's own status as a human being, which is only, we realize, a version of the larger culture's question concerning the Jews, the fact that Tzili's survival in this text depends very much on her animal instincts is not to be taken lightly.

Indeed, the novel does not forbear to stage one of its major climaxes in a burrow dug into a hill by the male protagonist Mark. This is a place of refuge and hibernation for himself and Tzili. It is a setting that replicates the conditions of Tzili's initial survival of her family's abandonment of her and the Nazi assault, when like a larva or chrysalis she emerges from the ruins. Lying "among the barrels in the shed, covered with sacking . . . she slept for a long time. When she woke it was night and everything was completely still. She poked her head out of the sacking . . . lifted the upper half of her body . . . kicked away the sacking . . . [and] stood up" (7–8). So, too, the "bunker" where Mark and Tzili hibernate protects them from detection and the elements. It produces the "warm, dark intimacy between them" out of which Tzili conceives her child (97). Giving birth to herself in the first instance, or at least emerging from childhood into adulthood, Tzili hibernates once again and becomes pregnant.

It is their rodent-like existence that prompts Mark to say that "man is not a mole." He rejects that existence (105). Yet it is the bunker that secures their survival, so long as they are willing to submit to its terrible, paradoxical logic—as did many Jews who went into hiding during the war, many of them in cellars. When Mark leaves, perhaps to die (we do not know what happens to him), Tzili also goes on her way, ultimately to lose her child and almost (though not quite) her life. For this reason it is difficult, to say the least, not to see these characters (the victims as well as the victimizers; indeed, in the case of Tzili, the victim of the victims) as bearing some significant relation to insects and other animals. Yet the scenes of Tzili and Mark in their burrow are among the most affecting and inspiring in the book. The text seems to be asking what if a human being is an insect after all? What kind of being is this creature called a human being, and does being an insect in any way compromise a human being's humanity? Might it, perchance, help define it?

It is impossible to read Appelfeld's refrain *man is not an insect* without being reminded of the Kafka text that surely stands behind it. It is useful to bring forward this companion text both to explore, through their similarities, aspects of Appelfeld's undertaking, and also to mark the important differences between the two writers.[5] Appelfeld himself, as we saw in Chapter 4, has commented on Kafka's influence on him, which, in Appelfeld's account, has to do with the discovery, early on in Appelfeld's career, that they spoke the same language. This language is not, of course, simply German. Rather, it is the language of the grotesque and the incomprehensible. This is the language that in and of itself raises fundamental questions about the humanness of human beings and the divine order of a profoundly unjust cosmos. "The Metamorphosis" nicely illuminates the shared territories of these two writers. Equally important, the Kafka text shadows forth the radical differences between them, placing Appelfeld more firmly in the tradition of Agnon than Kafka. For if Kafka's story opens up the unadulterated devastation of the world it figures forth, Appelfeld's lifts up off the grid of the naturalistic and the grotesque in order to provide a very different site for the interpretation of the human.

Although Kafka cannot yet be aware when he is composing "The Metamorphosis" of the role that the word *Ungeziefer* will come to play in the fate of European Jewry, Appelfeld is mindful of the significance. He also already has behind his text Kafka's uncanny prophecy (as we might call it) about human beings, who are not simply referred to as vermin (which is what the German *Ungeziefer* means), but literally are perceived to be such and are exterminated accordingly, as if word had become thing and metaphor were literally an action to be taken in the world. Kafka's fiction always and everywhere discovers the inexorable relation between language and ideology and between ideology and action—a knowledge that informs Appelfeld's *Badenheim* as well. But in *Tzili,* as in *Badenheim* and *The Iron Tracks,* Appelfeld also withdraws from the Kafkaesque logic to which he himself applies. He lifts up off the plane of the human and naturalistic onto the plane of the divine, where the human logic of *word equals thing* does not pertain. Again as in *Badenheim,* this move on Appelfeld's part has to do, as we shall see, with the difference between seeing and hearing as instruments of human perception and knowledge. The texts consistently grapple with the very delimited powers of human beings, as opposed to those of God, to actually create anything in the material universe.

Appelfeld's statement *man is not an insect* is already evidence of a difference between himself and Kafka. In the Hebrew translation of "The Metamorphosis," the word for vermin is *sherez,* which has a closer connotation to the German than to the English word *insect.* Yet Appelfeld does not choose the word *sherez,* a word that conveys the idea of creepy-crawly sliminess. Though his deviation from Kafka can be explained as his abiding by one prevalent interpretation of Gregor to be a sort of beetle or cockroach (conveyed by the Hebrew word *ḥaraq,* the word Appelfeld uses for insect), there is other significance to Appelfeld's selection. Like Kafka, Appelfeld entertains the possibility that humans might be insects. But if this is so, according to Appelfeld, humans are not necessarily a particularly disgusting form of bug. Furthermore, however much Appelfeld's stories tug away from the negation of the statement *man is not an insect,* nonetheless the equation is presented in the negative, emphasizing the non-insect at the center of the human bug.

Like Kafka, Appelfeld is concerned with the dual role implied in the human = bug metaphor. Writes Stanley Corngold, "the metamorphosis in the Samsa household of man into vermin is unsettling not only because vermin are disturbing, or because the vivid representation of a human 'louse' is disturbing, but because the indeterminate, fluid crossing of a human tenor and a material vehicle is itself unsettling. Gregor is at one moment pure rapture and at another very nearly pure dung beetle, at times grossly human and at times airily bug-like."[6] Yet even though we may feel sorry for the bug that is Gregor, whom we understand throughout the story to have all the attributes of a human being, in the final analysis we are presented in Kafka's story with an insect-eat-insect world. The reader is left with the impression that Gregor at least half-deserves his fate, and his family, which is also described throughout in animal imagery, is just as vermin-like as he is.

This is the general tenor of another text that might also usefully be brought to bear on Appelfeld's: Tadeusz Borowski's *This Way for the Gas, Ladies and Gentlemen.* Unlike Kafka's story, Borowski's is a response to the Holocaust, in which the author presents the range of tortures and torments that Appelfeld carefully excludes from most of his fiction. From the opening image of the thousands of naked men and women milling around the barracks in the volume's lead story, Borowski inundates the text with animal and insect imagery, all of which tend to produce a view of human beings not simply reduced by circumstance to inhuman behavior, but as realizing in their bestiality something essentially savage about human being itself. This outlook emerges in one form in the victim and in another in the victimizer.

This double, and doubly contemptuous, perspective reflects rather accurately Borowski's own status as witness. Though a prisoner himself, he also as an Aryan controls the fate of less fortunate prisoners. Hence his is a text filled as much with guilt as with expressions of suffering. He knows that he is not only one of the lucky ones, but that his efforts at self-survival are not entirely different from those in the German superstructure who incarcerated him. When he writes of the Greek prisoners as "huge human insects" and "pigs," we are meant to take these words, I think, as a condemnation of these prisoners in the same vein as the "rat-like, resolute smile" of the SS woman is a condemnation of the Nazis, or, for that matter, his referring to his own group as "sheep" or one of them as "growling" his words is intended to diminish them in our eyes.[7]

More painful, however, are the terms that Borowski uses to describe the Jews. His choice of words is surely intended to bring home to the reader both the objective horrors and the author's own inability to tolerate what he sees, such that he must somehow distance himself. His prose transcribes his immediate response to the scenes he is witnessing: "my head swims," he tells us; "my legs are shaky, again I feel like throwing up" (43). Nonetheless, even if we allow that the Jews arriving "inhumanly crammed" into cattle cars are propelled by conditions wholly outside their control into inhuman behavior and dehumanized form, and that Borowski knows this and wishes us to understand it, we are still confronted in the text with its own dehumanizing pictures of them: "breathing like fish cast out on the sand" (37) or "like a blind, mad river trying to find a new bed" (37).

These pictures tend to affirm rather than pull away from the Nazis' attempts to dehumanize Jews. Similarly, in presenting to us "trampled infants" as "naked little monsters" (39), the prose tramples them all over again; while the images of "hideous naked women, men twisted by convulsions," and "dirty, damp female bodies, the animal hunger, the inhuman labor" (44) convey alongside the damage done to human bodies the captors' view of them, which permitted them to treat human beings as garbage in the first place. Thus the reader, like the narrator, is put in the position of "feeling no pity." We, too, want them out of sight or, in repetition of what has already been done to them, "to beat them with [our] fists" (40). However we understand Borowski's reasons for producing his text this way (and there are clear reasons why he does this), for him the human being as bug or animal is a wholly negative equation.

This is emphatically not the case in *Tzili.* Here Appelfeld also exploits what is unsettling in Kafka's and Borowski's metaphor: its fluidity, such that it is difficult to distinguish man from bug; and its reversibility, that man is an insect and yet may not for this reason be less a human being. But Appelfeld does not mean this, as these other writers do, as unredeemed pejorative. And this is why the word *shereẓ* or vermin cannot serve the purposes of his text, and why he has to produce the analogy or metaphor in the negative. Human beings may squeak like bugs (like Gregor in the opening scene or like the fathers in Appelfeld's tales who grind their teeth); and they may even go to sleep one day and wake up, as do both Gregor and Tzili, transformed (both Kafka's text and Appelfeld's stress patterns of sleeping, waking, and dreaming). But, as the case of Tzili in particular insists, such a transformation will not only not make them any less human beings, but might well make them *more* human. Surely Tzili is the most human character in the novel, and her humanness is inseparable from her animal-likeness.

This is at least in part the case because of the way in which Appelfeld expands the frame around his world so that it includes not only the social and natural worlds that human beings inhabit, but also the realm of the divine. It is this additional frame, which Kafka's and Borowski's stories lack, into which Appelfeld deliberately places his own work, even before the story begins, by titling it, in the Hebrew, with a biblical allusion. The Hebrew title, the literal translation of which would be *The Coat and the Stripes,* immediately invokes the Joseph story and the coat of many stripes, which is both the sign of his chosenness and the cause of his betrayal *because* of that chosenness. The reference to Joseph's coat of stripes already suggests the other coat of stripes referred to at the end of the novel, the concentration camp garb of the Jews. Yet Appelfeld intends more here than to introduce some simple symbol of Jewish plight—whether straightforwardly or ironically. Indeed, thrown into a pit to re-emerge in multiple transformations, Joseph's own life story contains a significant component of insect-like hibernation and metamorphosis. Those contours of his life function, furthermore, as much within a divine scheme of things as within a human one.

I will return to the Joseph story later. At this point, I will stress that for Appelfeld, being insect-like is not necessarily an abomination; and that the revaluation he performs of the Kafkaesque metaphor may have something to do with the differently contextualized world of his fiction, in which human beings, animals, and bugs all exist within the larger entity of a transcendent or divine universe. Appelfeld's text, then, conspires in the question of Tzili's humanness not to refute that humanness but to produce in the reader a consciousness of those conditions without which we cannot apprehend humanness. That consciousness includes a concept of the divine.

At the center of the novel's critique of its characters and their world (which is our world as well) is the atheistic, rational–humanistic assumption that humanness might indeed be defined, and defined in very particular, knowable ways. This is the overriding assumption not only of the Germanic world Appelfeld displays in his fiction but of his cast of Jewish intellectuals as well (for example, the fathers in *The Age of Wonders, The Iron Tracks, The Healer,* and *All That I Have Loved*). Like many of the Jewish families in his fiction, Tzili's family is contemptuous of both religion and Jewish tradition. The Krauses are eager, through education, to secure an economic and social place for themselves in the non-Jewish world. Unlike the families in *The Age of Wonders* or *Everything I Have Loved,* however, and unlike the similarly named satirist Karl Kraus, who is mentioned explicitly in *Badenheim* and about whom Appelfeld himself had a few direct words to say, the Krauses are not intellectuals.[8] They have not in the least processed their position through some significant body of intellectual thought. Rather, they are shopkeepers whose cultural aspirations serve (in the manner of Badenheim) blatantly to expose the pretentiousness and shallowness of a certain kind of commitment to rational humanism. Indeed, the critique sweeps back to include figures like Kraus himself or the family in *The Age of Wonders.* It exposes rational humanism itself as a form of forgetting and perhaps even of pretension.

The reference to Karl Kraus, whose Jewish self-hatred is a commonplace in European intellectual history, is significant. Kraus was a brilliant satirist and culture critic in turn-of-the-century Austria. He distinguished himself as an adamant defender of German culture, not merely against the inevitable pull of that culture (as, perhaps, of all culture) toward the mediocre and the clichéd, but specifically against the threat posed by the Jews. His attack against European Jewry (much like Father's in *The Age of Wonders*) was mounted both in terms of the theology they professed and in what he saw as their ghetto mentality and their failure to absorb the highest principles of Western European culture. In a long passage discussing Kafka, which accompanies Appelfeld's comments on Kraus, Appelfeld himself points to the essential legitimacy of Kraus's position: the "emptiness of the Jewish petite bourgeoisie" that caused "sensitive people such as Otto Weininger and Karl Kraus [to fall] victim to self-'hatred.'"[9] "Through assimilation to redemption," Kraus directed his fellow Jews, sounding the appropriately Christian note, for eventually Kraus did convert to Roman Catholicism. This act of conversion is not irrelevant to Appelfeld's relation to Kraus. Kraus's rejection of institutional Judaism, with whatever auto-antisemitism his position may have expressed, in no way constituted a rejection of either God or religion as such.[10] Rather, Kraus rejected a particular institutional form that Appelfeld also finds wanting.

Even though *Tzili* is by no means a celebration of religious Orthodoxy (Jewish or otherwise), it is also (like *The Age of Wonders*) not a retrieval of the principles of the Enlightenment that had first encouraged Jewish hopes for integration into European culture. It is these principles that might have seemed merely to have gone astray in the Holocaust, as if the Holocaust simply marked a momentary and reparable disruption in the inevitable course of human cultural progress. But hyper-rational culture, which had lost its idea of the elemental being-ness of human beings, is itself one object of Appelfeld's critique. Tzili is the figure in this text for the elemental being that rational culture forgot, despised, and attempted to destroy. Such being, however, exactly because it existed outside the forces of the intellect that sought to annihilate it, not only survived the catastrophe but also provided a mirror by which to see what Western civilization had refused to see and acknowledge: the existence of being prior to and outside the power of the human mind to create—albeit not, tragically, to annihilate—it.[11]

In the one essay of his career in which Lionel Trilling directly addresses the issue of Western humanism and Judaic tradition, he provides the following definition of being, a definition that draws together the intellectual and religious impulses also at work, I think, in Appelfeld's text: "What does it mean when we say a person *is*?" asks Trilling in the essay entitled "Wordsworth and the Rabbis," written in 1950 and constituting Trilling's most sustained and significant response to the Holocaust. "Again and again in our literature, at its most apocalyptic and intense, we find the impulse to create figures who are intended to suggest that life is justified in its elementary biological simplicity, and, in the manner of Wordsworth, these figures are conceived of as being of simple status and humble heart: Lawrence's simpler people . . . Dreiser's Jennie Gerhardt . . . Hemingway's waiters . . . Faulkner's Negroes . . . and . . . idiot boys."[12] The difference between modernism and romanticism, Trilling suggests, is the difference between two diametrically opposed concepts as the organizing features of poetic identity: *self* and *being*. The modernist conception of *self*, Trilling suggests, is characterized by a violent inner-directedness. It derives from an idea of struggle as the site of self-definition, and it produces violent outer-directedness as well. It is intimately tied to the dynamics of divine grace as the only force capable of healing such inner division. As such, it is a quintessentially Christian definition. *Being*, on the other hand, implies the quiet affirmation of selfhood, both of one's self and of others. It inheres both in Judaism and in romanticism.

For this reason, Trilling identifies modernism's rejection of romanticism as a form of antisemitism.

In the veiled, subtle, and powerfully suggestive terms of a major modern critic of culture, Trilling locates as a major source of the catastrophe in Europe a cultural move that invisibly coincides with and perhaps even conceals and displaces the major trajectory of Western European theology in its rejection of and desire to convert the Jews. Christian antisemitism, Trilling suggests, had to do with an idea of internal division and strife that could only be healed through an act of divine intervention and redemptive grace. Resisting the self-affirmation of Judaism, which rejected the Christian savior, such a Christianity, in Trilling's view, placed itself in opposition to the idea of being itself. In this way, it could permit itself to forget the being-ness of those others whom it slaughtered.

Trilling develops his idea of being through an analysis of *Pirqei Avot,* the Jewish wisdom literature, which constitutes a part of the *Mishnah* (in the Babylonian Talmud, Seder Nezikin, Massechet Avot). This turns out to be the same text from which Appelfeld takes the liturgical passages that dominate the first two chapters of *Tzili,* to which he adds a kabbalistic dimension as well. In Appelfeld's scenario of frenzied Enlightenment aspiration and panicked response to the threat of antisemitism, the Jewish family is seen to embody, in miniature, the intellectual climate of modernism by which it was itself judged and found wanting. In a world that has forgotten its elemental connection to being, the slow-witted daughter Tzili is both an embarrassment and an endangerment to her family, which judges her by the same antisemitic standards as the rest of the world. Simultaneously, however, she is the family's double, indicating how the Jewish family is perceived by the outside world. That Tzili is mentally deficient, while the Jews are often detested for their opposite quality—namely, their intellectual superiority—only brings into sharper focus the degree to which the intellectual, cerebral definition of the human just masks a profound disrespect for and unwillingness to accept the primary claims of being itself.

Indeed, the idea that the humanity of a human being can be proven through intellectual achievement is exactly what makes the humanity of human beings susceptible to being disproved (by *humanity* I do not mean a human being's capacity to behave humanely, but the quality of being human, which characterizes human beings and by which we know human beings to be human beings). It is as if one's achievements in the world were concrete, visible evidence of one's humanness. The desire to prove the human takes us back to Stanley Cavell's idea of the difference between a genuine skepticism concerning the humanness of others—a skepticism that can never be done away with, because it asks truly unanswerable questions—and the radical desire to prove one's skepticism true and thereby to disown such knowledge as is possible to achieve.

It is a major feature of *Tzili,* as of *Badenheim* and other of Appelfeld's writings (*The Age of Wonders, The Healer, The Conversion* [*timyon;* lit.: *Abyss*], and *ᶜad sheyaᶜaleh ᶜamud hashaḥar* [Hebrew; *Till the Dawn's Light*], that the Jewish community replicates the culture that refuses to accept it. Therefore, even before the Jews are rounded up to be deported, the Krauses only barely tolerate Tzili's existence. And when the siege comes, they abandon her to her fate. The Jews in *Tzili,* as throughout Appelfeld's writings, are the very opposite of idealized, sentimentalized victims. Though they may be naive and innocent in their inability to defend or protect themselves, they are in no other way the proverbial lambs to the slaughter. Rather, they are voracious, even violent, in their desire and desperation. Appelfeld's question is not how the Nazis could have done this to God's chosen people. Instead, as we have already begun to see, his fiction ups the ante and asks the more disturbing question of whether the Nazi horror is any less horrible when its victims are, like *Badenheim*'s cast of grotesques or the maimed and flawed Krauses of *Tzili,* as defective as the Germans saw them to be, as disabled and inadequate as, perhaps, they saw themselves, or as we also may, in retrospect, judge them to have been. (This is another way in which the Joseph intertext works: Joseph was indeed unabidably arrogant, yet it was still abhorrent for his brothers to try to kill him.) In posing this vexed and disturbing question of the human, Tzili pushes the question to one sort of limit. For Tzili is indeed no gifted, or even ordinary child; she is unlike the child protagonists in *The Age of Wonders* or *All That I Have Loved,* whose sensitivity or innocence can stand neatly for the author's and thereby our own. Rather, in her severe dysfunction, Tzili raises exactly the question that the Nazis asked and answered vis-à-vis the Jews, which the text itself now comes to ask: the question *what is a human being?*

Innate Knowledge and the Performance of Human Being

Like many of Appelfeld's novels, *Tzili* tells the story of catastrophe outside the camps. It also narrates that story from the perspective of the child survivor, whose incomprehension and disbelief, on the one hand, and tenacity and capacity for survival, on the other, would seem the perfect lens through which to view the incomprehensible, inexplicable, but also somehow survivable horror of the Holocaust. Naomi Sokoloff, building on Alan Mintz's reading of Appelfeld, has described Appelfeld's technique as a "poetics of noninterpretive amazement," "a fictional discourse," in Mintz's words, "which registers rather than construes, observes rather than interprets."[13] This is surely true of Appelfeld's poetics and his reason for employing child protagonists in such works as *Tzili, The Age of Wonders, All That I Have Loved,* and *masa*ᶜ *el haḥoref* [Hebrew; hereafter: *A Journey into Winter*]. Yet, in presenting the child Tzili as a figure for the Nazi assault on the Jews, Appelfeld achieves another purpose as well. He shifts the focus from the destruction of Eastern European life and civilization to the far more elemental devastation wrought by the Nazis: the murder of more than six million individual Jews, whose claim to life rested on nothing more than their being human beings. And more: he pushes back the question of the human from its relevance to judging the Nazis, which, however horrifying, simplifies the question, to a more basic, universal, pervasive form of the question that preceded the Nazi atrocity. By so doing, Appelfeld disallows the possibility of crediting Nazism even with raising for the first time certain questions of the human.

The question *what is man?* precedes the major action of the narrative. Significantly, the question appears within a theological rather than a secular context. And the "answer" to the question, which isn't an answer at all in any ordinary sense of the word, does nothing less than save Tzili's life. As we shall see, this answer is intimately related to the text's refuting and then recasting the human rationalistic claim that *man is not an insect*—the claim that, ironically and in bizarre and horrific ways, led to the opposite conclusion, that some people were indeed vermin to be exterminated.

This is the catechism (adapted from *Perqei Avot*) that ends the first chapter of *Tzili*, a part of which is picked up again, in crucial ways, in Chapter 2: "What is man?" / . . . "Dust and ashes." / "And before whom is he destined to stand in judgment?" / "Before the King of Kings, the Holy One blessed be He." / "And what must he do?" / "Pray and observe the commandments of the Torah." / "And where are the commandments of the Torah written?" / "In the Torah" (5–6). (As with the story's title, the religious terms take on ironic secular meanings: many of those who wore coats of stripes literally did become ashes during the Holocaust.) As we have seen, one way *Tzili* calls into question the assertion that *man is not an insect* is by dramatizing, in particular through the character of Tzili, the ways in which human beings may well, in certain ways, be like insects after all; this comparison does not, however, in any way alter the fact that they are finally humans and not insects. Another way that the story reaffirms humanness is by accepting, by way of another vocabulary, that humans may also be only dust and ashes, "before the King of Kings, the Holy One blessed be He."

These two statements—*man is an insect / man is dust and ashes*—may just be paraphrases of each other. Yet the religious context is important. To be dust and ashes in God's world may not be the same, at all, as being an insect within a homocentric world defined on purely naturalistic and biological grounds. Whatever the case, the words of religious doctrine somehow enable Tzili to survive. This is the case even though the words are drilled into Tzili by a character who has no less contempt for her than do the members of her family and community and who is therefore no more to be admired than they are. I now quote the paragraphs that immediately succeed the catechism itself and then the passage that extends that catechism into Tzili's actual life experience, after the Nazi invasion:

> This set formula [*hanusaḥ haqavuaᶜ hazeh*] spoken in a kind of lilt, would awaken loud echoes in Tzili's soul, and their reverberations spread throughout her body. Strange: Tzili was not afraid of the old man. His visit filled her with a kind of serenity that remained with her and protected her for many hours afterward. At night she would recite "Hear, O Israel," [*qeriᵓat shemaᶜ*] aloud, as he had instructed her, covering her face.
>
> And thus she grew [the Hebrew says—significantly for our purposes—thus she

learned: *lamdah*]. But for the old man's visits her life [existence; *qiyyumah*] would have been even more wretched. She learned to take up as little space as possible [*hi lamdah leẓamẓem et middot gufah*]. She even went to the lavatory in secret, so as not to draw attention to herself. The old man, to tell the truth, felt no affection for her [*lo ahav otah*]. From time to time he grew impatient and scolded her, but she liked listening to his voice [*ahavah et qolo*] and imagined that she heard tenderness in it. (6)

* * *

In her fear she repeated [*meshannenet*] the words she had been taught by the old man [*shelimed otah hazaqen*], over and over again. The mumbled words calmed her and she fell asleep. . . . For a long time she lay supporting herself on her elbows, looking at the sky. And while she lay listening, her lips parted and she mumbled:

"Before whom is he [in the Hebrew the word is *you: ata*] destined to stand in judgment?"

"Before the King of Kings, the Holy One blessed be He." [This line does not exist in the Hebrew text] . . .

[I]n the meantime, the numbness left her legs, and she kicked away the sacking. She said to herself: "I must get up [*laqum*]" and she stood up [*qamah*]. (7–8)

Before trying to specify what, and how, and why Tzili learns from the old man's catechism, it is worth noting that the English translation deviates from the Hebrew in two significant ways. In the first passage, the final sentences might be rendered as "The old man, to tell the truth, did not love her. He merely tolerated her. And every once in a while his patience would snap. But Tzili loved his voice and thought she felt softness in it." The verb that is translated into English as *felt no affection* in the one sentence, and *liked* in the other sentence ("she liked listening") is, in the Hebrew, the same word in both cases: *ahav—loved.* This is not an insignificant choice of verb, since the prayer referred to in these passages, the *shemaᶜ*, contains in its extended form (and as it appears in the Torah itself) the devotee's statement of love for God as inseparably a part of the prayer (*Ye shall love the Lord thy God with all thy heart* . . .). I will return to the *shemaᶜ* later in my argument.

Similarly, in the second passage, in which the catechism is repeated, the English text also reproduces the answer to the question, "Before whom is he destined to stand in judgment?" This answer appears in the first citation of the catechism in both the English and Hebrew versions. It does not, however, appear in the repetition in the original Hebrew. Additionally, the asking of the question in the original itself differs from the English translation in that it asks, "Before whom do *you* stand in judgment?" rather than *he* (italics added). In the Hebrew, then, the question remains hanging, unanswered—until a few sentences later when Tzili does answer what has become her own question concerning her own behavior, by saying "to herself: 'I must get up,'" at which point, the text tells us, "she stood up" (8). I will return to this definitive juncture in the text shortly.

For the moment, what is important is that in Appelfeld's original Hebrew, the question is internalized as a question concerning not others but oneself. The purpose of this question seems less to render judgment on others or even to formulate some abstract theological principle than to provide a basis for self-regulating action. This willing subjection of the self to a kind of powerlessness somehow empowers behavior. It has to do with feelings of love, not justice or some other equally pragmatic, utilitarian idea of what regulates human conduct or value. The internalization of the catechism, its self-referentiality in these two different ways, is crucial to what the text is laying before us here in terms of a philosophy of the human and its relationship to God and religion.

What the two passages, each independently, but also, significantly, cumulatively, stress is how Tzili learns something from her religious catechism that she cannot learn from her secular studies. This something, the passages insist, somehow enables her to survive in the world, indeed to survive exactly that secular world whose lessons she cannot learn and which is also the source of her immediate imperilment. Through a painstakingly careful choice of vocabulary, the text (in the Hebrew) brings into vivid focus not only how radically different the child's two learning experiences are, but how they stand in diametrical opposition. Thus the text tells us, both in the passages above and in the ones surrounding them, that this child who "learns . . . by heart" her secular studies and immediately forgets them (2) does repeat and remember the catechism that the old man has taught her. She, who cannot learn what her family and community teach her at school, precisely can learn this catechism. "For hours she sat and studied. But all her efforts didn't help her," the text says of her secular education (2). Both this passage and the previous one, concerning her memorizing and forgetting her secular subjects, use, in the Hebrew, the same root *meshannenet* and *shinun* (7) that is used later in the text to convey her life-saving recovery of the catechism after the Nazi invasion (10 in the Hebrew text). The Hebrew text similarly uses forms of the same word—*lamdah* (learned [7]; also *limed/taught* [8])—to indicate her lack of success in learning at school what she does succeed in learning from the old man: *vekach hi lamdah* (9), the text informs us concerning the catechism; literally: "and thus she learned," which the English translates as "and thus she grew" (6). (The sentences "she grew" and "thus she grew" actually appear in the Hebrew text twice [*gadlah* and *vekach gadlah* (7) in relation to her literally growing up a member of her family as one more of the abandoned objects in the yard].)

This feature of repetition, which the text itself employs to contrast the two learning experiences, is not to be dismissed lightly. It calls our attention to an aspect of the catechism itself and to the sequence of passages that I have already quoted. Both the catechism and the passages in the novel constitute a set of repetitions, repeating the formulae—the catechism—that is their subject. It is as if the repetition is implicit in what the text calls, twice, the catechism's "set formula."

The idea of a formula [*hanusaḥ haqavua*ᶜ] is itself crucial to what the text presents both as the material and mode of learning (though the English chooses two different phrases by which to translate this—"traditional, unvarying formula" and "set formula"—in Hebrew the words are repeated verbatim near each other [5 and 6 in the English, 9 in the Hebrew]). The implication is that this particular lesson, which instills within Tzili both a will to live and the means by which to act on that impulse, is inseparable from how she learns it. She learns by repetition. To return to the imagery already alluded to—human beings as insects or bugs or animals—it is as if learning by rote and the process of internalization that memorization promotes produce something equivalent to what in the animal- and insect-kingdom is instinct or innate knowledge.

Let me put off for a moment tackling head-on what is surely the most elusive, paradoxical, and potentially off-putting aspect of these passages: the idea I am now developing, that human beings function by something akin to instinct and that this instinct is somehow, paradoxically, inculcated through religious liturgy. Instead, let us look more closely at the passages themselves. However we want to understand the process whereby Tzili gets up and saves her own life, the text does more than describe that process from the outside. Rather, through the repetition and manipulation of its words, in particular the three Hebrew roots having to do with *love, learning,* and, most important, *existence,* it virtually imitates the process of repetition and internalization it is describing. In this way, the passage produces a kind of subterranean groundwork of meaning, what we might think of as a linguistic picture or ideograph. Thus we are told that, even before the Nazi invasion, Tzili's *existence* [*qiyyumah*] is "protected" by the old man's words telling her to observe, to *perform,* the commandments (in Hebrew the word for "protected" is the unusual word *ḥofeh,* conveying the idea of sheltering as in the related word *ḥupah,* a canopy, specifically a bridal canopy; throughout the Bible the relationship of God and the Israelites is represented as a marriage). In Hebrew, the word for *performing* the commandments (as in the catechism) is *leqayyem.* It derives from the same root as *existence.* Were it not for the fact of the old man and his catechism, Tzili's *existence* would have been even more wretched, we are told. It is as if in performing the commandments one were performing, enacting, one's life (wedding oneself to it perhaps), much as animals and insects instinctually, atavistically, perform, enact, and in so doing, protect—save—theirs, as, for example, when butterflies burst their cocoons and fly away, which is what Tzili does when she flees after the Nazi invasion.

The second word used in relation to the commandments (in the text as well as in general Hebrew usage)—*lishmor, to observe or keep* (the commandments) —also means *to save.* Indeed, in observing or keeping the commandments, Tzili literally comes to save her own life. ("The family," we are told, "no longer *observed* the rituals" [4]; "they didn't *keep* the Sabbath" and "it had fallen to the lot of this dull child to *keep* the spark alive" [5]—all the verbs are the same verb, *lishmor*). The word *wretched/mivuzeh,* therefore, may suggest less what is wretched in its own terms, but what is rendered wretched by the actions and attitudes of others. This wretchedness, then, can be rendered less wretched by some internal attitude we maintain toward other people's disparaging of us.

Tzili's existence, her very being, is protected against the tendency of others to despise and debase it through her inner voice intoning a "set formula" of words. When after the catastrophe she tells herself, muttering the words of the catechism, to get up (and indeed she succeeds in standing up), the Hebrew word for both getting up and standing derives from the same root as the word for existence: *laqum/qam*. "Before whom are you destined to be judged?" Tzili asks herself (in the English, "stand in judgment"), and she immediately answers, "I must get up" and does get up (8). Though in the text these statements and events are interrupted by several sentences, in terms of Tzili's thought process, ensuing within the represented world, the one statement follows directly on the other. Her response to the asking of the questions is the knowledge that she must get up. It is also pertinent to what the text is enacting that what is stressed in those intervening narrative statements is the old man's insistence on the "proper pronunciation of the words . . . [which] insistence she remembered now" (8). In Jewish prayer, one is not supposed to read silently, but rather to mouth the words of the prayer, semi-audibly. Praying in Judaism, even when one is reading the text, is not a passive activity: it is an action, a performance.

However we want to understand what is going on in these passages, it is clear that the text does not content itself with merely describing or claiming something about its major protagonist. One standard complaint often lodged against the type of religious thinking presented in the catechism is that it asserts things that cannot be proven—for example, that humankind is dust and ashes standing before divine judgment. By presenting the performance and observance of the commandments as indistinguishable from the performance and saving of one's life, Appelfeld's text in its very words seems to be trying literally to perform the religious logic it is explicating. And it is trying to do this without violating the more natural bases of the human instinct to survive: to get up on one's feet and flee when danger presents itself. In fact, the passage seems to tie together the linguistic and the biological performances. It is as if words make things happen, including the most basic, elemental, life-saving of human activities.

There is in this text a decided continuity between something we might want to think of as human behavior—how we act or "perform" ourselves in the world (which is as much at the center of the secular education that Tzili cannot master as it is of the religious instruction that she can)—and something much more primitive, even biological, which is nothing more than the act of getting up on one's two feet. We might be tempted at this point to conclude that insofar as the knowledge that comes to the fore through the catechism communicates something essentially organic, which she ought to know anyway and for which we do not, therefore, need learning as such, religious instruction is indeed for the feeble-minded and childlike. In that case, perhaps Tzili's family was right to abandon her. And perhaps the Nazis were also right concerning those primitive prayer-wielding Jews who, even when secularized (like the Krauses), just could not seem to leave the liturgy completely behind. The Krauses did, after all, hire that old man to teach Tzili her prayers. Perhaps the Jews, especially the religious among them, did constitute a drag on modernization and progress.

Yet as I have already suggested and as almost every reading of this text will attest, Tzili is the most human person in this story, in every sense of the word. It is Tzili, after all, who acts in extraordinarily creative ways not only to save herself, but later in the story to save her lover Mark as well. Whatever it is that Tzili learns that saves her life, it is something, we come to feel, that others in her world (and ours) might benefit from knowing.

In the first instance, Appelfeld's text is demonstrating something about the place of instinctual or innate knowledge within the human animal. In particular, it shows how this inherent knowledge exists both inside human beings (in the same way that it exists inside other members of the animal kingdom) *and,* simultaneously, how it also exists outside them, externalized and encoded in texts. These texts simultaneously comprehend and express this instinctual knowledge in a particularly human way, as language. Another inherent or instinctual part of the human, the text shows, is the capacity or instinct for language itself. It is through this means that human beings can reinforce, or even when necessary recover and reintroduce to themselves, their own instinctual and life-saving knowledge. Indeed, insofar as both language and getting up on one's two feet have been taken as definitive signs of being human, it may be possible to argue that language is as instinctual as getting up. Language is perhaps the instinct that communicates to us other instincts, including such activities that we think of as primarily physical, like standing up.

An instinct for instinct? Though Appelfeld was likely not aware of recent developments in genetics suggesting that human beings may have a gene for learning instinctual responses (an instinct for acquiring instinct), the text, through its contemplation of Jewish tradition, seems to come to just this conclusion.[14] Indeed, we might think of the text itself, in its repetitious, incantatory structure (imitating the catechism that is its subject), as one more reflection of this instinct-learning process. By internalizing words, Tzili is able to make those words and their meanings organically a part of herself. She can transform them into something like what we understand innate knowledge or instinct to be for animals and bugs. The implication is that just as animals and insects know certain things without being taught, so too do the dust and ashes that are humankind also have internal knowledge, though this knowledge, or at least some aspects of it, may at various times and for various reasons have to be rendered internal through some process other than pure reproduction: let us say by linguistic or behavioral repetition instead of through biological reproduction per se. Just as animals and insects know in some non-linguistic way how to survive, so too do human beings know in some linguistic way how to acquire that same knowledge. Language means that innate knowledge can be instilled or revived or simply kept active by language from without: as, for example, from words that are spoken and read, generation after generation, by human beings, one to the other, as the words of ritual and prayer, or, as we shall see later, as stories.

One adverse consequence of secular culture, which, at the very least, religious learning corrects, is just this forgetting of the instinctual component of human life. This is to say as well that secular culture forgets that the life force *is* instinctual (not necessarily learned, but sometimes learned as well) and that human beings are all biological entities before they are anything else. Given the wholesale slaughter of millions of human beings by the Nazis (because they were Jews, gypsies, homosexuals), this is in itself not an inconsiderable contribution to moral thought. Tzili has to recover an instinct, a purely physiological propensity, that secular culture has robbed her of, in order to act, in defiance of culture, on that instinct. And the liturgy, at the very least, serves this purpose.

But insofar as this particular feature of human beings to get up on their two feet (*laqum*) is, by many accounts, itself a part of the primary definition of the human, as are the language skills that sometimes are required to retransmit that other more physical instinct, then standing up is not only a physical act. It is something different from such activities as eating or sleeping, which humans share with the rest of the animal kingdom. Rather, it is an enactment of the specifically human. This suggests that just as human beings know instinctually how to get up and survive (whether or not such instinct is learned), so too do they know instinctually (again in this double sense) that they *are* human beings and not beings of some other sort. And, equally important, they know this about *other* human beings as well. Human beings, in other words, both perform their definition of themselves the moment they stand up, *and* they signal this definition to others, who similarly stand up and declare their humanness to others.

Standing up is in this sense itself a language. And it functions in Appelfeld's text much like the face in the philosophy of Emmanuel Levinas. It issues a request by one human to another to be recognized as human. If the implicit question buried in a text like *Badenheim* is, as we have seen, what did the Nazis have to refuse to hear in order to torture and murder other human beings, the question posed now is: What did the Nazis have to refuse to see in order to see that other human beings were human beings? Not to be able to define human being is not at all the same as not knowing that another human being is a human being when you see one.

And this is how the text moves from instinct to ethics. Ethics, it is claiming, although not inborn (to know another human being is a human being is not the same as knowing how to treat that other human being), may nonetheless become a part of our instinctual knowledge through the internal–external way in which instinct functions within human beings. Hence we can understand the importance of the other forms of the root *quf vav mem* that have to do with performing not only one's existence but the commandments as well. For what makes human beings *human* beings, and not beings of another sort, is that their knowledge is *self-conscious.* It is this self-consciousness that ritual life re-enacts and transmits. The instinct to be human is not passive knowledge. Nor is it self-contained, for the self alone. It depends upon being performed, for others as well as for one's self.

What the religious definition preserves in its insistence on the biological elementality of human beings is that this definition of the human as dust and ashes pertains to all humans equally. It insists as well that *all* humans simply *know* this from within themselves. The text's careful and precise manipulation of its language, which makes the text itself almost indistinguishable from the same biological process that the catechism itself claims as basic to what human beings know, reinforces the idea that such religious formulae do not teach us something that we do not already know. Quite the contrary. They conform to a prior internal, inherent or innate, knowledge, which secular culture dangerously repudiates.

Human beings know as a part of their instinctual apparatus that they are human beings. They also know that other human beings in their midst are also human beings. The catechism, pouring back instinct from outside, in words that reverberate with that instinct because they are part and parcel of it, recalls this inherent knowledge when it declares that human beings are dust and ashes to be judged—at least concerning their human definition—not by each other but by God. It is God, according to the catechism, who, by contrast, defines human beings, not human beings themselves.

In this context, it is important to remember that Hitler had no more intention to rewrite moral law than Holocaust deniers seek to revise the foundations of historical evidence. Hitler therefore had to put the Jews outside the realm of ethics by declaring them not human. To do this, he had to argue that we know in some sort of scientific way precisely what human beings are (they are not, for example, insects or dogs) and then show that Jews (and gypsies and homosexuals) did not meet this definition. Hence Appelfeld's repetition of the claim *man is not an insect; man is not a dog.* Stripping away the cloakings of civilization, in the ghettos and camps, and performing medical experiments on them, the Nazis desperately tried to prove what they themselves knew to be false: that the Jews were not human. And the Nazis knew this in the same way they knew about each other that they were human—through the pain and suffering and humiliation they caused to disprove that humanness.

Human beings are not insects. Yet, they nonetheless stand in significant relationship to insects (as contemporary DNA studies have more than demonstrated). Human beings are also not God; yet they also bear some relation to God, such that they can be said stand in judgment before Him (which bugs and animals cannot do). Let us say that human beings are those creatures who are created in the image of God. The text evidences this in the name of the major protagonist, Tzili—*ẓel* being the Hebrew word for shadow or image, and reflecting another important and pervasive Hebrew phrase: *ẓelem elohim,* meaning the image of God (the name Tzili would be transliterated, in the system I am using, *ẓili;* to preserve clarity, I have remained with the spelling used in the English translation).

One definition of the human that emerges in *Tzili* can be expressed as *I stand therefore I exist.* (Perhaps for this reason the English translation renders the question "before whom is man destined to *stand* in judgment" even though there is no literal warrant for the word *stand* in the original.) This tautology recalls two other famous tautologies, both of which attempt to explain the existence of God. One is Descartes's famous cogito, by which he proves in one and the same declaration both his own existence and the existence of God: *I think, therefore I am.* The other is the name of God Himself, translated in the King James Bible as *I am that I am,* which is perhaps more precisely translated *I shall be that that I shall be.* By obliquely echoing these tautologies, Appelfeld's text suggests one final observation about the innate knowledge human beings possess concerning their humanness and the humanness of others, which knowledge, the text further indicates, is also embedded and transmitted in the written texts of the liturgy. This knowledge is that by standing up, performing the divine commandments, and performing one's existence (all of which converge in the human animal as its expression of its most basic, elemental humanness in a biological sense), one is also expressing something not wholly organic or biological, something transcendent, which, for want of a better word, we might as well call God.

Human beings, in other words, are also created in the image of God—*ẓelem elohim*—and human beings know this as well. In this text Tzili is the epitome both of self-knowledge and of the image and knowledge of God. Her name is the text's tetragrammaton for this: *tzili,* meaning my shadow, I am a shadow, I am a shadow of myself, I am a shadow or image of God. Indeed, the original Hebrew likely does better duty here than the King James translation. *I shall be that that I shall be* provides the future directedness and active quality of the divine name, which also characterizes Tzili and, through her, the Jewish people. In recovering the self-knowledge of the self as also divine, that in her very essence or Tzili-ness she is *ẓelem elohim,* Tzili does nothing less than save her life. Another Hebrew word embedded in her name is *lehaẓẓil,* to save.

What is important about the catechism, then, is not only what it tells Tzili about her and others' humanness in a biological sense. It is equally the way it conveys this information to her. The message comes not as technical data or information as in secular studies, but as incantation, prayer, and sound-sense corresponding to, and reminding her of, an innate knowledge she and her culture have somehow lost, with horrific results. What is equally important is that in reminding Tzili of these things—that all human beings are equally only dust and ashes—it simultaneously reawakens within her what is also innate or instinctual knowledge: that she is in and of herself, as Tzili, an embodiment of something non-material, something transcendent, something that in one major tradition of human thought is called God. Human beings know they are human beings. And that means that they know as well that they are *ẓelem elohim,* the shadow or image of something not purely material. That is what dust and ashes are, the shadow or image of something else. What is God but a shadow or image, something not substance and matter. The two seemingly divergent meanings of the term *ẓelem elohim*—dust and ashes on the one hand, and, on the other, the image of God—turn out to be one and the same thing. And both turn out to be *almost* identical with the being of God Himself.

This is what the text, almost magically or mystically, goes on to show us. Tzili at no time more fully expresses the *ẓel* or *ẓelem* of God than when she realizes herself as dust and ashes, as earthly being, the child of that first human being made of earth, Adam (in Hebrew the word for *earth* is *adamah;* we are *bnei adam* in Hebrew, the children of Adam, the children of the earth). Like the insinuation of the word—*qam/laqum/leqayyem/qiyyum stand up/perform/performance/existence*—into the language of the text, this idea of the human as a reflection of the divine as dust and ashes is also reflected in the language of the text. Again, it is as if how we know these things is inscribed, buried, inherent, both within us and within the every day words and names (like the name Tzili for example) by which we unselfconsciously describe ourselves and our existence (here the name Tzili takes on an additional meaning: it is a name that contains the sound or *ẓlil* of other words or meanings; sounds are also often echoes or, as it were, shadows, of other sounds). Thus, when we are told at the end of the first chapter that, under the influence of her religious studies, Tzili learned to contract her being, *leẓamẓem et middot gufah* (in the English: to take up as little space as possible), we might do well to consider, within the religious context established by the text, what contracting one's being might mean as a simple human activity. *Ẓimẓum,* explains Harold Bloom, "originally seems to have meant a holding-in-of-the-breath but [Isaac] Luria [who produces one important tradition of kabbalistic thought] transformed the word into an idea of limitation, of God's hiding of Himself, or rather entering into Himself. In this contraction, God clears a space for creation, a not-God."[15]

From the opening pages of the story, the assault against Tzili, by her family and her community, and well in advance of the Nazi invasion, has had to do with a failure to acknowledge her physical being in the world. "Since she was skinny and didn't get in anyone's way, they [the family] ignored her existence" (1–2). Yet later it is precisely her ability to remain "mute" and thereby "vanish" (1), to hold her breath as it were and disappear, that saves her life: "Tzili for some reason, escaped unharmed. Perhaps they didn't see her" (7). Able to hide among barrels and sacking, to burrow in the fields, and to blend into the non-Jewish landscape, Tzili is almost literally reduced to dust and ashes (as were many Jews quite literally reduced to ashes). But in so contracting her being, Tzili is nowhere more precisely imitating the being of God Himself, who, through the divine *ẓimẓum*—the contraction and withdrawal from the creation by which God grants the world (including human beings) its freedom—realizes the fullness of His *middot* (His divine attributes).

Secular humanism, in this text, fails even as paganism or idolatry. It forgets that from the religious perspective, what most characterizes the divine being is His willingness, which is a form of self-humbling or modesty, to withdraw from the scene of His own creation, to permit His creatures the free will that enables them to assume responsibility for themselves and their world. Humility and modesty, we are immediately told, also characterize Tzili's behavior. Just as Tzili's bodily contraction constitutes a kind of *imitatio Dei,* making Tzili's actions not merely mortal or less than mortal (animal-like), but also divine, so by recognizing herself to be no more than dust and ashes, she realizes in the very act of acknowledging her difference from God the divinity of her being, such that even her taking care of her private needs (*ẓorcheha*), those bodily contractions to which all of us are subject, *beẓinᶜah* (modestly or chastely), makes her less an embarrassed child than a holy being. Is more than simple run-of-the-mill potty training necessary for us to realize the restraint necessary not to shit on the world, as did the Nazis? Another bodily contraction that receives emphasis in this text is that of the uterus, as in menstruation and birthing: bringing life into the world is also a very ordinary human affair, but no less important for that reason, as we shall see later. What human beings need to do to realize their humanness is not to act as if they were gods but to fulfill their most basic human needs.

What follows in the next two chapters of the novel as Tzili "learns" to survive in a hostile, natural world becomes nothing less than the progress of a saint in the discovery of her holiness. This holiness, it turns out, is not a denial of Tzili's relation to nature, but the realization of it. In that realization is the recognition of the divine within the natural and the human, which is to say, the place of being itself within our definition of the human and the divine. Tzili achieves her humanness, which is to say her *ẓelem elohim,* her Tzili-ness, in being what God Himself achieves through his divine *ẓimẓum,* which is, in Bloom's words, being *not-God.* The human being, in being dust and ashes, becomes defined by being *not-God* in this sense. This is not the same as being *not-insect.*

The ideas of *ẓimẓum* and *ẓniᶜut* (contraction and modesty) are not without relevance for characterizing the text's own mode of being as text. In its restraint and reticence (Geoffrey Hartman's terms), the text too becomes an *imitatio Dei.* It is an embodiment of divine being in human (and I stress *human*) discourse. In this way, the text (like *Badenheim*) is itself a form of meditation or prayer, of which the addressee is not God but, as in the *shemaᶜ* itself, other human beings. This is prayer as a form of storytelling or narrative. The old man, we are told, teaches Tzili two things. One is the stories of the Bible. The other is prayer. In Jewish ritual the two are inseparable. And each has fundamentally to do with the same feature of repetition and internalization, the production of and correspondence to innate knowledge, which Appelfeld's text is reproducing. *Tzili,* like *Badenheim,* is a prayer of sorts, an extended version of the catechism with which it begins.

One must proceed cautiously here. "The tendency to speak of the Holocaust in mystical terms," writes Appelfeld, "to link the events to the incomprehensible, the mysterious . . . is both understandable and dangerous. . . . Murder that was committed with evil intentions must not be interpreted in mystical terms. A vile hand was raised against mankind; we do not have mysticism here, but a blow directed against the central pillar of the Ten Commandments" (39). Yet, as Appelfeld has also stated, "hesitat[ing] to say [what] one must: The apocalyptic horror of the Holocaust was felt by us as a deeply religious experience" (45):

> Anyone who lived through the Holocaust will never forget the cries of "Hear O Israel" which shattered the air and shook the earth. . . . What happened during the Holocaust was not ["*hazara biteshuva,*" a "return to religious observance"] but rather contact with an atmosphere permeated by a kind of mythic depth, the stratum out of which . . . faith arises. . . . Religious feelings during the Holocaust broke out on all sides, expressed silently, and in the sounds of song and prayer. . . . Mostly they were "illuminations" after days of hunger, danger, and despair, a sense of wonder about people or objects, a kind of contact with one's parents, self-consolation.

> For the children is was perhaps more "primordial"—contact with the trees in the forest, the moist earth, the straw, sucking fluids from the roots of the trees, the night skies. These contacts with a hostile space, for us, homeless and orphaned, had qualities that were beyond "discovery" or curiosity.
>
> I call these feelings religious, the fundamental religious sentiments . . . wonder for its own sake, without any ulterior intention: you and the world, with no separation. (*Beyond Despair,* 45–49)

What is unique about the *shema*ᶜ/*Hear O Israel,* and the reason one can imagine novels like *Badenheim* and *Tzili* as being prayers, is that it is *not* an address or supplication to God. Rather, it is a statement made by human beings to each other, declaring something *about* God, namely His singular, unitary existence, which He Himself articulates to humankind: *Hear O Israel, the Lord our God, the Lord is One.*[16] In and of itself this oft-repeated prayer, which is recited in varying contexts and in longer and shorter versions in the daily Jewish liturgy and at the moment before death, is simultaneously a human declaration and a quotation of a quotation of the divine word. "Hear O Israel," one Jew says to another, "the Lord our God, the Lord is one." And she or he says as well: "Hear O Israel" what God Himself has said to us, in that first and oddest of the Ten Commandments, the commandment that does not seem to be a commandment at all but a repetition of the tautology of the divine name: *I am the Lord thy God.*

The *shema*ᶜ quotes the divine voice itself as quoted and requoted by Moses in the Torah, where the *shema*ᶜ itself appears in full, in particular following the repetition of the scene of the giving of the Law and the citing of the Ten Commandments in Deuteronomy (which scene I have already discussed in relation to *Badenheim*). In other words, the *shema*ᶜ (like *halacha,* Jewish ritual, itself) is essentially a performative repetition. It is repeated in Appelfeld's text, as it is repeated by Tzili herself, as what every Jew who intones this prayer also repeats. For this reason, the *shema*ᶜ as a call to hear is itself a form of listening. And what is at the center of what it listens to amid all these human voices repeating these very same words is the word of God, as articulated in the first commandment. This is the commandment that states the truth, the truthfulness of which is performed through the declaration itself: *I am the Lord thy God.*

"What is man?" / . . . "Dust and Ashes." / "And before whom is he destined to stand in judgment?" / "Before the King of Kings, the Holy One blessed be He." / "And what must he do?" / "Pray and observe the commandments of the Torah." / "And where are the commandments of the Torah written?" / "In the Torah." Humankind enacts its humanness in the fulfillment of the commandments, by which human beings are told, both what they are not—*not-God*—and what they shall *not* do. A fascinating feature of the Ten Commandments is that only three of them are positive commandments, i.e., not put in the form of "thou shalt not." Of those three, two are concerned not with the realm of material culture but with the relationship of the human and the divine: I am the Lord thy God, the first commandment (which, as we have seen, is at the center of the *shema*[c]); and the third: Observe the Sabbath day, to keep it holy. Everything else in the Ten Commandments (except the commandment concerning one's parents) is in the form of a prohibition: what one is commanded not to do, which is not to steal, not to murder, not to make graven images, and so on. Like halacha, the commandments are meant to regulate the performance of life in material culture, and the condition on which such behavior of human beings toward other human beings is predicated is the existence of a realm that is the not-human. What is man? Dust and ashes. And what therefore can human beings learn? What *not* to do to those others with whom they share the time and place of a world of dust and ashes, of *not-God.*

In the tautology "Where are the commandments of the Torah written?" / "In the Torah" (which Tzili internalizes) is contained both the moral law of "thou shalt not" and the wisdom of the divine pedagogy, as contained in the divine name itself—*I am who I am.* This is the wisdom of indwelling knowledge and self-consistency. It exists for human beings in their realization that they are *ẓelem elohim* in the two senses of the concept already specified—as dust and ashes and as thereby responsible moral beings, capable in their being *not-God* of *not* doing harm to others. Toward the beginning of *Facing the Extreme,* Tzvetan Todorov suggests that "the most optimistic conclusion we can draw from life in (and outside) the camps is that evil is not unavoidable."[17] That evil is *not unavoidable* may be the major moral teaching of Torah itself, and not only in the Ten Commandments, but also in the stories it narrates: for the Torah contains far more than the Ten Commandments. It contains the entire story of the nation, in particular its exodus from Egypt toward the promised land. A central piece of that biblical saga is the story of the coat of many colors, as the Hebrew title of the novel *Tzili,* translated as *The Coat and the Stripes,* reminds us. The Bible stories themselves, it turns out, are also cast in the form of *thou shalt not.*

Literature as Midrash

Given its emphasis on the commandments and the Torah, it is hardly to be dismissed as insignificant that *Tzili* begins with a sort of "shalt not" of storytelling: "Perhaps it would be better to leave the story of Tzili Kraus's life untold [literally: "the story of Tzili Kraus's life it is perhaps forbidden—*assur*—to tell"]. Her fate was a cruel and inglorious one, and but for the fact that it actually happened we would never have been able to tell her story." Ostensibly (as we have seen) this comment responds to the prohibition concerning the writing of Holocaust fiction, which has seemed to many people an indecorous and frivolous response to the horrors that had transpired. Nonetheless, as the use of the religiously freighted word *assur* already signals us, storytelling may itself, as part and parcel of secular culture, constitute something of a forbidden activity. Making graven images is one of the very activities expressly prohibited in the Ten Commandments (we saw this already reflected in *Badenheim*), and what is secular literature but just that, a form of image-making? Were it not for the fact that human lives happen, that human beings exist, the text says in its own self-defense, then telling the stories of their lives would surely be forbidden.

We may take the author here as signaling his refusal of or resistance to religious dictate, though as we shall see in a moment, religious thinking—at least as expressed in the Torah—can be understood to proceed along the same lines. For Appelfeld, recording the fact of the uneventful eventfulness of human life—that lives happen, that human beings exist—restores to human beings their human form. Not only that, it teaches them the most important lesson to be taught concerning the human, that they live their lives in the performance of them, which performance also serves as nothing less than a definition of the human. This is for Appelfeld a religious as much as a secular lesson. Especially in the wake of the Holocaust (hence the double-duty done by that opening *issur/prohibition*), Appelfeld would remind us of the simple everyday humanness of human beings.

It is this enactment of the human that is demonstrated in story after story in the Old Testament—almost raising questions as to what sort of sacred text the Bible is. In the context of the catechism and its diffusion into the structure of Appelfeld's text, the way in which the biblical intertext is introduced into the novel, through its title, is significant: the book invokes, in order to retell, a story that is already known to its readers (even Tzili presumably knows this story), and it is known to them in the particular way of repetition we have been examining. A basic element of Jewish synagogue worship is the reading of the Torah, which entails the ritual repetition of the biblical stories week after week, throughout the course of the entire year, and beginning anew each year, and so on and so forth, year after year. The repetition works differently for Christian readers, for whom Old Testament texts are employed another way in the church service; yet in Christianity, too, the stories circulate and are known before they are invoked or alluded to. Appelfeld introduces his storytelling under the sign of an *issur,* and he lets it cast its shadow over his entire work. Perhaps, we come to feel, that *issur* is one more *ẓel* (shadow) that also has its origins in divine being itself, for the biblical stories are nothing if not tales of violation and sin, and yet they are divinely ordained nonetheless.

Given the fact that it is a story not to be told, it is not surprising that the story of Tzili proceeds through a series of trangressive acts, sexual and otherwise. This transgressiveness of the story, not only in terms of its large political ambience (i.e., the war itself), but also in terms of the mini-dramas enacted by its major protagonist (Tzili's illegitimate pregnancy, for example), could be understood, like Erwin's endless cycling of the rails, as confirmation of the dead-end stasis to which human civilization has arrived. Human life is an eternal round of violent acts and transgressive behaviors, arriving nowhere. Tzili, after all, loses her baby; and the ending of the novel promises only the most compromised relocation in the land of Israel, especially if the second novella printed with *Tzili* in the Hebrew publication, *The Immortal Bartfuss,* is to be taken as a commentary on it. Like many of Appelfeld's refugees from the war, now living in Israel, Bartfuss is anything but well-adjusted and happy.

Yet, concluding with the words of a lullaby being sung to Tzili, the book also hints at some sort of comfort. As in the case of reading *The Iron Tracks*, in order to reach this place of comfort, where human catastrophe recovers its relation to the divine (and, as the lullaby also suggests, with the mother), we have to journey the subterranean texts that this text conceals beneath its title and in the various image clusters throughout the book, in particular the biblical stories that drift, like prayer itself, throughout this text. These texts, as we shall see, are nothing if not transgressive. Not only do they record human transgressions against God, but they seem, in and of themselves, somehow not decorous, not "divine," as if overhung with *ẓel*.

Before I suggest how the biblical stories might figure in Appelfeld's novel, let me issue a warning similar to the warning I posted in relation to the psychoanalytic intervention into Appelfeld's fiction. *Tzili* in no way directly parallels or even directly invokes any set of biblical events, except, perhaps, through its title, the Joseph story. Even here, however, the allusion is strained, even tormented. Its purpose may well be less to invoke or allude to the biblical motif than to make visible a rupture between the Hebrew Bible and contemporary history—much as in the case of the biblical and prophetic texts that lurk beneath the language of *Badenheim*. As it turns out, however, the novel exposes a rupture implicit in the original text itself, which cracks covenantal history open at its core. It also signals the sharp divide between Jewish history and the Christian revelation that threatens to lure Judaism itself into visions of apocalypse and redemption. But to see the course the text travels, one must proceed cautiously and with care.

Tzili puts us in mind of several plots of divine salvation, in both the Jewish and Christian traditions. So doing, it locates, perhaps, the historical, textual links between Judaism and Christianity, which Nazism sought to sever. Indeed, it may even be recovering the origins of Judeo-Christian tradition within more pagan beliefs and customs. Even so, it does not draw these traditions together in order to declare the place of the Holocaust in messianic history, either Jewish or Christian or both. Appelfeld is quite explicit in his essays that this would constitute a kind of slander against the victims and a blasphemy against God Himself. It would also contradict the ending of the novel. As I have already indicated, even though the characters are poised on the brink of the promised land, the ending hardly reads as redemptive, though one must recall here that in the Five Books of Moses, the people also do not enter the promised land. They do so only later, and of course Moses himself never does realize the journey's finale.

In its emphasis on the moment before entering the promised land, the novel retreats from Christian allegory and Zionist messianism and rejoins more traditional Jewish historical narratives. So, let me for the moment recover some of the evocations of the divine that help lift this text off the axis of the purely natural and human, however much we will want, in the final analysis, to return to the natural, human world at the center of Appelfeld's thought. The text's biblical, religious allusions do not serve to trace a particular pattern of divine providence. Quite the contrary, even as they do not add up to an endorsement of one theological view or another, they mark a mystery of human existence, which rationalism and reason would dismiss, only at their own peril. Furthermore, they function to remind the reader that this mystery exists as much in a tradition of textual narration as within the world itself. Therefore, it is accessible not through some sort of primitive communion with nature, as if we might return to the world of nature with prelapsarian innocence and discover what civilization has covered over and destroyed. Rather, it is recoverable through the knowledge of those traditions, primarily biblical and liturgical, that have been invested, in Judaism at least, with telling the story of the divine within human history.

With its biblical reference staring us in the face in the Hebrew title, which is doubled in original Hebrew publication, since the title *hakutonet vehapassim/The Shirt and the Stripes* serves both as the title of the particular story concerning Tzili and also of the two-novel collection in which it was first published, the story immediately yields some superficial, allegorical, but nonetheless meaningful parallels to the story of Joseph and his brothers. *The coat of stripes,* which is translated in the King James Bible as the coat of many colors, is the sign of Joseph's chosenness. It is also the direct provocation of the sibling rivalry that proves his downfall. Of course there is already a marked difference between the original text and its literary inheritor. Although despised by her siblings, Tzili is the opposite of her parent's favorite child. Nonetheless, she is the one who is "chosen" (much to the old man's chagrin) to preserve the filament of faith, which the family has all but broken. Thus, even more despised than Joseph (by her parents as well as by her siblings), Tzili, like Joseph, is cast to her fate—almost, but not literally, into a pit—to suffer indignities and torments, like the chosen people itself.

The transformation of the terms in Appelfeld's title from the *coat of the stripes* to *the coat and the stripes*—i.e., the splitting of the coat from the stripes—itself constitutes an explication of the coat's meaning. This is reinforced later on by the explicit reference at the end of the story to the striped garments of the concentration camp inmates. Most readers of the Hebrew text will have already understood that allusion to be there in the title. It is the coat, which is the sign of Joseph's chosenness, Appelfeld's title reminds us, that occasions the brothers' revenge against Joseph. Chosenness, or at least the claims to it, may well account also for the nations' revenge against Israel. Both seem to be attempted fratricide sparked by envy. But the coat is also the visible evidence of the brothers' treachery by which they, erroneously, declare Joseph dead. Therefore, like the shroud of Christ later or like a prayer shawl, which is also, in its own way, a coat of stripes, the coat metamorphoses into the relic of a saint, which, while seeming to witness death, augurs salvation. (The Israeli flag is said to have been modeled on the prayer shawl and thus in a way on Joseph's coat.)

Like Tzili, Joseph submits to his fate. He contracts the dimensions of his somewhat overblown, overbearing being (Joseph is unabidably arrogant in the early stories) and survives his being thrown into the pit and sold into slavery.

Thus, he not only fulfills his destiny as the people's savior, but also enables covenantal history to continue to take its course. Joseph's sojourn in Egypt leads inexorably to the exodus into the promised land, though, significantly, as I have already noted, the people enter the promised land only after the end of the story itself, and Moses, of course, never arrives. A similar logic, the novel suggests, can be understood in relation to the Nazi violence against the Jews as represented by Tzili. Thrown into the pit by her family, sold as it were into bondage, first with Katerina and then with a series of Gentile peasants who beat and abuse her, Tzili finally makes her way to a caravan of refugees on its way to, but not arriving in, Israel.

As I have already suggested, it is difficult to take the end of the story as evidencing salvation and this chapter in Jewish history as one more installment in the unfolding of covenantal history. There are more reasons for this than the non-arrival at the end of the novel. After all, we all know, historically, that the children of Israel did enter the promised land, as did the Jews after the Second World War. Yet, losing the child she is carrying and becoming herself (in the book's final image) the child of a childless refugee singing Hungarian lullabies, Tzili serves equally to constitute an image of a regression backward out of biblical promise altogether, reversing the direction of covenantal history and arriving back in a world of elemental nature. Nature may be all that survives this Holocaust intact. The rupture between the coat and its stripes, signaled by the story's title, may not so easily be repaired. But this rupture, it turns out, like the non-arrival in the promised land, also has its counterpart in the original text. For an important feature of that text is that Joseph is not the direct progenitor of Jewish continuity.

However salvational history proceeds, Appelfeld's text is suggesting, its course is hardly direct. Even though Joseph occupies center stage in the story of the people's enslavement in Egypt, and therefore, subsequently, in the story of their exodus to freedom, Joseph is *not* himself a figure in the messianic line, either on the political or spiritual levels. There is no tribe named after Joseph. This honor bypasses Joseph and is divided between his two sons. Nor does Joseph in his own flesh and blood directly transmit to David and the promised messiah the line of Abraham, Isaac, and Jacob. It is Judah who does this, in the story embedded in the Joseph story, which interrupts it. This story is then taken up later in the biblical tradition in the Book of Ruth, which typologically and genealogically completes this story. Subsequently, the story of salvational history recovers its narrative momentum in the Christian inheritance of Judaism, in the Christ story itself. The story of Christ's birth and death is directly linked not only to Judah/Tamar and Ruth but, through the Pentecost, to the holiday in the Jewish calendar linked to Ruth, Shavuoth. Shavuoth marks fifty days following Passover. It marks as well the day of the giving of the Torah. In Old Testament covenantal history, in other words, Joseph is a figure of deferral. What happens happens around him and not through him. Indeed, in the minor tradition within Judaism that does subscribe to the idea of a messianic line emanating from Joseph, this line is imagined simply to precede and augur the more important and definitive Davidic line. Certainly within the Christian inheritance of Judaism, what matters is what happens between Judah and Tamar in the spaces of the Joseph story and not what happens to Joseph himself.

Before I suggest the kind of field of biblical allusion that is being constructed in Appelfeld's novel, and, in particular, the relevance of the Judah and Tamar story, let me examine a few oddities of the book that do not initially or necessarily have anything to do with God and the Bible. The first and foremost of these is the strange coupling of the attempted rape of Tzili by a peasant farmer and the onset of her menses. This association between rape and menstruation is furthered and deepened in the text by the description of the sensations experienced by Tzili's body as she begins to menstruate the first time and by the sexualized description of the corn fields just reaching their ripening where both the rape and the onset of her menses take place. These twinned features of the text carry over the imagery of sexual penetration from the attempted-rape scene as if, quite after the fact, Tzili were experiencing that rape after all, though not through any human agency. Thus, the word *qadaḥ* (16), *seethed* in the English (21), which describes the response her body to her menstruation, carries with it the sense of *drilled* or *bored.* Similarly, the word that describes how waves of pain woke her up or aroused her from sleep, *maqiẓim* (twice repeated) (16 in the Hebrew) incorporates (through the word *qoẓ*) an idea of pricking, quite consonant with the idea of the drilling or boring going on (21 in the English). As if this were not sufficient to alert us to something sexual in the events overtaking her body, the stalks of corn where she is lying are described as being *erect* (*zaquf* [16 in the Hebrew]; the pun on erection works in Hebrew as in English). "She feared her body," we are told, "as if something alien had taken possession of it" (21); more literally, she feared her body *as if something foreign had taken up its dwelling there.* The word *hishtaken*—to take up its dwelling—is crucial here (16 in the Hebrew). It derives from the same word as *shechina,* the Holy Spirit, while the word *nechar,* foreign, evokes the idea of *nochri,* a foreigner or stranger, a word that recalls the cognate used in the previous chapter by the attempted rapist, to describe his relationship to Tzili as one of *macarim,* acquaintances. Conveniently enough, the English translates this as "not strangers" (15; 13 in the Hebrew), picking up the way in which the root *nun qof reysh* is one of those words that conveys both its primary meaning and its opposite. Nor is it irrelevant in this context that the farmer's naming them "not strangers" and therefore entitled to engage in sexual intercourse, is linked to his having just identified Tzili as one of the daughters of the whore Maria. It is from the farmer that Tzili takes the saving idea of designating herself the child of Maria, a claim which builds on the fact that Maria is oddly distinguished by her close, sympathetic relationship to the Jews. Tzili is already, in this sense, the spiritual child of Maria, who marks the Christian/Jewish nexus embodied in Christ himself. Here it is useful to recall the doubling of the Madonna with another Mary, Mary Magdalene, who was not a virgin but a whore.

Emptied out of thoughts and memories and made hollow and empty, her "body . . . detaching itself from home" and "the seeds of oblivion already sown"

(26; the words for both *seeds* and *oblivion* coming from the same root as seed, *zera*ᶜ, which means male seed as well), and her menstruation described as a *vital* or *life-giving* wound (the word translated in the English as "not unhealthy" [26] is *ḥiyyut* meaning *life, vitality* [18 in the Hebrew]), Tzili becomes nothing less than the site of some sort of annunciation. The question is what sort and what this scene is doing here in this novel of catastrophe and devastation, especially since Tzili, even after she literally becomes pregnant through much more ordinary and human means, gives birth to no child, savior or otherwise.

One could, of course, take the text's linking of rape and menstruation and Tzili's subsequent, albeit figurative, rape by the landscape as purely ironic. The novel may here be subverting any connection between itself and whatever biblical materials, including the Joseph story, we might crazily imagine as hovering in the background of this highly naturalistic text. Certainly the imagery would seem, from the outset, to set at some substantial distance from the narrative itself any idea of redemption or salvation. Thus, for example, the link between menstruation and rape might be fitted into Naomi Sokoloff's more allegorical interpretation of the story as figuring through the vulnerable female child the vulnerability of the Jewish people itself. The association of menstruation with death, therefore, which the text makes explicit in Tzili's imagining, quite understandably, that her bleeding indicates she is going to die, could be said to gain further reinforcement through its connection with the threat of violent assault earlier on. Sexuality, which is an internal, biological marker of identity, and is no more to be denied or eliminated than menstruation itself, exposes women to violence. So does something about the Jews, though (as Sokoloff admits) it is hard to say exactly what this something is. (It is not irrelevant in this context that Jewish men were imagined within certain antisemitic circles to menstruate from their noses, an idea that is linked to a variety of fantasies concerning Jewish circumcision as evidencing a lack of virulence and masculinity.) Thus, what I am reading as a scene of annunciation might more readily be understood as a scene of death (by crucifixion?), which is implicit in the very being of this woman and this people. That Tzili's pregnancy, when she does finally become pregnant, terminates in abortion would seem to reinforce such an interpretation.

The problem with this reading, however, which nonetheless does, I think, inform the text in important ways, is that, despite the association with violence and death, menstruation marks the moment when Tzili moves from a position of defenselessness into one of increasing fertility and strength. This is explicitly noted in the text through its tracing of Tzili's accelerating skills of adaptation and survival. It is implicit as well in the texture of the text's natural setting. The text goes out of its way to establish the natural, physical contours of the world it is depicting, including the biological integrity of its major character, who survives by a native instinct (aided and abetted by that liturgy, of course, which she absorbs bodily into herself), uninformed by scientific knowledge. The natural setting of the story, the corn fields at harvest time, receives repeated emphasis throughout the opening chapters, as if the landscape itself were the major contributor to the survival of this woman. Whatever happens to Tzili in the corn field happens quite outside the world of human intercourse, except, of course, when she is joined there by Mark and later herself joins the refugees moving toward Israel.

Thus, in Yigal Schwartz's reading, which takes note of the dominant domain of this text—the child's experience within the natural world, including the transformations going on inside her own body—the story interprets the events of the war as a failed (or more precisely, given the text's own terminology, an aborted) rite of passage, in which the normal contours of socio-cultural history, urged on by irrepressible psychosexual process, are defeated by the radical rupture represented by the Holocaust itself (112–28). In this story, as in so many of Appelfeld's writings, the Holocaust externalizes and finalizes fault lines already in place within Jewish communal organization. Even if Tzili's entry into the world of non-Jews and nature is facilitated and sustained by the more conventional religious faith drilled into her by her less-than-sympathetic teacher, it may well be the case that her survival must nonetheless be understood as taking place in spite of or in defiance of or, simply, perhaps, in excess of her religious understanding. But if what is represented here is an aborted rite of passage, then it may also be the case that the text is self-subverting. The substitution of the world of nature for the world of community and God may be no substitution at all. With no world outside the natural world to receive her back when the process of her maturation is complete, her maturation is meaningless, as if sexual maturation were death after all. Reading the text as refusing theological meaning, which is to say, understanding Tzili's experience as refuting the idea of God and worship, delivers the text back to the original condition that might be understood to have precipitated the Holocaust both within and outside the family: a condition of godlessness. This godlessness first presented itself as a self-destructive hyper-rationality. Now it emerges as what only seems to be its opposite: a consummate and ultimately self-defeating paganism. As Schwartz has pointed out, Nazism's own connection to a heightened German romanticism of the *folk* is not to be forgotten in this context (112–28).

One could interpret these features of the novel by saying, simply, that the Holocaust has been so catastrophic a rending of the principles of both civilization and nature as to afford no avenues of recovery. And this is certainly one implied meaning of this text, which it would be folly to dismiss. And yet the text, again like almost all of Appelfeld's writings, is not without a hopefulness, which is incorporated into the very language of the text. Terrence Des Pres has argued that survival itself was an act of heroism in the Holocaust, and this idea seems to me very important to Appelfeld's novel. Tzili's survival is in and of itself inspirational. That human beings can survive the tremendous deprivations they are made to suffer is not a feature of the human to dismiss lightly. So, perhaps, human beings are insects after all, in some positive rather than negative sense, which is to say, perhaps we should not be so contemptuous of the insect or animal world and its capacity for survival. And yet, if that is all that Tzili teaches us, then survivability may itself collapse into the logic of the

Final Solution and reinforce it. After all, what did Nazi Germany want if not to ensure its physical survival, at whatever cost to its moral or ethical being?

So what else can we harvest from this text, glean from the fragments it strews before us as tantalizing reminders of other stories, other triumphs of the human?

Here it is pertinent that the story is set at harvest time, a fact it repeatedly emphasizes. Even without the route opened up by the Joseph story, we might be put in mind of the Book of Ruth, which may be the consummate story of the harvest told within the writings of the Old Testament. True the harvest in *Tzili* is a harvest of corn (*tiras*) and not, as in Ruth, of *shibbolet* (the Joseph story is also marked by a reference to *shibbolet* [wheat], Joseph's interpretations of pharaoh's dreams having to do with cows and grain). Corn as we know it was not a crop that existed in the ancient world. Thus the word *corn* in the King James Bible does not refer to modern-day corn but, rather, to wheat. But the idea that what is being referred to in the Book of Ruth is indeed corn is so much a commonplace in the Western literary tradition that Appelfeld could easily play on this in his own text. Even without this interpretation, however, an idea of harvest controls the imagery of the story. And it is not incidental to this configuration that the harvest story it may be invoking is associated, in the Jewish calendar, with the giving of the law at Sinai (Shavuoth; Pentecost in the Christian tradition). Like the Book of Ruth, *Tzili* has to do with the ability of a young girl, separated from her people, to move through a landscape of famine and death and survive on the leavings of other people's harvest (by "other people" I mean literally a people not her own, strangers or foreigners). Significantly, the passage that first records Tzili's gaining sustenance from the corn is also the first place in the text where the word *passim/stripes* appears, as if already linking the natural and the divine experience with the biblical stories, all of which intertwine in this text: "The darkness seeped slowly away. A few pale stripes appeared in the sky and turned a deeper pink. Tzili bent over to rub her feet and sat down. Unthinkingly she sank her teeth into a cornstalk. A stream of cool liquid washed her throat" (10).

Also significant is that Tzili's rejoining her people comes through what some people might well identify as illicit sexual relations, when Tzili (like Ruth laying herself down at her husband's kinsman's feet) sleeps with, and becomes pregnant by, the one surviving male of his family, a suggestively named (from the perspective of the Christian motifs of this novel) Mark. It is the Book of Ruth that explicitly picks up the genealogy of the Davidic line established through an earlier act of sexual transgression, the sexual intercourse between Judah and Tamar which, as I have already noted, almost without rhyme or reason, interrupts the Joseph story. This is the genealogy that is recalled in the opening passages of the New Testament (i.e., in Matthew), in the record of Christ's ancestry, on his father's side, which is both cited and canceled/transcended since, of course, Christ has no earthly father, only a divine one.

The immaculate conception remembers these earlier moments of sexual transgression, in which the woman, submitting to what might seem like sexual violation, returns biblical history to its proper course. It also redeems these earlier moments through the bypassing of sexuality altogether: in a relationship between human sexuality and the divine which is replicated or hinted at in the Christ narrative itself through the doubling of Mary by the prostitute Mary Magdalene. The immaculate conception, of course, marks the inception of the new law. At Pentecost, fifty days after the crucifixion at Passover, and coinciding with the Jewish Shavuoth, the Holy Spirit (the *shechinah*) once again descends to dwell among humankind.

There is nothing to prevent our taking these fragmentary gleanings of biblical texts ironically. They may do nothing more than hammer one last nail into coffin of covenantal history. Indeed, reading Tzili's experience against the biblical stories may serve only to bring into view the text's investment in a natural world order and/or paganism, which precede and/or resist Judeo-Christian civilization and its deforming intellectualization of human experience. Tzili is no savior in her own right. Nor does she produce any issue that might be thought either to carry on the line or redeem it. But for exactly the same reasons—that Tzili's biological development does not save her, except in some very limited, biological way—the text's withdrawal into the world of nature under the banner of the biblical text, which it announces as its title, can also be understood not as a retreat out of the Judeo-Christian tradition but as a reinterpretation of that tradition.

Very deliberately *Tzili* constitutes a midrash on—an interpretation of—the Joseph story. It re-examines the relationships between religion and nature, which is to say between God and the world of His creation. Whatever else the story intends by placing Tzili within the natural world and refiguring her survival as a biological or physiological rather than a purely spiritual experience, it also situates her within a schema of providential history, which forces us to rethink the meaning of providential history, in particular in its intersection with naturalistic, sociological human experience. What do we understand by the indwelling of the spirit, whether we imagine that spirit, as does Christianity, as literally producing a divine savior, or whether, as in Judaism, we understand it as interacting with and informing human history in some less embodied, less incarnate form?

Nowhere is Christianity more creative in its adaptation of Jewish texts than in its idea of the immaculate conception, which is no less an anti-typological rethinking of the inception and birth of Isaac than the crucifixion is of *ʿaqedat Yitzhak*—the binding of Isaac. In Judaism, even before Christianity, the human enactment of divine history takes its insemination from an intercourse with the divine. How else explain Sarah's conceiving and giving birth well past the years of her reproductive capacities? As to many a barren woman in the Bible, an angel appears and a child is born. We are dealing here with more than a figuring of the miracle of birth. The progress of human history, in Judaism, proceeds through God's permission that it do so: through His willingness, in His dealings first with Abraham (as later, perhaps, with Jacob) that the child be conceived and, later, not sacrificed. In kabbalistic interpretation, this emerges as God's withdrawal of Himself from the world (his *ẓimẓum*) such that the world of humankind and nature may proceed through a volition of its own and not by its coercion or superimposition by God.

This might be one way of thinking about divine grace. The natural world, in this view, is not a world controlled by God. Nor is it a world outside and independent of God, such that whatever divinity we may feel to inhere in nature is internal to itself, as in, say, deistic or pagan interpretations. Rather it is a world which is informed by God in the suspension of His will to dominate the world. It is a world granted its freedom and permitted to exist in some degree of violation or forbiddenness or transgression, which no degree of personal, human sacrifice (either of self or other) can redeem. And this is the difference between the Christian universe and the Jewish one. No immaculate conceptions or virgin births. No saviors, human or divine. No redemption, no apocalypse, no second coming. No human beings who are not *not-God*, for what is Christ but a refutation of the human as dust and ashes, which opens up the possibility of a human being who is more divine than human, a kind of Nietzschean superman.

Tzili refutes this Christian teleology, which it sets in relation to the Old Testament history Christianity would subsume and overwrite. And it places itself in *the* story that leads to the people's *historical* rather than transcendental experience, which culminates in their almost-arrival in Israel and *not* in the birth of a messiah. Only the transmission of history, with its inevitable acts of transgression—from the garden of Eden through the patriarchs and down onto Moses' striking of the rock—carries the story and definition of the human, insisting on the human–divine relation without confusing the categories of human being and God.

In Judaism, to return to where this chapter on *Tzili* began, human beings are dust and ashes, not in a physical world of animals and insects, and not literally as human beings reduced to ashes in the crematoria, but in a divine universe, in which our affinity with the being of other beings (sentient as well as nonsentient, conscious as well as unconscious) is the condition from which we begin our metamorphosis into beings of another order, still not divine saviors or gods. As Emmanuel Levinas points out, in his essay on *ʿaqedat Yitzhak* and Kierkegaard, when Abraham, who later stays his hand and does *not* kill the son, intercedes for Sodom and Gomorrah, the dialogue virtually begins with "I am but dust and ashes." It is this other dialogue between Abraham and God that occasions Levinas's remark, in contradistinction to Kierkegaard's claim that the story evidences the existence of "God above the ethical order," that "perhaps Abraham's ear for hearing the voice that brought him back to the ethical order was the highest moment in this drama."[18] In Judaism, human beings never reach the condition of divinity toward which they aspire. And therefore, turned back on being only human, they realize divine purposes only through the ordinary and mundane work of everyday being. And tell its story.

Story as Prayer

In the moment of final extremity, on the verge of death, Jews traditionally intone the *shema*ᶜ. In so doing, they speak concerning their mutual lives in material culture, not to God, but to other human beings. This is more or less what literature is: the speaking of one person to another, about the many things there are for human beings to speak of. In such tellings of stories as in the enactments of the lives they tell, human beings perform their definition of the human—*leqayyem* that definition, as suggested in the liturgy at the beginning of the novel. There is no other definition. And there is no other way to "learn" what a human being is except to listen to the performance of such self-definition as human beings achieve. This is the beauty of storytelling, as much within the synagogue ritual of Torah reading as anywhere else. Indeed, such performance is what makes it possible, in Appelfeld's writing, to think of fiction as a sort of prayer: specifically the prayer I cited in relation to *Badenheim*, specifically alluded to in *Tzili* as well: the *shema*ᶜ.

Prayer is fundamental to Appelfeld's vision of the moral human life, not institutional Judaism per se, or even the entirety of the Jewish liturgy, but prayer as something basic and fundamental to the human experience of life—something akin to language, which is itself performative and not passive. Here as elsewhere Appelfeld is influenced by kabbalistic thinking. To quote again the passage from Harold Bloom that I quoted in Chapter 3:

> As a theory of meaning, Kabbalah tells us that meaning *is* the hurt[,] that meaning itself is hurtful. For Kabbalah tries to restore the primal meaning that God intended when He gave Torah to Moses. But Kabbalah treats Torah as alphabet, as language itself. God gave writing, which was almost primal, except that writing was what we now would call a compulsive sublimation of a more primal instruction. The primal *act* is that God *taught;* the primal *teaching* is *writing. Zimzum* is therefore in the first place Instruction. *Ein-Sof* instructs Himself by concentration and *what* he teaches is then apparent in the *tehiru* (vacated space) as the letter *yod.* God teaches Himself his own Name, and so begins creation.[19]

Not accidentally for Appelfeld, this linguistic quality of the divine is especially evident in the language of the Torah itself, Hebrew. In his interview with Philip Roth, Appelfeld quotes a line from the Mishna, "Silence is a fence for wisdom," and goes on:

> The Hebrew language taught me how to think, to be sparing with words, not to use too many adjectives, not to intervene too much, and not to interpret. . . . If it weren't for Hebrew, I doubt whether I would have found my way to Judaism. Hebrew offered me the heart of the Jewish myth, its way of thinking and its beliefs, from the days of the Bible to Agnon. (*Beyond Despair,* 72)

For Appelfeld it is the Hebrew language, not the Jewish liturgy, that forges his relationship to the Jewish people and their history, textual as well as political, human as well as divine. It is the Bible as much as the later writings of authors like Kafka and Agnon, that constitutes the literary lineage into which he writes. Thus, the advice rendered to the protagonist Kuti in *A Journey into Winter*, by one of those typical rational humanist Jews that everywhere populate Appelfeld's fiction, may be taken as quite the opposite of Appelfeld's own philosophy of what produces a writer. "Believe me," Herbert Sturm says to Kuti, "copying verses [from the prayer book] won't teach you to write, grammar and composition will teach you that, and also works of philosophy and the masterpieces of literature." And Sturm repeats his wisdom twice more in the short compass of the final chapters of the novel, now specifically in relation to the question of Kuti's becoming a writer in the literary sense of the word: "You must learn grammar, composition, and style," he instructs him. "Of one thing I am sure: verses of prayer won't teach you to write"; and finally, in the most explicit and telling formulation of all: "If you want to be an author, you must learn grammar and composition; you must read books of philosophy and the masterpieces of literature. Hebrew letters and verses from the prayers will not avail you. We live in an age of reason and science" (204, 205, 208).

Of course, the moment we come to the claim of "reason and science," just at the moment that the Holocaust is about to descend on this little band of Jews, we know not to trust this character's wisdom. Therefore, the word that Sturm uses to designate literary masterpieces (*sifrut mofet*) calls our attention to something else in the text, the appearance of the word *mofet* long in advance of its appearance here, in a very different, indeed antithetical context. It is the *ish mofet*—the illustrious one—who gives Kuti the assignment in the first place to copy out verses of prayer. Indeed, Sturm himself has been to the *ish mofet* and has received this very advice, which he rejects. Like the emphasis in *Tzili* on the pronunciation of the prayers, copying out the letters is actively to engage them, to enter into the performance of them, and thus to discover in words an avenue into nothing less than life-saving action.

A Journey into Winter tells the story of Kuti, an orphan with a serious speech impediment, who by the age of thirteen is left (reluctantly) by his adopted mother to shift for himself. Of remarkable physical prowess, despite his speech handicap, Kuti (much like Tzili) does quite marvelously on his own, working at a convalescent home/resort hotel, which caters to those who have come to seek the wisdom of the same *ish mofet* whose advice he himself has sought concerning his stammer. This is what the rebbe says to him:

> "Every morning, when the Jews stand at their prayers, write in your notebook in clear letters the first passage of the morning prayers; and during the afternoon prayers transcribe into that same notebook the first passage of the afternoon prayers; and also for the evening prayers, do this. Do this regularly, morning, afternoon, and evening. Endeavor to write in clear letters and check that you haven't left any letters out. Thus will your prayers be entered with those of the Jewish people." After a pause, he added: "Your notebooks you should keep in a clean place." (60)

Kuti follows almost to the letter, as it were, the rebbe's instructions, copying the letters of the prayers faithfully day by day. He also tends to his chores, sends packages of food to his stepmother, and pursues a rigorous program of physical exercise. And as the war begins to close in, and he and the other workers and guests at the hotel band together to mount armed resistance to the Ukrainian and German armies, lo and behold he also begins to lose his speech impediment.

One might attribute Kuti's increasing fluency of speech to his increasing physical and emotional competence, not to mention the war effort itself, which, as the same depressive guest who dismisses the rebbe's advice as irrational says, is one way out of depression and self-concern. But it is hard not to see Kuti's control both over his words and over his body (of which speech, as we have seen, is in Judaism a necessary part) as not being fortified by this strange sort of praying he performs three times a day, this praying which is not prayer in the traditional sense but the sheer physical motion of transcribing the letters of prayer. As Kuti himself reveals in his conversation with Sturm, he also is not quite sure whether the rebbe's instructions have cured him of his problem. And yet, even as he is expressing his doubt, he realizes that somehow he has surmounted his handicap. The very words he speaks to his skeptical interlocutor come out easily and fluently.

Like Tzili memorizing by rote the words the old man teaches her and finding in them the strength to get up out of the ruin of her world and save her life, so Kuti, simultaneously exercising his body and exercising his writing hand, inscribes the prayers within himself. By so doing, he makes himself into a heroic figure who is also a member of the Jewish people. Moses, as the rebbe himself points out, was also a stutterer. And we might say, insofar as Moses is at very least the transcriber and in this sense the author of what are referred to as the Five Books of Moses—the Torah—he was a great writer as well. The Ten Commandments, we do well to recall in this context, were engraved, physically carved, in stone: divine words are as concrete and physical as they come, and they are very much a part of the material creation, to be learned the way anything physical is learned—through the body.

Thus, the assignment given Appelfeld's child protagonist in *A Journey into Winter* by the rebbe recalls as well the instruction given to Helga in his earlier novel *The Healer* to overcome her nervous breakdown. "The soul is hungry for the letters," the rebbe tells Helga's mother. "He raised the prayerbook slightly and opened it to the second page. 'These are the holy letters. . . . The girl must be taught these bright, holy letters. Three times a day, morning, noon, and evening.' " And indeed Helga, like Tzili, does learn to recite the *shemaʿ*, " 'Hear, O Israel' at night," as does Appelfeld's namesake Erwin in *The Ice Mine*, as we shall see (40–43, 141).

As the emphasis on the bright holy letters of Hebrew and the teaching of these letters to children by rebbes who are more affiliated with Kabbalah than with traditional Orthodoxy already begin to suggests, whatever prayer is for Appelfeld that it should occupy so central a place in his work, it is by no means the apparatus of organized religion, not even of Judaism as opposed to Christianity. Indeed, like Theresa in *The Age of Wonders,* Helga in *The Healer* is throughout the text associated with Christian worship, in positive as well as negative ways (103, 112, 150, 160, 167, 198, 206). This corresponds to the pervasive sense of Christian and even pagan sanctity that permeates *Tzili* and other of Appelfeld's texts, in which, for example, Christian housekeepers become the vessels not only of Christian but of Jewish worship as well (see, notably, *The Conversion,* in which the protagonist, a convert to Christianity, is led back to Judaism by his Christian housemaid, with whom he falls in love).

"Take her to a convent," Helga's father Felix says contemptuously to her mother, to which her mother responds, "We're Jewish. . . . We don't worship idols" (112). Yet Felix himself is defended from an antisemitic incident by a Jewish woman who has converted "because the Church gives life meaning" (206). Furthermore, by the time he has returned home, his house has been transformed by his Christian housekeeper into a Christian sanctuary. In the end, Felix rips from over the head of his bed the "two awkward pictures . . . Jesus at his mother's bosom and the other . . . a crucifixion." But this hardly brings either redemption or relief. "[T]hat act, accomplished with his last strength, prostrated him on the pillows like a corpse, and he immediately sank into sleep" (220). These are the last words of the book. Uprooting himself from Christianity has no more salutary effect than his uprooting himself and his family from Judaism.

Yet there is a difference for Appelfeld between a return to Judaism and the conversion to Christianity. This has nothing to do with the difference between these two religions as religions. Rather it has everything to do with what is inevitably, almost genetically, Jewish inheritance, as portrayed in *The Age of Wonders* as well. "A person must return home," the rebbe tells Helga and her mother in *The Healer.* "Return, children, return. The inheritance of the Lord yearns for you" (142). However far the Jews have drifted from their Judaism, this (more than Israel now or Europe then) is their homeland ("What's that?" Helga's brother Karl asks her; "A Jewish prayerbook, haven't you seen one?" to which Karl answers "Not from up close" [53]). "We constantly retreat before that cruel invader," says the rebbe, leaving imprecise exactly which invader he means, "'though we no longer have anywhere left to flee.' The old man spoke in a whisper, but Henrietta caught every word. The subject was clear to her as though that language had been hers from time immemorial. He spoke of the urgent need to withdraw into bright warm homes. 'The outside is a lie. A lie'" (141). The word *language* here refers to more than Hebrew, and the rebbe himself is represented in the text as speaking the several languages of the Jews, including German. But Hebrew in this text, as in *A Journey into Winter, The Iron Tracks,* and *The Age of Wonders,* is the mother tongue of the people, the somewhat silent, mystical, kabbalistic, feminine language of the Jews.

To pray, then, in these texts is neither to commit oneself to some institutional form or liturgical pattern, nor even necessarily to address a deity: as we have already seen, the *shema*ᶜ is spoken to fellow Jews, not to God. Prayer, spoken in what the rationalistic father in *The Healer,* so like the other fathers in Appelfeld's fiction, calls the "ancient ghost language" (112), is what bespeaks home. By this, Appelfeld means the Jewish homeland of history and tradition without which the self is forever stranded in what is called in *The Age of Wonders,* picking up, as we have seen, the same language of ghosts, the "familiar strangeness" (219) of "familiar exile" (216) of the alien places where Jews reside (including, we must add, modern-day Israel).

All our human existences, it would seem, are haunted by one set of ghosts or another. The question will be whether we will learn the ancient ghost languages in which such phantoms speak, and whether, translating and comprehending what they are saying to us, we will be able to speak words of our own that are not simply doomed to mystify and obscure meaning. Writing in the ancient letters that he, like his protagonists, had to learn as a second language, Appelfeld recovers the language not of a national homeland but of the homeland of self—a self that exists at home with the other selves who also speak this language, not to God, but to one another. That, for Appelfeld, is prayer, and it is conveyed as much by *sifrut mofet*—the masterpieces of literature—as by any liturgical tradition, although those masterpieces of literature must include as equally illustrious the text known as the Hebrew Bible. Not to acknowledge that text as one of the texts by which Jews speak their existence is not to acknowledge the existence of the Jews altogether. Prayer, for Appelfeld, is the affirmation of human being, one human being by another, as *ẓelem elohim* in both senses of the term we have examined. Thus is Appelfeld's novel as a novel in and of itself also a prayer, which literally—in letters—conjures the existence of the child whom society has decided to abandon, perhaps even murder. As in *The Iron Tracks* (and in psychoanalytic speaking and in prayer) so in *Tzili:* words make things happen.

By way of concluding my discussion of *Tzili,* let me return to several passages we have already examined in order to see how the language of the novel "literally" produces Tzili's human form, her aliveness. And produces it in a particular language: for even though Tzili's world is not a Hebrew-speaking world, the text that articulates her being is.

As we have seen, the assault against Tzili, by her family and her community, and well in advance of the Nazi invasion, has had to do with a fundamental failure to acknowledge her being in the world. "Since she was skinny and didn't get in anyone's way, they [the family] ignored her existence" (1–2). Tzili is "mute," and her words "vanish." She is neither seen nor heard. Yet, like the words of the final paragraph of *Badenheim,* the words *illemet* [mute], *ne*ᶜ*elmot* [vanish], and *hit*ᶜ*almu* [ignored], which are here used to describe Tzili, have more than a descriptive or connotative function. Rather, they construct a subterranean field of sound-sense that both imitates, and yet, even more importantly, works against the material culture it cites. The culminating feature of the sound-sense of the passage is the child Tzili herself, whose name, we recall, evokes, among other things, sound.

In the first instance the text's sound-sense serves to bury Tzili, just as surely as has the family, within a cultural context that is as invisible as what it buries. It identifies this condition, which is the condition of all of our lives in culture, as the embeddedness of consciousness within words or beliefs or concepts, which consciousness cannot make visible to itself. For this reason, the family's attitude toward Tzili is, we are told, not once but twice, a faith, the word *emunah* in the original Hebrew text ending one sentence and almost immediately beginning the next. This faith, we are told, "unite[s] the mother in the shop and her daughters at their books" (3). It also unites the family with the community at large, which shares the family's view of Tzili, which turns out to be the community's view of the family as well. Given the family's lack of faith in the religious sense, which the opening chapter explicitly and repeatedly cites, and given the coincidence of their view of Tzili with that of outside world, the family's faith in Tzili's deformity or deficiency, their lack of faith in her humanness, can only represent the substitution of one faith for another, the family's concession to the cultural prejudice that surrounds them. As in *The Iron Tracks,* this is faith as ideology, where the ideology in question is specifically antisemitism.

At the same time, however, that the text is registering the collective and finally murderous denial of Tzili's being as contained in the very fabric of the culture's being, in language, it is also launching the process whereby her invisibility and muteness are undone and her existence rendered manifest. The text literally transcribes Tzili's existence, not simply by exposing what is hidden to view, as if there is, after all, something to be seen behind or underneath culture, the knowledge of which could serve to render culture visible and thereby remediable. Rather, the making Tzili visible, the making her exist, occurs through the text's verbal construction of its own independent, alternative perception, which, in the case of this text, has the effect of producing Tzili's existence from within her family's, and later the Nazis', denial of it. Tzili comes alive for us, almost as a kind of song, sung or chanted by the language of the text.

Language is a crucial element in *Tzili,* as it is in *Badenheim.* However concrete and elemental Appelfeld's vocabulary, however much he resists the pull toward metaphysical or metaphorical language, he does not, as I have insisted before, write realist, descriptive fiction. As the renaming of *Badenheim, Resort City* to *Badenheim 1939* in the English translation, so the titling of *hakutonet vehapassim/The Shirt and the Stripes* as *Tzili: The Story of a Life* obscures the text's high degree of intertextual investment. But even prior to the allusive power of the title, and in anticipation of and parallel to it, the language of the text acts to unsettle, if not virtually to explode, the deadening, one-to-one referentiality of its words, which might be imagined, appropriately enough, to keep the story nailed to the coffin of the suffocating reality it depicts (like Erwin's language at moments in *The Iron Tracks* or Bruno's in *The Age of Wonders,* when the protagonist's words become repetitive and monotonous).

Anyone who has heard Appelfeld read his own texts aloud will immediately understand what I mean concerning the musicality of his writing. It can be glimpsed as well in the text's proliferation of sound repetitions and irregular and imperfect rhymes. Thus Tzili's name, dancing around the Hebrew word *ẓlil* (sound, note), is itself musical; and this musicality is not divorced both from her divinity (*ẓelem elohim*) and her powers of divinely invested self-salvation (*haẓalah*).

This musical quality is also, as in *Badenheim*, part of the text's worshipfulness, marking the same move from the visual to the aural fields that locates the divine element within *Badenheim* as well. This divine element emerges from within the difference between imagining the possibility of human acts of literal, material creation, such as describe modernist rational culture, and some other form of human creativity, which is a form of listening and obeying. If Appelfeld's text comes into existence in defiance of an *issur*, a prohibition, which it nonetheless acknowledges, it does so in order to accept the difference between human and divine creativity. What human beings (*ẓelem elohim*) create is only the echo or shadow (*ẓel*) of what God creates. As human creation, it listens and responds to the divine creation.

In other words, to understand the Holocaust, not only in terms of its consequences and from the position of those who suffered it, but (as it were) before the fact, from what first produced the conditions that enabled a Holocaust to occur, one needs to understand human action and belief—consciousness—as already embedded in words, the meanings of which we for the most part fail to make conscious to ourselves. Aesthetic and rhetorical artifice make visible the invisible motions of culture. They restore to sight what has disappeared, at least on the verbal level. But this is not the work of creativity in the divine sense, as if human beings could make or construct a world. Rather, it is a severely reduced and delimited restoration, as in *tiqqun ᶜolam*. It only mirrors or echoes the creative power of God. Appelfeld's methodology is compensatory. Though his objective exceeds simply making the events of Holocaust believable by concretizing and personalizing them, still the linguistic generation of Tzili's existence through the sound and sense repetitions of the very words by which she was denied that existence is intended, not literally to create her, nor even to resurrect her (as if literature had this divine power), but rather to do the limited and imperfect work of literature. This is nothing more than the work of restoration by which a person is, to paraphrase Appelfeld from his words quoted earlier, given back his or her human form in the highly diminished form of language. Appelfeld's Tzili, evoked in language, is the echo or distant sound of herself.

To restore and to give back: these ways of describing the modest acts of fictionalization are crucial to Appelfeld's definition of his art. They also define its religious ambience, its kabbalistic worshipfulness. Already in the second sentence of the novella, preceding the many words describing Tzili's non-existence, which also construct her presence in the language of the text, is one of those Appelfeldian words that punctuate many of his writings, the word *ilmaleʾ*—meaning, *were it not for*. This is the word that at first seems to establish the text's legitimacy in terms of its connection to real, historical events, outside of and prior to the text. But this assertion, we immediately recognize, is at once undermined by the fact that the text is not documentary but fiction. *Ilmaleʾ*—were it not for—these words on the page, including the word *ilmaleʾ*, Tzili, who is nothing but a fiction, would not exist at all, which is to say that the many real Jewish children, of whom Tzili is also the shadow and the sound, would also not exist for us, in any form whatsoever, were it not for the writer's words making them appear. Indeed, the word *ilmale*ʾ, as in and of itself a piece of language anticipating the sounds of the words for *mute* and *vanish*, already, in advance of the appearance in these other words in the text, reverses both of the other words' potential to annihilate. Tzili exists on the page quite independent and defiant of the attempts to render her mute and make her vanish.

Yet, at the same time, these words, being words, reverse the fantasy that words are capable of restoring to sight and sound real children, who have been rendered invisible. Human beings do not have the power to create what they clearly have the power to destroy. Therefore, within the fictive world that the text constructs, the text acknowledges the simple truth that Tzili exists despite the family's denial of her, quite independent of what they do or do not want to recognize about her. A "quiet creature," "like a squirrel," whom her siblings would on occasion pluck out of the dirt and deposit in the house, Tzili may seem to her family and community no more than a "servant girl," to be ordered about and contemned. But as one of God's creations, Tzili exactly exists. She is already a being: the word for this in the text is *yiẓẓur/creature*, from the word to create; the first book in kabbalistic tradition is *sefer yeẓirah/The Book of Creation.* "Every now and then her mother would remember her and cry: 'Tzili, where are you?' 'Here,'" Tzili would answer, echoing the cry of both Abraham and Moses to signal their attendance upon God's will (2). However invisible and non-existent to her family, Tzili is always present to herself, very much "here," where, in the context of the literary text, the word *here* has the effect of locating her simultaneously in three worlds: the natural world, to which (within the world of the text) she is already associated and will become more connected as the story unfolds; the world of God invoked through the catechism, which bridges her world and the world of the reader; and the world of the text itself, which is the "here" and now of our experience of her. Whatever the creative power of this text, it is represented within the text itself as only a dim reflection of the life force it reflects. This is, finally, the text's religious decorum, its recognition of the difference between the human author and God.

The word *ilmale*ʾ responds twice to the prohibition against writing the text. The problem is not, simply, that fictional invention and aesthetic form so compromise the brutal horror, which generates the narrative, that only a relationship to factuality can in the least reclaim such a text from its scandalousness. The additional problem is that the creative power of the author, which is already sullied by its having been conceived and empowered by the very force it wishes to oppose, is further compromised by the godlike role the author seems to assume, presuming to produce life *ex nihilo,* as if the text might restore to life what has been destroyed. The power to create and the power to destroy are not symmetrical and equivalent forces in Appelfeld's world. If man does, indeed, enjoy the power to destroy, he does not have the power to create. Indeed, if the power to destroy represents the fatal reversal of the fantasy of creativity, authorship may become only another way of taking life and death into one's own hands.

That is, the text's power to create, especially since the text is fictional and not documentary, may represent nothing other than a repetition of the Krauses' and their culture's own anti-Judaic belief in humanism and the powers of the human mind. Even before the Nazi devastation, this logic had acted to deny the child her existence. In engaging in such an act of creative eventfulness as I am claiming for this text, the text must violate a prohibition even more fundamental than that prohibiting the telling of the story of this particular narrative. This, as we have seen, is the commandment against producing idols and images. The text will consent to do this, but only through making clear that such creativity as it expresses is an act of worship, not of self-deification. The text knows what and Whom it reflects.

In its every attempt to discover a proper relationship to the trauma, the text finds itself caught in a transgressive position that it must parlay into an act of reverence. Each transgressive facet of the text's undertaking re-enacts rather than erases the transgression it seems to come in to correct, much like the biblical texts of transgression, which the novel recalls and which are themselves the substructure of Judaism and Christianity both. Inventing what did not exist before, the story not only transgresses the taboo against fictionalizing and aestheticizing the brutal facts of history, but it also presents itself as the godlike power capable of restoring what has been destroyed. The trangressive power of the text exponentially increases, which, in the moral calculus that the text expounds, means that it comes to constitute its own kind of assault against the victims. If the Nazis forgot the Ten Commandments, so had the Krauses and the Jewish community, which had already sought to create man in their own image, which was an image the Jews shared with the surrounding, antisemitic culture.

In not forgetting the link between the Nazi assault against the Jews and the Jewish assimilationism and self-hatred that preceded the Holocaust, Appelfeld has seemed to some (as we have seen) either to be blaming the victims outright for their victimization or to be so committed to the teleology of Jewish history, culminating in the founding of the State of Israel, as to not pay sufficient attention to the implicit logic of his thought. All of this, I suggest, is reversed by the careful placement of the narrative under the sign of an *issur* (a prohibition). Appelfeld, I suggest, is exactly noting the human impulse that characterized victimizers and victims alike because it characterizes all human beings—the desire (including his own) to be creative beings. At the same time, however, he also clearly marks and keeps visible the line separating human being from God, human logic from divine logic, and thereby the creative power of the divine from the imitative and non-recuperative capacities of art.

Appelfeld will write fiction, whether it is a forbidden activity or not. But he will acknowledge what fiction is, and what it cannot be. And he will accept the moral and religious burden his craft imposes. If the text's initial presentation of itself as, from its inception, a transgressive act, has to do, in the first instance, with its violating a set of related taboos against the telling of the story, the telling itself incorporates that prohibition as part and parcel of what constitutes human, as opposed to divine, art. Appelfeld's is in every way a very human novel. It is, in and of itself, an enactment of the human and thus as textual performance is an answer, not to be paraphrased in other words, to the question, *what is a human being?* To that question this text proposes a one-word answer: Tzili. But in saying that name—Tzili—the reader, responding to the words of Appelfeld's text, owning Tzili as our own (the Hebrew ending represented by *i* signaling *my: my Tzil*) indeed as a sort of *ẓel* or shadow of ourselves, articulates his or her own being as well, that sound and shadow of the human and the divine in which the *I* of everyone of us is and will be.

6 Imagination, Memory, and the Storied Life: *The Story of a Life*

In his conversation with Philip Roth, Appelfeld had the following to say about the autobiographical aspects of his writing, in particular in relation to *Tzili:*

> I have never written about things as they happened. All my works are indeed chapters from my most personal experience, but nevertheless they are not "the story of my life." The things that happened to me in my life have already happened, they are already formed, and time has kneaded them and given them shape. To write things as they happened means to enslave oneself to memory, which is only a minor element in the creative process. . . .
>
> I tried several times to write "the story of my life" in the woods after I ran away from the camp. But all my efforts were in vain. . . .
>
> . . . [T]he moment I chose a girl, a little older than I was at that time, I removed "the story of my life" from the mighty grip of memory and gave it over to the creative laboratory.[1]

Conveniently for our purposes, *Tzili* is subtitled in the English translation: *The Story of a Life. Sippur ḥayyim—The Story of a Life*—is the name Appelfeld himself gives to the autobiography he published in 1999.

Anyone interested in the "creative laboratory" in which Appelfeld produced his fiction over the last forty years will find the autobiography a goldmine. Not only does the text provide the autobiographical bases for many of the events that find their way into the fiction (in particular in *Tzili*), but, far more importantly, it locates the themes, images, and language that have become the heart of Appelfeld's fictional enterprise. Yet to go digging in the autobiography for the origins of this or that phrase or image in the fiction, however tempting, will hardly do justice to what is a fascinating literary text in its own right. (I myself have had to exercise severe restraint to keep from citing the autobiographical origins of various moments in the fictions I have been explicating.) Although *The Story of a Life* is a memoir, and therefore is bound by convention to narrating more or less "historical" facts, the text does battle with the same "mighty grip of memory" that Appelfeld tackles in his other writings. Appelfeld's large self-reflexive, literary subject, we might say, is how one produces fiction, which is to say literature, out of memory without reducing fiction to autobiography.

Concerning the autobiography, which eschews the chronology, inclusiveness, and other markers of traditional autobiography, Appelfeld expounds as follows:

> This book is not a summary of a life. It is, rather, an attempt, a desperate attempt if you wish, to reconnect the separate stalks of my life to the living root from which they have sprung. The reader would do well not to seek in these pages for a

precise and orderly account of a life. Much has been lost, eaten away by forgetting. What remains seems at the moment as nothing at all. And yet, despite that, when I have placed fragment upon fragment I have felt not only that the years had discovered their integrity but that they had achieved, as well, some sort of meaning. (8)

This meaningfulness has fundamentally to do with the production of fantasy. Such fantasy which resists the "mighty grip of memory," however, also *depends* on memory, which has itself to be rescued from the mighty grip of another force equally problematic: oblivion or forgetfulness. One of Appelfeld's great insights, and a major subject of his fiction, is the place of fantasy within human existence, along with the question of how fantasy must be retrieved from its twin enemies and help-mates: remembering and forgetting.

The Story of a Life, therefore, is not autobiography in the sense of being an accurate, complete record of personal historical events. Rather, it is the story of how one particular human being, the author himself, endowed his life with meaning, or more accurately how he discovered the meaning that his life contained, by simply being a human life. The Holocaust threatened to annihilate more than the remembering by which we human beings come to apprehend the continuity in which meaning resides. It jeopardized the equally important capacity to fantasize by which we project that meaningfulness forward and imagine and construct a future. Nonetheless, the first stage of the battle is the retrieval of memory. In Israel, this has meant for the survivor not only a personal, psychological struggle, but an ideological battle as well. The watchword of Israel in the 1950s, in which Appelfeld first tried to make sense of his life, resonated all too closely with the survivor's own deepest psychic inclinations, which were to forget the past.

"Forget, strike roots, speak Hebrew"

For the immigrant orphan refugee child, without even a viable language of his own, the "struggle" to become a writer (to use the term Appelfeld takes from Kafka) proved an almost insurmountable task. This was especially the case since the national dictate commanded the new immigrant not to remember the past: "Forget the diaspora and strike roots in the soil," Appelfeld and his generation were admonished; and Appelfeld concedes: "we came to the country to build and be rebuilt. 'To build and to be rebuilt' meant for most of us the annihilation of memory, total self-transformation, and absorption into the land itself" (105). In order to wrestle with memory, Appelfeld had first to free himself from the national ideology that set out to construct a new Jew and a new Jewish reality.

Much of *The Story of a Life* is given over to fierce battle between the writer and the public injunction to "forget, strike roots, speak Hebrew" (126). Try as he might, Appelfeld is incapable of making himself over into an "Israeli" as defined both by the literature and by the national consensus of the new country. "Searching" for himself and his identity "in the young men who peopled [the] novels" of the major authors of the day, Appelfeld finds instead "a foreign world, populated by self-confident youths, soldiers, officers, and farmers working the open fields. . . . I read and read, but the more I did so, the clearer it became to me that this pretty, rational life of work and warfare and love would never be my lot in life, not even if I were to attain the unattainable." They were certainly not destined to become the subjects of his fiction, though "in my first stammerings," Appelfeld recalls, "I was a farmer working the Judean hills, a member of a kibbutz, a fighter in the Palmach, a watchman in the vineyards. Everything but myself" (137).

What Appelfeld brings to the surface in his autobiography is not simply his inability to step into this new identity, but his often self-tormenting and not completely self-comprehending refusal to do so:

> What could I do? Entwined in my very being was a refusal to demolish the old Hebrew and build a new life on his ruins. The thought that a man must annihilate his past in order to build a new life had seemed to me even earlier a warped conception, but I hadn't dared to declare my bourgeois ideas, even to myself. On the contrary, I blamed myself for my diaspora mentality, my middle-class way of thinking, and, of course, my incorrigible egotism. (105)

Many of the most affecting passages in the autobiography have to do with the refugee child's loss of everything he has known: family, home, landscape, and language—all the aspects from which most of us, quite unselfconsciously, construct a self. In the case of the budding writer, this means creating a self fashioned in language, of which he possesses none. I quote several pertinent passages from Chapter 18 (*eighteen* in Hebrew being the word *ḥay; alive, living*) of the autobiography, which form the crux of his representation of immigrant muteness:

> The year is 1946, the year of my aliyah to Israel. My diary is a pastiche of words written in German, Yiddish, Hebrew, and even Ruthenian. I say "words," and not "sentences," because I wasn't yet capable of stringing words into sentences. These words are nothing more than the arrested cries of a fourteen-year-old youth, bereft of language, who had lost all the languages he had spoken. The diary served as his secret hide-away. Here he tossed together the remnants of his mother tongue, and the pieces of his newly acquired vocabulary. "Tossed together" is not a metaphor. It is literally a picture of my soul. (99)

> The first year in Israel wasn't for me an exodus but rather a harsh withdrawal, deeper and deeper into myself. . . . Scenes of home and its language grew dim and faded away. But the new language wasn't quick to take root. There were, of course, young people who adopted Hebrew expressions easily, rattling off words like a native. For me, however, for whatever reason, the pronunciation of even a single word required the utmost exertion. Sentences were out of the question. (101)

"My mother tongue was German, the language beloved of my mother," Appelfeld explains in the same chapter; but "whoever spoke in his mother tongue was rebuked, boycotted, and sometimes even denounced" (99–100).

One broad field of battle on which *The Story of a Life* wages its struggle for identity and authorship is this ideological battlefield on which Israeli life in the 1950s was being conducted. This terrain of forgetting, furthermore, had its internal counterpart in the immigrant refugee himself, who either preferred to forget or, at very best, found himself incapable of remembering. "When we finally reached Israel," Appelfeld records in the introduction,

> oblivion had fortified its place in our soul. In this sense, Israel was a kind of continuation of Italy. Here oblivion found fresh ground. To be sure, the dominant ideology of those years reinforced that fortification, but the command to vouchsafe forgetting did not come from without. Sometimes scenes of war would filter through the barricades and encasements and claim their right to be witnessed. But they were powerless to breach the pillars of forgetfulness and the powerful desire to live. Life said to us: forget, adapt. The kibbutzim and the moshavim were marvelous incubators for breeding oblivion. (7)

This might seem all well and good: the national ideology and the dictates of the psyche are reinforcing each other in the interests of a new life both for the individual and for the nation. But, of course, as Appelfeld's fictions so expertly dramatize for us, and as we all quite know, forgetting is easier said than done; and what the mind manages to rid itself of on the conscious level often reemerges through other more bodily inscribed forms of remembering. Witness the experiences of Erwin in *The Iron Tracks* or Bartfuss in *The Immortal Bartfuss.* Furthermore, as Appelfeld shows us in a novel like *The Age of Wonders,* even nations possess the equivalent of a return of the repressed or what Kierkegaard identifies as sentimentality. Indeed, sentimentality turns out to be an extremely pertinent word (paradoxically) to describe the rugged, heroic but memory-less native Israeli literature of the pre-state and early state periods.

But this is only one half of the double bind in which the immigrant survivor found him- or herself. The dominant ideology said to *forget,* which is exactly what the survivors' internal psychological apparatus also commanded (or itself accomplished), even if the individual, in point of fact, was incapable of forgetting. At the same time, however, within the larger Jewish world, and to some degree within Israel itself, at least among certain survivors there was a contrary dictate exactly to remember, so as to commemorate the six million and also to insure that a second Holocaust would never occur, either in Israel or abroad. This injunction, compelling in and of itself, also carried very precise instructions on how to remember. Covering ground very familiar in Holocaust studies, Appelfeld writes:

> Testimony was considered the only legitimate form of expression. Fiction was thought an affront. But I didn't even have anything to testify to. I didn't remember the names of people or places, only the sounds and shapes of darkness. Only in time did I come to understand that these were the raw materials of literature, the marrow of story-telling, and from them it would be possible to fashion an inner tale. I say "inner" because at that time only historical narrative was valued, as if therein was contained the truth. The concept of an inner narrative hadn't yet been born. (97)

In *The Story of a Life,* Appelfeld confronts directly the same prohibition against fictionalization that he cites at the very beginning of *Tzili.* Indeed, Appelfeld reports that among the earliest criticisms of his fiction was exactly this rebuke against casting the events of the Holocaust as fiction, or worse (as in his earliest undertakings) as poetry.

Yet Appelfeld's defense of his decision to write fiction is somewhat disingenuous. "Those who were already adults during the war," he explains,

> took in and remembered place names and people and at the end of the war they could sit down and enumerate and describe them. And thus they will certainly continue to do till the end of their days. But for the children it wasn't the names of things that got absorbed but rather something entirely different. For the children memory became a reservoir that nothing could drain. Over the years it only renewed itself and grew more vivid. Not a chronology of events, but an endlessly metamorphosing surfeit, if I may be permitted to put it this way. (85)

Just as Appelfeld claims in defense of his writing *Tzili* that the story is documentary and not fiction—when of course it is very clearly fiction—so here he defends his decision to write fiction against the same prohibition by claiming that he has no memories as such. To be sure, Appelfeld does not know from personal experience the stuff of history textbooks: names and dates and events. He does, however, remember his own experience, which, for most survivors, constitutes the raw material of the narrative. Appelfeld's choice to write fiction and not testimony is not in the least a decision born of necessity. Furthermore, whatever autobiographical circumstances led Appelfeld toward fiction rather than to some other form of narrative, what emerges through the course of most of his writings, in his antimimetical style as much as in any other way, amounts to nothing less than a defense of fiction-writing per se, in particular in relation to the Holocaust. The fantasizing imagination, Appelfeld comes to realize, was itself one of the victims of the Nazi onslaught. Like every other objective of Hitler's annihilation, this one, too, must not be permitted to succeed.

This is perhaps Appelfeld's major insight, both in *The Story of a Life* and in the novel that preceded it into print: *Ice Mine.* The Holocaust disrupted more than the continuity of the survivor's biography. It did more than erase, or withhold, the names and dates and places and events by which the chronology and the material substance of a life are constituted, even for adult survivors who were more capable than children of reconstructing the factual past. Rather, it tore to shreds the stories or narratives by which each of us invests our life with meaning, by which we make it live, into the future as much as in the present. This is exactly the capability so fatally lacking in a character like Erwin in *The Iron Tracks* or Bartfuss in *The Immortal Bartfuss.* The Holocaust (and perhaps Jewish history itself) tended to discredit the provinces of imagination. It is one major achievement of Appelfeld's art to restore art itself as part of what defines human being.

If one insight that emerges through the pages of Appelfeld's writing is that the enormity of the Holocaust effectively perpetuated the continued eradication of the individuality of the human beings who perished there, another lasting consequence of the catastrophe, Appelfeld shows us, has been to discredit the possibilities of Jewish imagining. Yes, there is poetry after Auschwitz, Appelfeld would say, keeping Adorno in mind.[2] Along with the utter uniqueness and specificity of the human beings who dreamed their lives in their own special ways, Appelfeld would also restore—both in his fiction and in his autobiography, and both to the individual and thereby, just as importantly, to the people—the possibility of imagination altogether. The inseparability of the individual and the group, as of memory and imagination—the ways in which each is constituted through and by the other—is also for Appelfeld an important aspect of what produces literature. It is also a major subject of the autobiography. But for Appelfeld it is the individual, speaking his or her individual thought in the individual words that constitute language, that is the vehicle of art.

The Story of a Life does not simply tell the story of a life. Rather, it narrates the life of storytelling. It concerns the ways in which life is a story, and how, without its storied quality, it ceases to be a life at all. In order to prepare the way for this central insight of Appelfeld's autobiography, as of his other of his writings, let me take a detour through one more of his more purely fictional works. This novel has at its center another Erwin. One of its major subjects is the place of imagination within human existence.

The Interpretation of Dreams: *Ice Mine*

"Over the course of the years," Appelfeld tells us in the autobiography,

> I have tried, more than once, to touch again the wooden bunks of the camp, to taste the watery soup that was our only food. My efforts have produced only a cacophony of words, inaccurate and falsely conceived, their cadences broken, the images either too pale or too vivid. The most profound experiences, I have learned, can all too easily come to ring untrue. Even now I cannot touch that white heat. (49)

The novel published at roughly the same time as *The Story of a Life, Ice Mine* does touch that "white heat," which Appelfeld is incapable of touching in the autobiography, even though to do so he has to turn that heat to (white) ice, at least in the title. Indeed, *Ice Mine* seems almost intended to fill in the gap in the autobiography. Through his namesake protagonist-narrator Erwin he records the very experience he leaves out of *The Story of a Life.*

To a large extent, the novel presents what has become the familiar fare of most Holocaust writings, except Appelfeld's: the ravages of hunger and cold and the other physical deprivations and sufferings inside the camps, the ever-present threat of death, the psychological despair and disorientation, and the irrationality and perversity of *l'universe concentrationnaire.* It also, however, incorporates what is the hallmark of Appelfeld's writing: the variety of human responses, including fantasies of denial and hope, by which different human beings managed this situation of extremity. However human beings became reduced by their experience to the bare bones of human subsistence, they continued to survive as individuals, with all the variations that define a human population. Therefore, a leitmotif of this novel, which seems in certain ways almost inappropriate, is the daydreaming and fantasizing that go on in the camp.

One of Appelfeld's major insights into the Nazi devastation, and the large contours of his contribution in *Ice Mine* (as in *The Story of a Life,* as we shall see) is that insofar as the Nazi annihilation aimed at the destruction of the persons who would constitute the future of the people, it destroyed, or more precisely, threatened to destroy for those who miraculously survived its terrible onslaught, the capacity to fantasize and daydream and imagine. As psychoanalysts (such as Donald Winnecott) have pointed out, it is this ability to mobilize one's imagination in the service of the future that to a large extent permits a meaningful future to come into being. To cite Appelfeld's own terms for this in the interview with Philip Roth, to remain within the "grip of memory," which preserves "things that happened" in the "shape" in which they "happened," is to be "enslaved to memory."

Though imagination and fantasy might seem, initially, to be the enemies of memory, they are in the final analysis what enable memory to be delivered into —and simultaneously to remain in the service of—a viable future. Properly conceived, indeed, memory has to be understood as already incorporating imagination: there is a difference, Appelfeld suggests in the autobiography, between remembering as a physical activity performed largely by the body and remembering as a mental activity that transpires in the brain. Both go by the name of *memory,* but they are by no means the same phenomenon. And it is only *memory* of the more cerebral kind that can release us from the stranglehold of the past and make the past available as the life force of the future. In order to do this, however (and this is one of the central ironies of remembering), memory will have to avail itself of the bodily forms of remembering, which resist consciousness. How does memory in the bodily sense, then, become memory in the more intellectual, imaginative, and, finally, literary sense?

As one more of Appelfeld's many fictional envisionings of the "grip of memory," *Ice Mine* provides perhaps the most cogent exposition in Appelfeld's writing of the significance of imagination for the survival not only of individual human beings, but of the very definition of what makes us human in the first place. It is clear from *Ice Mine* that the fictionalizing imagination is not merely an ex post facto instrument of recollection. Rather, it was an ongoing resource within the camps themselves. It operated even as the annihilation was occurring, constituting its own form of resistance to dehumanization and death.

Sometimes, it is true, imagination represented a form of escapism that was either dangerous or unethical, and sometimes both (as in the case of those starry-eyed optimists everywhere populating Appelfeld's fiction, who remained perilously committed to German culture or to Communism). Sometimes, however, it did not. Sometimes imagination, in the form of what the text calls "dreaming," by which it means something closer to daydreaming than to dreaming proper, becomes the very instrument of survival itself.

In this, his most severe rendition of life in the camps, Appelfeld quite extraordinarily provides a paradigm of the place of imagination, not only within the more leisured, artistic self-contemplations of human beings (artists or mere mortals), but also within the very forces, instinctual and spiritual both, that, as is the case in *Tzili* as well, declare and preserve their humanness. Thus *Ice Mine* opens with a scene of death in which death is not, as we might expect, the consequence of brutal murder (instances of which exist in abundance in the world of the ghettos and the camps and which Appelfeld does not forbear to show us elsewhere in this text), but of the much more subtle and agonizing death of the will to live.

"We are here two-and-a-half months," the text opens, in the lyrical prose/matter-of-fact poetry in which Erwin the narrator-protagonist writes; "and," he goes on, "it is an eternity. The day slowly separates out into minutes and seconds, but even such tiny fragments of time as these do not pass on their own. Time stands still here. It drizzles and seeps into you, a single hour as swollen as a year of life." The "here" of the world of the concentration camp remains eerily nameless, its "time" oppressively without measure: it is *here* and *now* that *there,* in the past, these events are transpiring in a kind of eternal present.

The "sights" of the war, Appelfeld tells us again and again in the autobiography, continue to "inhabit me with intense clarity, and there are times," he says specifically of the forced march to the labor camp, that "it seems to me that the journey that went on for about two months still goes on today, fifty years later, and I am still limping along" (93). In *Ice Mine,* the days unravel into tiny units of time that pass in an instant. Yet each instant seems itself a year, an eternity. Furthermore, time no longer remains outside human existence. It is no longer what frames and structures and enables life to proceed by getting outside itself, self-reflexively to measure and take the measure of itself. Rather, time is what life has become reduced to: "a life" "not of expectation," as the text goes on to say, "but of hours" (7). Time squeezes out desire. It freezes imagination.

Thus, the death that occupies center stage in the first chapter is death by starvation. This starvation is no metaphor but is quite literal. Yet the literal itself goes beyond mere physical fact. The victim's comrades, the text informs us, are willing to help feed him. Given their limited rations, this act is nothing less than a form of heroic self-sacrifice. But the self here has lost its will to survive. It is unwilling to feed itself, unwilling to nurture its will to live, and unwilling, therefore, to take sustenance from others. "Hunger," we are told, "is the death that precedes death." And using the same word that he employs in the opening paragraph to describe time's absorption into the bones, Appelfeld continues, "hunger seeps into your bones and dissolves the soul. First the strangling of your words, then the bloating of your face, and finally the faltering footsteps. It isn't long till you are swathed in haze of delusion. . . . Most individuals thus caught in delusion's web cannot release themselves. Day by day, hallucinations detach him from his surroundings and shackle him to those whom he has left behind"

(9–10). Fantasy here is the black magic of memory, not of imagination, and as in *The Iron Tracks* and *The Age of Wonders,* it is lethal.

Like that of most survivors, Erwin's own survival is as much a matter of luck and circumstance as anything else (in the autobiography, Appelfeld calls his own survival a miracle). Yet it is represented throughout the novel as accompanied by a process of mind in which imagination comes to provide the vital narrative structure that is absent in the world of the camp itself and without which human being cannot sustain itself. It is this internal narrative structure (a rudimentary form of what Appelfeld in the autobiography will call an "inner" narrative) that the camps have done their utmost to obliterate, substituting units of time for the narrative events that time ordinarily produces. Therefore, Erwin's dreams, many of which are waking dreams—daydreams—punctuate the text. They carry not only the weight of Appelfeld's story, but the burden of Erwin's ongoing life and consciousness as well. Since the novel has not yet been translated, I take the liberty of providing a rather lengthy quotation from the text:

> Our dreams, it seems, are very similar to each other. Always there is a deep wide river separating us from our loved ones. The river is so wide that it doesn't even occur to you that you might be able to cross it. Sometimes a boat appears, but it is so small and so flimsy that any wave can easily capsize it. Strange, but our dreams are intensely interesting to us. There are those who argue that the presence of a lot of water in a dream is a sign that we do not have much longer to live and we will soon be swallowed up by the [River] Bug. Another opinion holds the opposite: that the presence of a lot of water is a sign and a portent that we will soon be released to be reunited with our loved ones.
>
> One of the prisoners, one of the artists of survival, who interprets our dreams, is Paul. Were we able to listen to him or, more to the point, could behave as he does, our lives would be much easier. His theory is built principle by principle. The first is indifference. Take every calamity with composure, as if it weren't intended for you, as if it doesn't affect you; and if the tribulation is exceedingly great, say to yourself: life is but an illusion, and when this illusion passes away, so will the pain. The body can be broken, but not the soul. The soul is eternal and dreams are the language of the soul. We have to learn from our dreams and obey them; they are signs that endeavor to guide and protect us.
>
> Whenever one of us complains about a bad dream that seems to torture him with his imminent departure from this world, he looks him straight in the eye and says: "Tell me what was shown to you in the dream."
>
> "The Bug tries to devour me."
>
> "But the fact is, it didn't devour you."
>
> "But isn't it a suggestion that in the future it will devour me?"
>
> "The suggestion is that you must not be afraid. If you overcome your fear, you will not be devoured."
>
> "Madman" he is pronounced by more than a few, who keep their distance from him. But there are those who are charmed by his equanimity, by the way he takes his repose and slumbers, and by his amazing generosity. He is one of the only individuals who is capable of taking a portion of bread and giving it to someone else, in exchange for no rations in return.
>
> His skeptics again reach the same verdict. "Also that is mad," they say. (92–93)

A feature that gets lost in the translation is that the words for *capsize, devour,* and *mad* all derive from the same root: *tet reysh pe,* meaning to devour. This is the word used prominently, and famously, in the Joseph story to describe Joseph the dream-interpreter's "death" by wild beasts in the pit: "*tarof toraf yosef,*" exclaims Jacob when he is brought the bloodstained coat of stripes, which, we have seen, features as a key image in *Tzili,* where it also bridges biblical and Holocaustal contexts. In *Ice Mine,* the same defiance of the illogic of covenantal history that operates in *Tzili,* also prevails. It is no less than mad to imagine surviving the horror of the camps. Certainly it is madness to risk one's own death by giving one's rations to another. Yet without these fantastical, crazy gestures one is doomed, like Dr. Hollander in the first chapter, to certain death. Such a death is first of all the death of the imagination.

To live requires imagining oneself alive. Camp conditions force the men to distance themselves from their own interior life force. "If it weren't for the dreams," Erwin tells us, "we would already be men without souls. It is the dreams that return us for a moment to our souls" (84)—*souls,* Erwin says, not the past. These dreams, though not intended in the Freudian sense as distillations of the day's events intermingled with older fantasies and fears, nonetheless do, like Freudian dreams, function (as in the above example) to protect the dreamer from the intrusion of destructive waking knowledge. They are also (paradoxically) fairly self-conscious works of the imagination, constructions like stories that register future rather than past events. It is almost as if the story is reviving the ancient understanding of dreams as prophesies (as in the Joseph story) rather than recollections.

Early in his experience Erwin thus dreams of returning home to his mother. In the dream, his mother is represented, inexplicably, as not inquiring after his absence. Instead, she stands there drawing pictures, fulfilling her own early artistic ambitions, which were thwarted in the actual years of her adult married life. The dream is a fantasy within a fantasy. And it issues in lifesaving advice. "Everyone for herself," says Mother; "and finally I am for myself. Why are you so surprised?" (79). To be sure, the dream registers the son's painful sense of exclusion and loss, even of anger (which so subtly, almost imperceptibly, pervades Appelfeld's fiction) against the parents who were powerless to save him. But it also manages these emotions by imagining the life he is no longer living as still going on, as changing and moving forward, and, just as importantly, as granting him license to also pursue his own dreams, regardless of them. Be for yourself, his mother tells him, which, given his situation, is exactly the right advice for a mother to give. As in so much of Appelfeld's fiction, it is the mother who is associated with art and thus with the son's artistic abilities. In *The Story of a Life,* as we shall see, this centrality of the mother takes the form of a prolonged emphasis on the mother tongue, literally the language that Appelfeld's mother speaks.

As Erwin's dream life develops and becomes more elaborate, he invents an entire alternate world for himself. Even as he is living his life in the camp, he is writing himself another life as a fiction, in defiance of the prohibition or judgment that this is an insane thing to do—a verdict that recurs after the war in the form of rules concerning what can and cannot be written about the Holocaust. Erwin's violation of the taboo against fantasy no less than helps save his life. What imagination provides is a someplace else through which one can see and cope with the place one is in, another self by which one can refashion one's own self.

Wolfgang Iser's description of the case of fiction-making generally can serve us in good stead here:

> Staging in literature makes conceivable the extraordinary plasticity of human beings, who, precisely because they do not seem to have a determinable nature, can expand into an almost unlimited range of culture-bound patternings. The impossibility of being present to ourselves becomes our possibility to play ourselves out to a fullness that knows no bounds, because no matter how vast the range, none of the possibilities will "make us tick." From this we may infer a lead as to the purpose of literary staging. If the plasticity of human nature allows, through its multiple culture-bound patternings, limitless human self-cultivation, literature becomes a panorama of what is possible.[3]

For Appelfeld, as for Iser, the panorama of the possible has ethical and religious connotations as well.

Thus, a short time after his dream about his mother, Erwin dreams about the rabbi who married him, who now inquires how his Jewish learning has fared in the years after their first meeting. Erwin explains, reasonably enough, that he has been in a labor camp and has had no time to study. The reader's first response to the imagined conversation is to have contempt for the rabbi (which is to say for religion generally), who has no inkling concerning Erwin's suffering. But set as it is within the story of one of the other prisoner's mad but very poignant longings for his wife and leading into Erwin's own sudden revelations concerning his mother, the fantasy conversation has another, more nuanced consequence. This is the text:

> "And there didn't chance to be there any devout Jews?"
> "Yes, but our lives there weren't lives."
> "Did you at least observe their observance?"
> "A little."
> "And what did you learn from them?"
> "Butzi impressed us all with his sturdiness and with his faith, but to say that we loved him would be an exaggeration."
> "Then I see that you have learned nothing at all," he said. (124)

This strange scene turns stranger still in the subsequent passage, when suddenly Erwin discerns his mother standing on the sidelines of the exchange between himself and the rabbi. After a few moments of reflection about his parents' unhappy marriage, Erwin reports the following, which links this dream to his previous one concerning his mother:

> Mother doesn't question and doesn't intervene and her life now seems even more submissive than it was before, but her desire to paint is apparently undiminished,

even in this difficult hour. I want to paint, her resigned face says, and if you will give me a brush and paints and paper I will paint and never stop. All these years I have vanquished sights to a place within me and now I can't keep them any longer. Hearing her words, or rather her muteness, Father says, "Now, in the middle of the war, when everything is turned upside down and we have nothing, you want to paint?" Hearing his words, Mother shrivels up and disappears.

All night long the cannons thunder and also in the morning light volleys of light shoot through the skies, but the officers don't cancel the morning exercises nor the cry "Labor frees, labor purifies." . . . Honig hands me a scrap of paper and a pencil. "Aida," I write, "If by chance we never meet again, know that everything was as it had to be, always yours, Erwin" and I let loose the note to the winds. [Aida is Erwin's wife.]

The next chapter, which begins immediately after these words, starts:

> Butzi approaches me and murmurs, "Say *qeriʾat shemaʿ*"
> "I don't know it," I say shaking.
> "Say, *shemaʿ yisraʾel adonai elohenu, adonai eḥad.*" . . . It is difficult for me, but I make the attempt and I say it. (124–25)

And the chapter ends with Erwin's saying the *shemaʿ* "in a loud voice," which becomes, we are told, "louder still" (127).

What we have in this extended passage is a picture (reminiscent of the role of the catechism in *Tzili*) of the lifesaving infusion of fantasy (of which prayer forms a component) into waking life. Just as Erwin discovers permission for his self-preservation in the first dream of his mother, so here he finds legitimacy, not only for the practicalities of such self-preservation but, in addition, for the fantasy life on which such self-survival is built. Thus immediately following his dream, and against the background both of the threat of the war's closing in on them and of the perversion of logic and sanity that governs their lives in the camp, Erwin writes and sends his note to Aida. This note, which will never of course arrive, contains a message to himself as well. And it occasions his saying his own name, thereby stating and affirming his own identity.

His action repeats and reinforces an earlier moment in the text in which fantasy and concrete action go hand in hand. In this scene, the men are digging a tunnel to another barrack, an activity that not only keeps them spiritually alive but, unlike Dr. Hollander's death-dealing vision of home in the first chapter, also provides them with meaningful and lifesaving access to their loved ones. "Since we have begun tunneling," reports Erwin, "our mood has changed, as if the barrier between us and our loved ones has been lifted. We dream and remember our dreams. Yesterday I saw Aida and she is telling me that the note I sent her had arrived. 'But why the despair?' she asks; 'Why have you lost your faith in life after death?'" (110).

If the motto of the camp is a perversion of the idea that "Labor frees, Labor purifies," the tunneling and dreaming and praying that take place in the text not only redeem from their distortion this wisdom, but they also discover the many modes in which human labor consists. For the work of the human is both mental and physical, secular and religious: there is an intimate relation between believing in this life and believing in life after death. Immediately following Erwin's dream of the rabbi in Chapter 30, Butzi, as if he has been inside Erwin's dream with him, teaches Erwin the *shema*ᶜ, which Erwin then recites, with increasing vigor. The worship of God which he hasn't had the presence of mind to observe—in the sense either of watching it in others or performing it himself—he now observes, in the more technical, *halachic* sense of the word as well, as used in *Tzili* too: to observe the commandments.

Now we can understand the reasons for Appelfeld's choice of diction, in the above passage, when he calls "devoted Jews" ᶜ*ovdei el* in the Hebrew, paralleling the phrase ᶜ*ovdei elilim* ("idol worshippers"). Like idol worship, from which it is also to be distinguished, so too is the performance of the commandments, in every sense a performance, as we saw in *Tzili*. As such, it is an almost pagan celebration of human labor, including worship of the imagination, as men and women express their internalized pictures of the world in painting and words. It is forbidden to make engraved images; and it is absolutely essential. At the end of the very next chapter, which is also (though they do not yet know it) the very last day of their incarceration in the camp, it is the observant Butzi who performs the ultimate act of self-sacrifice. Without realizing it, in defending his own life, he saves the lives of the others as well.

Save one life and save the world, advises a Jewish saying. That life, it appears, could be one's own, if one is writing the scene as fiction. As in *Tzili*, and in line with kabbalistic thinking in such matters, it is performance in some literal sense as opposed to some more verbal or abstract form of worship that is important. And this performance corresponds as well to the performance of heroic deeds, including the courage it takes to believe and to imagine and to create art, even in the midst of every reason to call this mad, *meturaf*.

Dredging the Streams of Memory: Telling the Life's Story

In Chapter 26 of *Ice Mine*, Erwin engages in a long conversation with Aida, in which she argues for life after death, and he rejects her idea. But, of course, this conversation—which he tells us, at the end of the chapter, so "fortified" him that he didn't feel the sergeant's whip on his back rousing him from his reverie (112)—is a ghostly conversation. In Aida's word, as imagined within the vision, it comes from "afar" (111). Therefore, in and of itself it constitutes testimony to at least one sort of "life after death." This is the life of the mind, which is not the life lived but the thought of that life, which is itself life-sustaining. Such life is not simply memory. Erwin's conversation with Aida is not remembered, even if it makes use of details Erwin remembers from the past. Rather it is a fantasy, a waking-dream. It is another version of the "interior narrative" to which Aida's mother, much like Erwin's, retreats during her imprisonment in the ghetto.

This other mother, Aida informs him in the imagined conversation, has also withdrawn further and further into herself. What she tells them of, from there, is her "internal life" (111). Aida's father, like Erwin's, has no patience for this. He is even embarrassed by it. But "dear God, what is there to be embarrassed by?" Aida exclaims, defending what comes to be a decidedly female knowledge; "she is already in the world that is altogether good" (112). These words conclude the reverie and the chapter. They produce within Erwin a vital feeling of inner strength. Yet that whip does land on his back. While a temporary dulling of pain may be in the service of his survival, nonetheless he had better "jump to his feet" (112) if he is to make good the gains of fantasy. Realism must anchor the flights of imagination on which reality itself depends. How does one produce a life story as a story that not only lives, but furthers life as well?

One major subject of *The Story of a Life* concerns the rights of memory and a foreign-born, diaspora identity even after the Holocaust and within the new Israeli nation. Another is the right to fantasize, to daydream, even in harsh disrelation to the realities that appear to have primary claim on one's attention. For Appelfeld, memory and imagination are each other's handmaidens. Together they invest human life with what it is that makes life meaningful, what makes life live. Without them, life becomes only so many hours and days. This is not simply the inevitable consequence of the work camp, but one of the Nazis' intentions.

Therefore, Appelfeld observes, even before he has begun to tell his Holocaust story in *The Story of a Life,*

> There are times when memory and imagination reside together as one, each nestled inside the other. During those submerged years, it was as if they were vying between them. Of the two, memory seemed the more solid, the more substantial. Imagination had wings. Memory clung fast to the familiar. Imagination soared in the unknown. And while memory soothed and comforted me, imagination tossed me relentlessly hither and yon, abandoning me, in the end, to despair. (5)

What Appelfeld comes to realize is not only that remaining within the confines of memory constitutes its own form of danger, but that, in some circumstances, imagining is not a surrender to weakness but its own form of courage. Appelfeld's insight here parallels that of Terrence Des Pres concerning survival, as noted in Chapter 5. In the Holocaust, Des Pres reminds us, just staying alive became a manifestation of heroism. So for Appelfeld, both during and following the catastrophe, imagining was a similar act of resistance and defiance. Hence the vignettes to which some of finest pages of the autobiography are devoted: the magnificent portraits of the great dreamers of his early childhood, his grandfather, his Uncle Max, Gustav Gottesman who was the head of the school for the blind, and the brothers Rauchwerger, who constantly risk life and limb (one of them actually dies) in order, like Butzi in *Ice Mine,* to remain true to their imaginings. In his own early memories of himself, Appelfeld is also one of this company of dreamers, as, in the first chapter, remembering detail by detail his vacations with his parents and his visits to his grandparents, the child plots wholly new adventures on the living-room carpet with toy animals and teddy bears.

Memory, this passage makes clear both in its subject matter and in its structure, leads, in the normal course of things, directly into fantasy, and fantasy is the vital organ of the present and the future. For this reason, those descriptions of the dreamers of his early acquaintance are also, we realize, intended to replicate textually, and thereby to recover the activity of the young child. They are also intended to suggest how that province of childhood is absolutely fundamental to the most important moral work of adult human beings. It is this work of imagination that is performed both by the subject of Appelfeld's sketches and by the sketches themselves.

To imagine, Appelfeld understands, is dangerous. It means risking the dematerialization and defamiliarization of the world, encountering the unattainable and the frightening. And, as is the case for characters like Erwin Siegelbaum (the Erwin of *The Iron Tracks*), it may well catapult an individual into despair. No wonder so many of Applefeld's protagonists remain safely if painfully tethered to memory (and bodily memory at that). For this reason, the autobiography is anything but an exercise in memory per se.

It is not that Appelfeld is naive concerning the dangers of imagination. One of the opening sketches of the autobiography, dealing with his indigent Uncle Robert who squandered away his money in pursuit of wild visions, already cautions us against its overindulgence. And quick to follow is the more severe example of the crazed optimists who refused to relinquish their love of things German and, even in the jaws of disaster, "interpreted everything to the good" (32). Problems of decorum and ethics adhere to the work of the imagination even under the best of circumstances. Nor does Appelfeld advocate abandoning memory for some purely imaginary, fictional realm divorced from the historical circumstances of human life. In the first place, even if *The Story of a Life* is not exclusively a defense of the legitimacy of the immigrant Israeli's European past, it is that as well. As Appelfeld dramatizes so compellingly in *The Age of Wonders*, Jewish amnesia is not a recent phenomenon, and the Israeli defense of the new Jew as against the old Hebrew repeats rather than puts to rest the same Jewish self-hatred that this Israeli ideology thinks it is opposing. But what Appelfeld realizes is that there is no real remembering without imagination. There is also no art or significant human life.

Therefore, Appelfeld would recover the world of his past, not for its own sake but in order to reconnect it to the present, which is the place of fantasy and dream as well as memory. Appelfeld's intention is not simply to explain the present, as if the past were an historical archive containing the key to unlocking contemporary realities. Rather, he wishes to re-establish in the present the realm of dreaming, fantasizing, and projecting a future, which memory can either prohibit or advance—depending precisely on how we manage the tricky realm of their interrelation. For often what we mean when we speak of the survivor's inability to remember is the person's inability to remember in this particular way of imagination. Indeed, it is clear that survivors (like Bartfuss, for example, or Bruno, or Erwin Siegelbaum) remember all too well, both on the level of bodily, traumatic re-enactment and in terms of concrete image pictures that prohibit any form of interpretative distance. This sort of remembering produces what in Kierkegaard's terms is labeled sentimental "recollection" or in Freud's vocabulary, the deadening return of the repressed. And both sentimentality and hysteria, Appelfeld realizes, can occur as much on the textual as on the physiological level. This is one of the primary insights of the autobiography, which sets the basis for Appelfeld's own very differently penned excursions into the past.

Although written and spoken forms of remembering, such as documentary and testimony, give the appearance of being freed from the hysteria of bodily re-enactment, Appelfeld nonetheless understands that they remain just as imprisoned within the traumas of the past as the hysterical body itself. In many ways, a text like *Badenheim,* which is made to speak from within the moment of mounting catastrophe, speaks a hysterical language. The same is true of *The Iron Tracks,* which in many ways follows the iron tracks of its protagonist's repressions. Such use of language is obviously not evidence of Appelfeld's inability to mount a non-hysterical narrative, since in other texts he writes from outside the hysteria of others (albeit in sympathy with their hysteria). Rather, it is part of the writer's effort to demonstrate how speaking and writing do not, ipso facto, exceed the hysteria of human behavior.

"At the beginning of the fifties," Appelfeld writes in the autobiography,

> when I started to write, the long stream of words concerning the war had already begun to flow. Many recounted, witnessed, testified, and judged. People who had promised themselves and their dear ones that after the war they would tell everything, did indeed fulfill their promises. Thus were compiled the booklets, pamphlets, and volumes of memoirs. Much pain is invested is those tomes, but also much that is clichéd and beside the point. The silence that reigned during the war and for a short time afterwards was swallowed up in a sea of words. (97)

> Only after the war did words once again emerge. People returned to questioning and wondering, and the people who weren't there demanded explanations. The explanations were ridiculous and pathetic, but the need to explain and to interpret was apparently so deeply submerged in us that, even knowing of how little value it was, you couldn't stop yourself from explaining and interpreting. Clearly these efforts were part of the attempt to return to a normal social existence, but what can you do? the effort was absurd. Words do not have the wherewithal to stand up against great catastrophes. They are weak, pathetic and quick to falsify. (96)

Or as he puts it still elsewhere in the autobiography:

> The years from 1946 to 1950 were years of abundant chatter. Ideological life produces words and clichés. Everything is talk. Sometimes it seemed to me that everyone had been educated at a school for talking and I was the only one who hadn't studied there. Not only at home, but on the street and in gatherings, they talked. Also the literature was full of words. (112)

1950s Israel—both on the parts of the survivors and the native inhabitants—is caught in the grips of a hysteria in which words are not the antidote to neurotic behavior but its very manifestation and form. Unfocused feelings sunk in past experience overflow in words that clarify nothing.

Appelfeld knows that his only way out of such hysteria (both public and private) is to recover, not only language (which is a primary goal for the young man "bereft" [99] not only of the many languages he spoke but of language as such), but some relationship to language that, for want of a better word, and in order to invoke one major trope of Appelfeld's text, we might as well call *silence*. *Silence* is what the public speaking of the 1950s replaced and what the budding artist (indeed the nation itself) must recover. We have already encountered in relation to Appelfeld's fiction this apparent paradox of silence as a form of speech. In *The Story of a Life*, Appelfeld fleshes out (almost literally) what he means by this. For the speaking of the language of silence turns out to be nothing less than the recuperation of language itself, the recovery, intact and uninterpreted, of the objects, scenes, and images in which quotidian reality itself consists and which is the primary, or at least initial, function of language to conjure. This is the art of contemplation or reflection or acknowledgment, of which *The Story of a Life* is itself both an embodiment and a large-scale defense.

Literature, Appelfeld is adamant, is not (as the Israeli academic establishment would have it in the 1950s) a "platform for the investigation of social issues" (135). Rather, its vitality and its human relevance reside in its ability to reproduce human scenes and human faces, as recorded not mentally or even linguistically, but bodily, in the silence of the physical. Literature, in other words, depends for its subject matter on the corporeal memory of the body itself. But what is purely hysterical re-enactment in such characters as Erwin Siegelbaum and Bartfuss and Bruno, or its equivalent, the hysterical language of both the founding land-of-Israel writers like S. Yizar and Moshe Shamir and the immigrant survivor-authors of testimony and history, becomes in Appelfeld's writing the respectful, restrained, silent enactment—in language—of the life that in reality is itself an encapsulation of such reverence and restraint: life unmolested by human interpretation. It is useful here to quote again a statement I cited in the Introduction: "I had never been enamored of pathos and big words. I continued to like what I had always liked. Contemplation. Conjuring wordless reflections. Evoking the stillness of objects and a landscape that seeps into you without imposing anything" (145). This quiet, unimposing absorption and conjuring produce the literature toward which Appelfeld directs his efforts. Such memoried imagining, producing a storied life, begins with the work of memory defined in a certain way.

The Silent Face of Fiction

"Memory," Appelfeld tells us, by which he means that portion of the human brain we imagine as the place where mental pictures are stored, "is the organ of remembering. But the cells of my body, it seems, remember more" (83). What this means about remembering, and about the poetics that Appelfeld thereby constructs, is no less than definitive both for his fiction and for his philosophy of art. Memory, Appelfeld realizes, cannot proceed in the absence of the body, which is to say, in the absence of the concrete literal encapsulation of what were, in the past, literally concrete experiences and events. Leading into his recollection of what is perhaps the most painful episode recorded in the book, and as an example of what he *cannot* remember even as he is, of course, now remembering it, is the forced march with his father to the work camp. I quote at length from this stunning passage, and provide some additional passages as well that emphasize what may be the major insight of Appelfeld's poetics, the relationship of bodily remembering to remembering of the more cerebral kind:

> The Second World War went on for six continuous years. Sometimes, though, it seems to me as only a single long night from which I awoke somebody else. Other times I think, it wasn't me who was in the war but someone else, someone very close to me, who some time in the near future will tell me exactly what happened: for I myself do not remember what happened, or how.
>
> I say, "I don't remember," and that is the simple truth. What inhabits me from those years are mostly intense bodily sensations. Hunger for bread, for example. . . .
>
> In the course of the war I was in hundreds of different places, railway stations, remote villages, riversides. All these places had names. I cannot recall a single one of them. . . .
>
> Everything that happened is sunk into the cells of my body but not in my memory. Memory is the organ of remembering. But the cells of my body, it seems, remember more. . . .
>
> I say, "I don't remember," yet I remember a thousand myriad details. Sometimes the aroma of a certain food or dampness in my shoes or a sudden noise is enough to deliver me back into the midst of the war, and then it seems to me that the war isn't yet over, that without my knowledge it goes on, and that when I awaken I will know that, from the time that it began, it never came to a close.
>
> . . .
>
> Sometimes the way I am sitting or standing conjures before my eyes a railroad station crammed with people and packages. There is much squabbling, children are being beaten, and hands beg over and over again, "Water, Water." Suddenly without warning hundreds of legs rise up and of one accord charge a barrel of water that has rolled into the hut. The sole of a large foot stomps on my frail midriff and cuts off my breathing. It is hard to believe, but that very foot is still imprinted in my body, to this day a fresh wound, and for a moment it seems to me that I can't move from my spot for the pain. (83–84)

Or earlier in the text:

> More than fifty years have passed since the end of the Second World War. I have forgotten much—places, dates, the names of people. Yet, in every part of my body, that experience still lives. Every time the rain falls, and the cold and the wind rage, I am returned to the ghetto and the camp and to the forests where I spent so many of my days. Memory, it would seem, has roots that dig deep into the flesh. Sometimes the mere scent of building straw or the screeching of a bird is enough to catapult me into a distant and deeply inner landscape.

. . .

> My arrival in the forest, I do not recall. I do, however, remember the first moment I stood there, face to face with trees laden with apples outrageously crimson. I was so startled, I immediately backed away. Those first steps backward my body remembers better than I do. Every time I twist my back a certain way, or turn aside, I picture the tree with the red apples. (49–50)

The question is how this body memory, to which Appelfeld refers not only in these passages but throughout the text, differs from the hysterical bodily reenactments of his fictional protagonists. The difference is not simply the fact of their being rendered in words, as we have already seen. "All during my years at the university," Appelfeld tells us,

> I wrote poetry, poems that constituted the whimpering of an abandoned creature who spends long years searching to discover his way home. Mother, Mother, Father, Father, where are you? Where are you hiding? Why do you not come and rescue me from my sufferings? (135)

This early Appelfeld has more in common with his fictional protagonists and with other refugees who write witness testimony and memoirs than with the mature writer himself.

What saves him from this "sentimentality," as he calls it, is "fiction." Fiction for Appelfeld is a particular, physical and concrete way of using words. "By its very nature," he goes on in the very same passage,

> fiction demands concreteness. Emotionality and intellectualization are things it does not favor. Only an idea or feeling that emerges from within the concrete exists in fiction. . . .
>
> Like others of my generation at the University, I read Kafka and Camus with a thirst. These were the founding prophets from whom I sought to learn. And like all primary education of the young, so mine tended toward extremes. I was so captivated by the dreamlike and foggy, that I didn't perceive that Kafka's mists were constructed of minutely detailed, tangible, and precise descriptions, which anchored the fog in its fogginess and lent the mysterious its familiarity, rendering it a commonplace,—if I may make recourse to Max Kadushin's well-known remark.
>
> Russian literature saved me from the pitfalls of the mist and the symbol. From Russian literature I learned that there is no need of either one: reality, if correctly described, by itself produces the evocatively symbolic. Indeed, every specifically contextualized object is itself a symbol. (135)

Russian realism provides a literary model that even Appelfeld's masters (Kafka, and later Agnon) fail to provide, at least (as we shall see) till he has learned to read them in a certain way (to become a writer Appelfeld must also become a literary critic). The symbolic valence of the object, in its materiality, objectively rendered (so to speak), recognizes and vibrates with the already meaning-making constitution of reality. The concrete, non-sentimental, non-hysterical text (like Appelfeld's own, and, as he comes to realize, the fictions of Kafka and Agnon as well) recognizes this, as it patiently acknowledges and expresses both the inviolable realness of the world itself and the meaningfulness, nonetheless, of reality's insistent autonomy.

In many ways, Appelfeld's philosophy of language recalls the objectivism of a writer like Hemingway. But whereas Hemingway, for example, directs his attention toward an immediate present, making the reader see a world virtually before his very eyes, Appelfeld directs our gaze, through his, backward toward the landscape of a vanished past. This landscape, already shadowed by distance, is further rendered through the memory of a child, for whom mature perception is as distant as the landscape itself. In other words, Appelfeld would write concretely about a world that no longer enjoys concrete existence and that was experienced when its concreteness was inaccessible to mature reflection. By turning to fiction, Appelfeld confronts the double dilemma that in many survivors led to the production of such memoirs and pamphlets as remained caught in the emotionality of the moment. By imagining a past rather than skirting what cannot be recalled, fiction becomes a way for him to concretely capture the trauma of the past.

Like the neurotic reactions of characters like Erwin in *The Iron Tracks,* which, as we have seen, are not only expressions of dysfunction but also a sort of silent poetry (if only we attune our ears to hear it), Appelfeld's prose embodies and re-enacts (silently, which is to say, without commentary or emotionality) the trauma of which it would speak. But unlike the silent language of the traumatized body, it does so through what the author self-consciously constructs as the inherent meaningfulness of the world, including the enactments of that traumatized body. This meaningfulness is eminently accessible to being translated into words, even if, to remain true to the experience it would record, those words must retain the silence surrounding their origins.

Essentially Appelfeld constructs, or perhaps recovers, the mother tongue of the writer, which is not German (the author's own literal mother tongue) or any other native language that he or any other writer might acquire (whether in childhood or later). The mother tongue of the writer, any writer, turns out to be the language of fiction itself. This language of fiction (in whatever literal language it happens to be written) is a language unto itself, like the language of one of Appelfeld's prototypes of the artist in *The Story of a Life,* the child singer Amelia. "She didn't sing in any known language," he tells us,

> but rather in a language all her own, a language compiled of words recollected from home, sounds from the pastures, and noises from the forest, all of them blended with monastic chants of worship. People would listen and cry. It was difficult to know what she was singing about. It always seemed as though she were recounting a long saga, laden with hidden import.

And the text continues:

> Sometimes there would arise among us an emissary whose mouth overflowed with words from before the war. These words were as lacking in taste as stale grains of wheat. Only in the speech of little children did some sort of freshness reside. (79)

This "freshness" has to do with the necessary reinvention of language itself after the war.

This is the case not only because language had been violently ripped from the throats of the survivors, making their case different from that of ordinary immigrants or refugees (Appelfeld provides a particularly violent example of this in relation to the two child survivors in Chapter 11). Rather, it has to do with the fact that the German language had, after the war, come under something of an ethical, aesthetic question mark. As Appelfeld confesses in relation to his beloved mother tongue, as much as German is the language of his mother, more associated in his mind with her than with the Germans, nonetheless it is also the language of his mother's murderers. The language is tainted, and this presents the writer with an almost insoluble dilemma.

But as the word *freshness* and the fact that only children spontaneously acquire this new language suggest, what is needed is not simply a different language to replace the mother tongue. Rather, what is required is a more or less precise equivalent of a first language—a language such as children normally and naturally acquire in childhood and that is thereby linked to their primary, original experiences—a blend of the sounds and noises and words they hear. This is a language that has to develop organically, for a fact about language acquisition is that children do not *learn* language in the same sense that they learn math or science. It is not taught to them, but, rather, it is made available for them to absorb—again a feature of Tzili's experience of the catechism in *Tzili*. In this definition of language acquisition, the mother, who not only speaks language to the child, but also, as much in her silence as in her words, protects and loves the child during this time of acquiring language, is, for Appelfeld, crucial. The mother is not the child's teacher in any direct, pedagogical way. Rather, she facilitates the process whereby the child takes in the world. Like nature itself, she is the nurturing environment in which reflection and contemplation—the primary tools of literature and life both—take place.

A large portion of *The Story of a Life* concerns Hebrew as that language that cannot, at least not initially, constitute a mother tongue, because it is a language taught rather than made available. Indeed, it is a language that is anything but that unimposing process of reflection and contemplation. The Hebrew language is uncompromisingly, even violently, imposed on the new immigrant as an ideologically determined condition of his or her new existence. From the time of his arrival in Israel, Appelfeld struggles to learn this Hebrew and convert it into the requisite mother tongue. Eventually, he succeeds in this undertaking, as his fictional output more than affirms. But the Hebrew in which Appelfeld writes is *not* the official Hebrew of the dominant culture. It is a Hebrew recovered in spite of the politicization of the language.

In a way, the land of Israel and later the new nation see the refugees and survivors of the Holocaust in the way we ourselves might choose to see some of Appelfeld's protagonists, like Bartfuss, Erwin Siegelbaum, and Bruno: as broken, neurotic individuals in need of repair. Their only salvation, we might feel, would be in their coming to see themselves as we do, from the outside, with what we imagine is reparative interpretive distance. Then they could undertake their own transformation, according to the program that we of greater sanity would provide them. Thus would they emerge as healthy, vigorous, farmer soldiers, such as the heroic protagonists portrayed in the national revivalist fiction. To some degree, Appelfeld sets up the analytically inclined reader (let's say, like myself) to fall back onto the very premises of ideology that greeted the writer during his early years in the country. This ideology ironically has no place for the European refugee (including the author), whom the state was presumably fashioned to save. The reader is tempted, in the name of good mental health, to impose a pattern of normalcy on individuals whose behavior, at very least, is incomprehensible, perhaps even demented.

Needless to say, it is the purpose of the texts to caution us to resist this desire to cure the protagonists. And they instruct us in how we might do this without what is equally unacceptable as a response to human suffering: remaining silent and passive. People cannot be taught to be sane. This is one of the great insights of Freudian psychoanalytic theory and one of the reasons that finally, when all is said and done, it is extremely pertinent to reading Appelfeld's fiction. Sanity (whatever it is) can only be acquired from within, as a realization and a choice to which an individual comes privately, on his or her own. Outside forces might, however, like the mother herself, illuminate and facilitate the way, especially to what might become an individual's new mother tongue.

If people cannot be "taught" a mother tongue, where by teaching we understand the sort of instruction that dictates or imposes, they can be put in the condition of acquiring one. The world can be made into a home in which we can learn to speak. One of the ironies that vividly emerges through the pages of Appelfeld's autobiography is how the war years did not necessarily ravage the individuals (including the children) who survived it. In some cases, as with the brothers Rauchwerger or some of the child prodigies Appelfeld describes (including, perhaps, the author himself), the war actually nurtured creativity and the capacity for moral thought. Appelfeld comes back to this notion again and again in *The Story of a Life,* as, for example, when he describes as a time of love his season with the abusive Ukrainian peasant Maria.

The question the autobiography, like the fiction, puts to the reader is: how do we come to understand other people's languages, including the traumatic languages of the body? How do we translate those languages into a language of our own, which simultaneously respects what remains inaccessible in the other's discourse and yet which still does not forfeit the possibility of comprehension and even intervention and assistance? One way, which Appelfeld emphatically rejects, is to force other people to translate themselves, to express themselves in our language, according to our precepts and definitions.

And yet Appelfeld's dysfunctional protagonists are indeed dysfunctional. And the writer with no real language, who writes, when he writes at all, in sputtering fragments and incoherent whimpers, is not going to be able to find modes of self-expression that are satisfying to himself or that in any way make his experience real to us. So the question the text puts to its author (as opposed to its audience) is: how do we ourselves learn to speak and write in such a way as to invite other people into our world, to make our reality theirs as well? This is the question any writer must confront.

However much the reader, or the host culture, might wish to lend an attentive ear to the suffering newcomer, that individual must, eventually, learn a language, and that language must become (especially for the professional author) like a mother tongue. What, according to *The Story of a Life,* are the specific features of a mother tongue that not any particular language will do in its stead? The question is not different, it turns out, from the question of what literary language is. And this returns us to the issue of the centrality of silence both as a feature of the mother–child relationship and of the mother's language and as what characterizes the language of literature.

Though the fact that a major portion of the child's wanderings during the war took place in the absence of language altogether might seem to constitute an additional problem for the budding author (there was no one with whom to speak, his true language might betray him, and his language is rudimentary at best), this lack of language turns out to be the fortunate accident that enables him to produce for himself a new mother tongue, which preserves close affinities with the literal mother tongue of his literal mother. Like trauma itself, the child's experience is inscribed bodily. Therefore, it recalls what is the most basic feature and primary function of any language: to refer to the concrete entities known as reality. And it probes deep back into the past of the mother–child relationship before their mode of communication came to be conducted in words. In bizarre ways, the forests are for Appelfeld a place of birth, or more properly, perhaps, rebirth. But whereas the rebirth of a character like Erwin Siegelbaum remains inaccessible to his own consciousness, Appelfeld's becomes the occasion for his assumption of authorship.

"Whoever was in the ghetto or the camps or the forests knows silence from within his body," Appelfeld explains; "war is an incubator for hatching watchfulness and silence. . . . My mistrust of words I brought from there. . . . During the war what spoke weren't words but faces and hands" (95–96). Appelfeld's point is not, simply, that the conditions of wartime impose a particular burden, though they do that, too. Rather, proceeding through organically derived imagery, Appelfeld retrieves the origins of all speech in the infant's silent observations of the world. "We are accustomed," writes Appelfeld later in the same chapter, "to circumscribe great catastrophes in language so as to protect ourselves from them. My first written words were hapless cries of despair, seeking to recover the silence that had enfolded me during the war. With the understanding of a blind man I knew that within that silence resided my soul. If I could manage to retrieve it, perhaps I would be restored to proper speech" (97).

To be restored to true speech is neither to yield to the chatter that simply cloaks trauma in reassuring noise, nor is it to cry out in despair in some sort of pathetic appeal to silence to return to you. Language, he understands, can as easily as action become a protective wrapping, serving the needs of repression, whether it proceeds through rational explanation or by frantic ranting and raving. "Without language," he comments, "human nature is frankly exposed. . . . Those who were outgoing and of an imposing disposition [who learned the language rapidly] knew how to turn the situation to their advantage. Their words became orders, their voices booming above the rest, dominating every unoccupied space" (101).

Eventually, naked nature recovers words, and those words imitate the nature of the speakers. Even those who remain withdrawn from speech (the taciturn introverts like the author himself) expose themselves in hiding. They express themselves in a silence that communicates nothing at all: "My early writing," he tells us, "limped and faltered. The trials and tribulations of the war years weighed on me heavily, oppressively. I wanted to repress them even further, to construct a new life on the back of the old" (97).

What Appelfeld has to discover is the verbal construction of silence, its language. For this reason, the Hebrew of Israel in the 1950s, which is alternately ideological and sentimental, can never be anything more than a "step-mother" (103). It is for the writer sheer noise. Even the more literary, written Hebrew that he discovers through his teachers and soulmates Dov Sadan, Leib Rochman, and Shai Agnon, who are the fathers of his new mother tongue, cannot suffice. This other Hebrew, of Hasidism and Kabbalah, at least contains one of the languages of his youth (Yiddish). But it is not yet the language of the mother. This he discovers in the language of fictional discourse itself, which translates contemplation back into the objects that inspired reflection in the first place.

This language, needless to say, also has its fathers, specifically in the persons of Kafka and Agnon and the Russian realists. But its real progenitor is his mother. This is quite literally the case for Appelfeld, since it is his mother who bequeaths to him the talent for contemplation. The "tendency toward reflection," Appelfeld explains, "I apparently inherited from Mother. Mother loved to contemplate the world. Frequently I found her standing by the window lost in thought. It was hard to know if she was observing the landscape pictured through the window or attending to something that arose from within her inmost being" (124). Appelfeld's inheritance is genetic and figurative both.

It is paradoxically while in the army, that bastion of patriarchy where Appelfeld hopes (quite literally) to discover his manhood, that Appelfeld recovers the link to his mother and to her language, and through them to the child whose memories the mature writer will go on to speak. "In order to surmount my distress," Appelfeld explains, "I adopted a stratagem that I already knew from childhood. I began to contemplate things closely" (122). This return to contemplation restores the past in exactly the language the past spoke. "Already in childhood I had loved to observe the world," he goes on, celebrating "the pleasure of blending in with everything that happened along my way" (122). This habit of mind is restored both during the years of the ghetto and during the wandering afterwards in the forests:

> I didn't survive the war because I was strong or because I fought for my existence. I was more like a tiny animal finding temporary shelter in a random burrow, sustained by whatever the moment happens to provide. Danger made me a child attentive to his surroundings and to himself. It didn't make me sturdy. For hours I would sit in the forest contemplating the underbrush or tracing the flowing of a brook. Reflection made me forget the hunger and the fear. It restored me to household scenes. Those were my most pleasurable hours, if one may be permitted to speak this way concerning what was after all war. This child on the verge of being forgotten in a savage foreign land, perhaps even killed, once again became his mother's and father's child, wandering with them the long summer country roads, an ice cream cone in his hand, or swimming with them in the river Prut. These blessed hours preserved me from spiritual annihilation. Also later, on the trek after the war and during the youth aliyah, I would sit and watch and contemplate scenes and sounds that connected me to my former life, joyful that I wasn't just one more anonymous face among the thousands.
>
> . . .
>
> During my army service I learned how much my childhood experience in the ghetto and camps was a part of me. . . . [T]he army actually revived scenes of the ghetto and the camp. Perhaps because I once again found myself trapped and threatened. I envied my friends who, though they had also come from the camps, obliterated memory and freed themselves of the past. . . . For me, as if to spite me, the ghetto and the camp renewed themselves and became ever-present. If during the days of the youth aliyah it sometimes seemed to me that the past was sinking out of view, descending into the abyss, now, during my army service, sights I hadn't seen in years emerged from within the recesses of consciousness. Those visions, to my astonishment and dismay, were as clear as if they hadn't happened years ago but only yesterday.
>
> . . .
>
> . . . It was as if the life I had lost during the war, the memory of which had begun to dissipate, came alive in, of all places, the army. . . . In the army I came to know with utter lucidity that the world I had left behind—parents, home, street, and town—was still alive, dwelling within me, and everything that had happened in the past or was about to happen in the future was tied to the world from which I had taken root. The moment I understood this, I was no longer an orphan who dragged his orphanhood behind him. I was a man with a grasp of the world. (126–28)

A man in the company of other men, first in the army, later at the university, and finally at the club for refugees (which constitutes the subject of the concluding chapter of the autobiography), Appelfeld recovers himself by recovering his mother and relearning her language of silent contemplation.

These silent origins of language, which are the only means by which he can restore his own history, turn out to have an ethical component as well, which makes them particularly apt for the literary project on which Appelfeld embarks: the evocation of the Jewish world that the Holocaust destroyed. "For me a fluent string of words," he writes, "is suspect. I prefer stammering, for in stammering I hear the friction and the discomfort, the endeavor to refine words of their dross, and the desire to impart to the listener something from within." And he explains:

> The war deepened the old saying that man is judged by his deeds alone. . . . During the time of the war it was not words that spoke but faces and hands. From a face you learned how much the person next to you was willing to help you or whether he was about to scheme against you. Words didn't facilitate such understanding. The senses were what brought you the necessary information. Hunger returns us to our instincts, to the language before language. Whoever reached out to hand you a piece of bread or a sip of water when you were already weak and on bended knees, that hand you will never forget. (96)

The essence of Appelfeld's fictional craft, as he looks into the face of the past and tries to acknowledge the unutterable pain he sees reflected there—his own as well as that of others—is what we might call a form of stammering in images (recalling his character Kuti in *A Journey Into Winter*). The struggle is for more than the perfect image to express his meaning, though this is a large part of the endeavor of authorship. As he himself puts it, "the themes, the subject—they are the consequence of his writing, not its essence. During the time of the war I was a child. That child grew up, and everything that happened to him and in him continued into his adult years: the loss of home and language, the suspiciousness and the fear, the inhibitions concerning speech, the strangeness. Out of these feeling I weave the tale. Only the right words produce a literary text, not its subject" (113–14). Rather, those "right words" which convey those particular "feelings" are vehicles of acknowledgment: they dig back into the sensual world to produce a picture of reality that respects the integrity of the original events, and their inaccessibility to our interpretation and translation.

Terrence Des Pres has suggested that for many survivors "bearing witness [is] less a 'literary' act and more a 'biological necessity.'"[4] Appelfeld does not represent the Holocaust in the abstract, as a theoretical problem or idea that can be explored discursively, through meditative or metaphorical, philosophical, historical, or intellectual, language. Rather, he represents the event as primarily a physical, even a bodily one, experienced by and thereafter inscribed on the flesh of the person who has endured it. For this reason, Appelfeld transcribes the experience in language that, as nearly as possible, reproduces the experience graphically, on the page.

Hence, we have the simplicity of Appelfeld's prose style, its lack of adornment and its fidelity to figuring forth, unqualified, almost to the point of allegorical reduction, the stark dimensions of the devastating logic of its world. Nouns and verbs drive the text forward; there is no compromising the representation through metaphorical displacements, adverbial or adjectival modification, or the usual layerings of subjectivity that lift the literary text off the ground of the here and now and set it into metaphysical spin. The text sputters and stammers in acknowledgment of the suffering that remains outside our capacities, not only of representing it, but even of identifying and sympathizing with it. To cite again Emmanuel Levinas's essay on Kierkegaard:

> In his evocation of Abraham, he describes the encounter with God at the point where subjectivity rises to the level of the religious, that is to say, above ethics. But one could think the opposite: Abraham's attentiveness to the voice that led him back to the ethical order, in forbidding him to perform a human sacrifice, is the highest point in the drama. That he obeyed the first voice is astonishing: that he had sufficient distance with respect to that obedience to hear the second voice—that is the essential. Moreover, why does Kierkegaard never speak of the dialogue in which Abraham intercedes for Sodom and Gomorrah on behalf of the just who may be present there? Here, in Abraham, the precondition of any possible triumph of life over death is formulated. Death is powerless over the finite life that receives a meaning from an infinite responsibility for the other. . . . It is here, in ethics, that there is an appeal to the uniqueness of the subject, and a bestowal of meaning to life, despite death.[5]

The finite life in its relationship to the infinite responsibility for the other, not only as such responsibility is manifested in deeds, but as it is performed in words as well, is, I suggest, Appelfeld's large subject and the achievement of his writing.

By acknowledging the Holocaust, rather than discoursing about it, Appelfeld reminds us that human existence is to be defined in its enactment, which performance we will either respect or degrade in the responses we mount. To invoke again Todorov's statement, that what we learn from the Final Solution is that human evil is not unavoidable, we might say that Appelfeld's fiction "teaches" us that what is to be learned from life is to be learned only in our unimposing contemplation of it, as it is rendered both in other people's actions, and in their words. It is to speak silently of what we cannot understand. And to listen in our speaking to the silent speech of others.

Notes

Introduction

1. The most comprehensive analyses of Appelfeld's fiction, which do not limit themselves to his Holocaust writings, are: Lily Rottok, *A Precarious House: The Narrative Art of A. Appelfeld* (Tel Aviv: Hekker, 1989) [Hebrew]; Gila Ramras-Rauch, *Aharon Appelfeld: The Holocaust and Beyond* (Bloomington: Indiana University Press, 1994); Yigal Schwartz, *Individual Lament and Tribal Eternity: Aharon Appelfeld: The Picture of His World* (Jerusalem: Keter, Magnes, 1996) [Hebrew]; translation: *Aharon Appelfeld: From Individual Lament to Tribal Eternity,* trans. Jeffrey M. Green (Hanover, N.H.: Brandeis University Press, 2001); and Gershon Shaked, *Hebrew Fiction 1880–1980,* vol. 5 (Tel Aviv: Hakibbutz Hameuchad and Keter Publishing House, 1998), 235–73 [Hebrew]. Works more focused on the Holocaust fictions include: Alan Mintz, *ḥurban: Responses to Catastrophe in Hebrew Literature* (Syracuse, N.Y.: Syracuse University Press, 1996; orig. pub. 1984), 203–38; Lawrence Langer, *Admitting the Holocaust: Collected Essays* (New York: Oxford University Press, 1995), 125–37; Daniel R. Schwarz, *Imagining the Holocaust* (New York: St. Martin's Press, 1999), 248–70; Lea Wernick Fridman, *Words and Witness: Narrative and Aesthetic Strategies in the Representation of the Holocaust* (Albany: State University of New York Press, 2000), 33–52. I want especially to thank Gershon Shaked, Yigal Schwartz, and Jeffrey Green for introducing me to Appelfeld—both the man and his writings; and to acknowledge their help in this, my first foray into writing about Hebrew fiction.
2. For a fuller account of the history of Hebrew fiction from the 1880s on, see Gershon Shaked, *Modern Hebrew Fiction,* trans. Yael Lotan, ed. Emily Miller Budick (Bloomington: Indiana University Press, 2000).
3. Susan Gubar, *Poetry After Auschwitz: Remembering What One Never Knew* (Bloomington: Indiana University Press, 2003). For a good general statement on "The Problematics of Holocaust Literature," see Alvin Rosenfeld, *A Double Dying: Reflections on Holocaust Literature* (Bloomington and London: Indiana University Press, 1980), 12–34. Most critics cannot avoid the subject of how and whether to represent the Holocaust in literature.
4. Appelfeld's major survivor novels include *The Immortal Bartfuss, The Iron Tracks,* and *The Age of Wonders* (which I will be discussing), and, more recently, *laylah veʿod laylah* [*Night after Night*] and *pitʾom ahavah* [*Love, All of a Sudden*].
5. On "The Holocaust in the Jewish American Literary Imagination," see my essay in *The Cambridge Companion to Jewish American Literature,* ed. Michael P. Kramer and Hana Wirth-Nesher (Cambridge, Cambridge University Press, 2003), 212–30. Many Jewish American writers of the current generation who deal with the Holocaust seem to me to exhibit the influence of Appelfeld on

their writing, in particular his tendency toward a Kafkaesque grotesque coupled with a minimalism and lyricism. I am thinking here of writers such as Aryeh Lev Stollman, Thane Rosenbaum, Nathan Englander, and Anne Michaels.

6. Aharon Appelfeld, *Beyond Despair: Three Lectures and a Conversation with Philip Roth,* trans. Jeffrey Green (New York: Fromm International Publishing Company), 21–22, 39, 80.

7. Emmanuel Levinas, *Proper Names,* trans. Michael B. Smith (Stanford, Calif.: Stanford University Press, 1996), 3–4.

1. Acknowledgment and the Human Condition

1. Lawrence L. Langer, *The Holocaust and the Literary Imagination* (New Haven, Conn.: Yale University Press, 1975), 2–3 and Alvin Rosenfeld, *A Double Dying: Reflections on Holocaust Literature* (Bloomington and London: Indiana University Press, 1980), 5, 13. See also Sidra DeKoven Ezrahi, *By Words Alone: The Holocaust in Literature* (Chicago: University of Chicago Press, 1980), 10–20. The studies by Langer, Rosenfeld, and Ezrahi are among the earliest and best studies of Holocaust literature; they set the terms for the scholarship that follows, and they survey, by examining many different works of Holocaust literature, covering many different genres and national literatures, both the modes of imaginative representation of the events and the bases for developing a theory of this form of fiction.

2. Gershon Shaked, *Hebrew Narrative Fiction, 1880–1980,* vol. 5 (Hakibbutz Hameuchad and Keter Publishing House, 1998), 243 [Hebrew].

3. The best discussion of the religious aspects of Appelfeld's work is Yigal Schwartz, *Aharon Appelfeld: From Individual Lament to Tribal Eternity,* trans. Jeffrey M. Green (Hanover, N.H.: Brandeis University Press, 2001).

4. I have dealt with the relationship of skepticism and anti-mimetic modes of representation, specifically in historical fictions, in my two studies of American historical romance: *Fiction and Historical Consciousness: The American Romance Tradition* (New Haven, Conn.: Yale University Press, 1989) and *Engendering Romance: Women Writers and the Hawthorne Tradition, 1850–1990* (New Haven, Conn.: Yale University Press, 1994).

5. See especially "Knowing and Acknowledging," in *Must We Mean What We Say? A Book of Essays* (rpt. Cambridge: Cambridge University Press, 1976; orig. pub. 1969); 238–66, and *Disowning Knowledge in Six Plays of Shakespeare* (Cambridge: Cambridge University Press, 1987).

6. Deborah E. Lipstadt, *Denying the Holocaust: The Growing Assault on Truth and Memory* (New York: Macmillan, 1993).

7. James Young, *Writing and Rewriting the Holocaust: Narrative and the Consequences of Interpretation* (Bloomington: Indiana University Press, 1988), 24.

8. Peter Brooks, *Psychoanalysis and Storytelling* (Oxford: Blackwell, 1994), 55–56.

9. On documentary fiction, faction, and the nonfiction novel, see Barbara Foley, *Telling the Truth: The Theory and Practice of Documentary Fiction* (Ithaca,

N.Y.: Cornell University Press, 1986) and Mas'ud Zavarzadeh, *Mythopoeic Reality: The Postwar American Nonfiction Novel* (Urbana: University of Illinois Press, 1976).

10. Jeffrey Moussaieffe Masson, *The Assault on Truth: Freud's Suppression of the Seduction Theory* (New York: Farrar, Straus and Giroux, 1984).

11. Nicholas Rand and Maria Torok, *Questions for Freud: The Secret History of Psychoanalysis* (Cambridge, Mass.: Harvard University Press, 1997).

12. *Testimony: Crises of Witnessing in Literature, Psychoanalysis, and History,* ed. Shoshana Felman and Dori Laub (New York: Routledge, 1992).

13. See Walter Benn Michaels, "'You who never was there': Slavery and the New Historicism, Deconstruction and the Holocaust," *Narrative* 4 (1) 1996, and Alain Finkielkraut, *The Imaginary Jew,* trans. Kevin O'Neill and David Suchoff (Lincoln, Nebr.: University of Nebraska Press, 1994).

14. Geoffrey H. Hartman, *The Longest Shadow: In the Aftermath of the Holocaust* (Bloomington: Indiana University Press, 1996), 158.

15. Cathy Caruth, *Unclaimed Experience: Trauma, Narrative, and History* (Baltimore: Johns Hopkins University Press, 1996), 17.

16. Dominick LaCapra, *Representing the Holocaust: History, Theory, Trauma* (Ithaca, N.Y.: Cornell University Press, 1994), 209–210.

17. Elizabeth J. Bellamy, *Affective Genealogies: Psychoanalysis, Postmodernism, and the "Jewish Question" after Auschwitz* (Lincoln: University of Nebraska Press, 1997), 17–18, 31.

18. Dominick LaCapra, *History and Memory after Auschwitz* (Ithaca, N.Y.: Cornell University Press, 1998), 40.

19. Paul de Man was an important Yale University deconstructionist, who was discovered to have had ties with the Nazis in Belgium. See *Responses: On Paul de Man's Wartime Journalism,* ed. Werner Hamacher, Neil Herz, and Thomas Keenan (Lincoln: University of Nebraska Press, 1989).

20. Stanley Cavell, *Contesting Tears: The Hollywood Melodrama of the Unknown Woman* (Chicago: University of Chicago Press, 1996), 94–96.

21. Introduction to *The Collected Stories of Isaac Babel,* ed. Lionel Trilling (London: Penguin, 1961; orig. pub. 1957), 13–14.

22. Adam Phillips, *Promises, Promises: Essays on Psychoanalysis and Literature* (New York: Basic Books, 2001), 20, 24–25.

2. Literature, Ideology, and the Measure of Moral Freedom

1. Michael André Bernstein, *Foregone Conclusions: Against Apocalyptic History* (Berkeley: University of California Press, 1994), 61. Other readings along these lines include: Gila Ramras-Rauch, *Aharon Appelfeld: The Holocaust and Beyond* (Bloomington: Indiana University Press, 1994), 135–42; Daniel R. Schwarz, *Imagining the Holocaust* (New York: St. Martin's Press, 1999), 252–59; and Lea Wernick Fridman, *Words and Witness: Narrative and Aesthetic Strategies in the Representation of the Holocaust* (Albany: State University of

New York Press, 2000), 33–52. I want to thank Michael Kramer, Avigdor Shinan, and the readers and editors (especially Marshall Brown) of *MLQ* for helping me revise different drafts of this chapter.

2. Alan Mintz, *ḥurban: Responses to Catastrophe in Hebrew Literature* (Syracuse: Syracuse University Press, 1996; orig. pub. 1984), 214.

3. Geoffrey H. Hartman, *The Longest Shadow: In the Aftermath of the Holocaust* (Bloomington: Indiana University Press, 1996), 161. Though Hartman does not use this expression specifically to refer to Appelfeld, it is harmonious with his discussion of Appelfeld, 89–91.

4. See Gershon Shaked, "Appelfeld and His Times: Transformations of Ahashveros, the Eternal Wandering Jew," *Hebrew Studies* 36 (1995): 87–100; Yael S. Feldman, "Whose Story Is It, Anyway? Ideology and Psychology in the Representation of the Shoah in Israeli Literature," *Probing the Limits of Representation: Nazism and the "Final Solution,"* ed. Shaul Friedlander (Cambridge: Harvard University Press, 1992), 223; Bernstein, *Foregone Conclusions,* 55–56; and Mintz, *ḥurban,* 204–205.

5. For likeminded critiques of the book see Ruth Wisse, "Aharon Appelfeld, Survivor," *Commentary* 76 (1983): 74–76; Yael Feldman, "Whose Story is it, Anyway?"; and Michael Ignatieff, "The Illusion of Fate," review of *Foregone Conclusions: Against Apocalyptic History* by Michael André Bernstein, *The New Republic* (February 13, 1995): 29–32.

6. Bruce Robbins, "Death and Vocation: Narrativizing Narrative Theory," *PMLA* 107 (1992): 44; Louise O. Fradenburg, "Criticism, Antisemitism, and the Prioress's Tale," *Exemplaria* 1 (1989): 111; Regina M. Schwartz, "Nations and Nationalism: Adultery in the House of David," *Critical Inquiry* 19 (1992): 131–34, 149–50; and Stephen Greenblatt, *Marvelous Possessions: The Wonder of the New World* (Chicago: University of Chicago Press, 1991), ix; see also Daniel Boyarin and Jonathan Boyarin, "Diaspora: Generation and the Ground of Jewish Identity," *Critical Inquiry* 19 (1993): 693–725 and Jonathan Boyarin, *Storm from Paradise: The Politics of Jewish Memory* (Minneapolis: University of Minnesota Press, 1992), 116–29.

7. For a useful summary of these issues, see David Hawkes, *Ideology* (London: Routledge, 1996), as well as the scholars cited: for example, Slavoj Žižek, "How Did Marx Invent the Symptom?" *Mapping Ideology,* ed. Slavoj Žižek (London: Verso, 1994), 296–331; Louis Althusser, "Ideology and Ideological State Apparatuses (Notes Towards an Investigation)," also in *Mapping Ideology,* 100–40; Jacques Derrida, *Of Grammatology,* trans. Gayatri Spivak (Baltimore: Johns Hopkins University Press, 1976); Terry Eagleton, *Criticism and Ideology: A Study in Marxist Literary Theory* (London: Methuen, 1976); and Michel Foucault, *The History of Sexuality,* trans. Robert Hurley (New York: Vintage Books, 1990).

8. See James Young, "Against Apocalyptic History," *Prooftexts: A Journal of Jewish Literary History* 15 (3) (September 1995): 282–91 and Ignatieff, "The Illusion of Fate."

9. Gary Saul Morson, *Narrative and Freedom: The Shadows of Time* (New Haven, Conn.: Yale University Press, 1994), 6; cf. 117–72.

10. *The Dialogic Imagination: Four Essays by M. M. Bakhtin,* trans. Caryl Emerson and Michael Holquist (Austin: University of Texas Press, 1981), 324.

11. Dominick LaCapra, *Representing the Holocaust: History, Theory, Trauma* (Ithaca, N.Y.: Cornell University Press, 1994), 27.

12. See again James Young's review of Bernstein's book.

13. Bakhtin, "Forms of Time and Chronotype in the Novel," in *The Dialogic Imagination,* 253. See also Stanley Cavell's discussions of voice in "Knowing and Acknowledging," *Must We Mean What We Say? A Book of Essays* (Cambridge: Cambridge University Press, 1976; orig. pub. 1969), 238–66; *Disowning Knowledge in Six Plays of Shakespeare* (Cambridge: Cambridge University Press, 1987); and "Skepticism and a Word Concerning Deconstruction," *In Quest of the Ordinary: Lines of Skepticism and Romanticism* (Chicago: University of Chicago Press, 1988), 130–36.

14. David K. Danow, *The Thought of Mikhail Bakhtin: From Word to Culture* (New York: St. Martin's Press, 1991), 25.

15. See Sacvan Bercovitch, "Games of Chess: A Model of Literary and Cultural Studies," *Centuries' Ends, Narrative Means,* ed. Robert D. Newman (Stanford, Calif.: Stanford University Press, 1996).

16. *Pentateuch and Haftorahs,* ed. Dr. J. H. Hertz (London: Soncino Press, 1972); all biblical quotations from this text.

17. Franz Kafka, *The Trial* (Harmondsworth: Penguin, 1985), 243.

18. "Discovering America: A Cross-Cultural Perspective," in *The Translatability of Cultures: Figurations of the Space Between,* ed. Sanford Budick and Wolfgang Iser (Stanford, Calif.: Stanford University Press, 1996), 149.

19. Franz Kafka, *Selected Short Stories,* trans. Willa and Edwin Muri (New York: Modern Library, 1952), 254–55.

20. Immanuel Kant, "Analytic of the Sublime," *Kant's Critique of Aesthetic Judgement,* trans. James Creed Meredith (Oxford: Clarendon Press, 1911), 91, 98, 111.

21. My ideas here are indebted to Sanford Budick, *The Western Theory of Tradition: Terms and Paradigms of the Cultural Sublime* (New Haven, Conn.: Yale University Press, 2000).

22. *Aharon Appelfeld: From Individual Lament to Tribal Eternity,* trans. Jeffrey M. Green (Hanover, N.H.: Brandeis University Press, 2001), 105–42.

23. See also *History and Memory after Auschwitz* (Ithaca, N.Y.: Cornell University Press, 1998), 27ff.

24. Cf. Bernstein, 58.

25. Susan Handelman, *Fragments of Redemption: Jewish Thought and Literary Theory in Benjamin, Scholem, and Levinas* (Bloomington: Indiana University Press, 1991) and David Patterson, *The Shriek of Silence: A Phenomenology of the Holocaust Novel* (Lexington: University of Kentucky Press, 1992).

26. Isaiah Berlin, *Four Essays on Liberty* (Oxford: Oxford University Press, 1982; orig. pub. 1969), 118–72. Cf. Wayne C. Booth, "Freedom and Interpretation: Bakhtin and the Challenge of Feminist Criticism," in *Bakhtin: Essays and*

Dialogues on His Work, ed. Gary Saul Morson (Chicago: University of Chicago Press, 1986), 145–50.

27. Rabbi Joseph B. Soloveitchik, "Kol Dodi Dofek: It Is the Voice of My Beloved That Knocketh," *Fate and Destiny: From Holocaust to The State of Israel* (New York: KTAV Publishing House, 1992, 2000), 1.

3. Fear, Trembling, and the Pathway to God

1. Nicholas Abraham, *Rhythms: On the Work, Translation, and Psychoanalysis* (Stanford, Calif.: Stanford University Press, 1995), ix.
2. Coetzee, "Whither Dost Thou Hasten?" *The New York Review of Books* (March 5, 1998): 19.
3. A text that surely stands behind these comments is the famous speech by Himmler, in which he acknowledges the natural recoil experienced in seeing "a hundred corpses lie side by side or five hundred or a thousand," and then goes on to say: "to have stuck this out, and—excepting cases of human weakness—to have kept our integrity, that is what has made us hard"—quoted by Dominick LaCapra in *History and Memory after Auschwitz* (Ithaca, N.Y.: Cornell University Press, 1998), 28. LaCapra is quoting from Shaul Friedlander's own quoting of this passage in *Memory, History, and the Extermination of the Jews of Europe* (Bloomington: Indiana University Press, 1993).
4. Silence as a major and repeating motif in Holocaust fiction generally and Appelfeld's writing in particular is a dominant feature of the scholarly landscape. In this context see especially: David Patterson, *The Shriek of Silence: A Phenomenology of the Holocaust Novel* (Lexington: The University Press of Kentucky, 1992); Sara R. Horowitz, *Voicing the Void: Muteness and Memory in Holocaust Fiction* (Albany: State University of Albany Press, 1997); Lea Wernick Fridman, *Words and Witness: Narrative and Aesthetic Strategies in Representation of the Holocaust* (Albany: State University of New York Press, 2000), 33–85.
5. Cathy Caruth, *Unclaimed Experience: Trauma, Narrative, and History* (Baltimore: Johns Hopkins University Press, 1996), 7, 64.
6. Elizabeth J. Bellamy, *Affective Genealogies: Psychoanalysis, Postmodernism, and the "Jewish Question" after Auschwitz* (Lincoln: University of Nebraska Press, 1997), 45.
7. Bjørn Killingmo, "Conflict and Deficit: Implications for Technique," *The International Journal of Psycho-Analysis* 70 (1989): 68–69.
8. See again Sara R. Horowitz's discussion of the trope of muteness in Holocaust fiction—in *Voicing the Void.* Appelfeld's texts may actually be intended to reverse what may well have been part of the purpose of the perpetration of the Nazi violence, which was, as Horowitz points out, to render the victim voiceless. See in this context Lea Wernick Fridman's *Words and Witness,* in which she argues that texts like Appelfeld's do not fall silent so much as construct a narrative structure around what cannot be said (33–52).
9. Gershom Scholem, *Kabalah* (New York: Jewish Publication Society, 1975), 3.

10. Harold Bloom, *Kabbalah and Criticism* (New York: Seabury Press, 1975), 22–43.

4. The Conditions That Condition This Utterly Specific People

1. Stanley Cavell, "Being Odd, Getting Even," in *In Quest of the Ordinary: Lines of Skepticism and Romanticism* (Chicago: University of Chicago Press, 1988), 124.
2. Aharon Appelfeld, *Beyond Despair: Three Lectures and a Conversation with Philip Roth,* trans. Jeffrey M. Green (New York: Fromm International Publishing Corporation, 1994), 39.
3. "Repetition," in *Fear and Trembling and Repetition,* ed. and trans. Howard V. Hong and Edna H. Hong (Princeton, N.J.: Princeton University Press, 1983), 131–32.
4. Nicholas Abraham and Maria Torok, *The Shell and the Kernel,* ed. and trans. Nicholas T. Rand (Chicago: University of Chicago Press, 1994), 131–32.
5. On the function of the child protagonist in Appelfeld's fiction, see Naomi B. Sokoloff, *Imagining the Child in Modern Jewish Fiction* (Baltimore: Johns Hopkins University Press, 1992), 129–51, in which she specifically deals with *Age of Wonders* and Sokoloff, "Tzili: Female Adolescence and the Holocaust in the Fiction of Aharon Appelfeld," in *Gender and Text in Modern Hebrew and Yiddish Literature,* ed. Naomi B. Sokoloff, Anne Lapidus Lerner, and Anita Norich (New York: The Jewish Theological Seminary, 1993), 71–89.
6. See, for example, Rochelle Furstenberg, "'Before' and 'After' the Holocaust: Aharon Appelfeld's 'Age of Wonders,'" *Hebrew Studies* 4 (1978): 7–11.
7. On the text as being about Jewish literary tradition, see David Suchoff, "Kafka and the Postmodern Divide: Hebrew and German in Aharon Appelfeld's *The Age of Wonders* (*Tor Ha-pela'ot*)," *Symposium* (Fall 1994): 1–20.

5. Religious Faith and the "Question of the Human"

1. Tzvetan Todorov, *Facing the Extreme: Moral Life in the Concentration Camps,* trans. Arthur Denier and Abigail Pollak (New York: Henry Holt and Company, 1996).
2. Anne Michaels, *Fugitive Pieces* (New York: Vintage Books, 1998), 166.
3. Quoted by Todorov in *Facing the Extreme,* 123; the quotation is taken from *The Reawakening,* trans. Stuart Woolf (New York: Collier-Macmillan, 1965), 214.
4. Stanley Cavell, *The Claim of Reason: Wittgenstein, Skepticism, Morality, and Tragedy* (Oxford: Oxford University Press, 1979), 377–78.
5. An earlier story that makes use of Kafka's "Metamorphosis" is his "*Hahishtanut,*" in *On the Ground Floor.* For a discussion of this story and its relation to Kafka see Alan Mintz, *ḥurban: Responses to Catastrophe in Hebrew Literature* (Syracuse, N.Y.: Syracuse University Press, 1996), 221–23.

6. Stanley Corngold, *Franz Kafka: The Necessity of Form* (Ithaca, N.Y.: Cornell University Press, 1988), 56.

7. Tadeusz Borowski, *This Way for the Gas, Ladies and Gentlemen,* Trans. Barbara Vedder (New York: Penguin Books, 1976; orig. pub. 1959), 35, 41, 48, 45.

8. *Badenheim 1939,* trans. Dalya Bilu (Boston: David R. Godine, 1980), 62: "If anyone deserved the title of a great Jew, according to Fussholdt, it was Karl Kraus: he had revived satire." Fussholdt is one of the characters in *Badenheim,* an intellectual who spends most of his time during the encroaching tragedy correcting the proofs of his latest book. Insofar as Appelfeld's *Badenheim* is itself satire, the passage cannot be passed over lightly. For Appelfeld's own comments, see *Beyond Despair: Three Lectures and a Conversation with Philip Roth,* trans. Jeffrey Green (New York: Fromm International Publishing Company), 6. For a positive appraisal of Kraus, see Walter Benjamin, *Reflections: Essays, Aphorisms, Autobiographical Writers,* trans. Edmund Jephcott; ed. Peter Demetz (New York: Schocken Books, 1978), 239–76.

9. Appelfeld, *Beyond Despair,* 6.

10. See Edward Timms, *Karl Kraus, Apocalyptic Satirist: Culture and Catastrophe in Hapsburg Vienna* (New Haven, Conn.: Yale University Press, 1986), 237; discussion, 237–49.

11. On Appelfeld's attraction to the primitive and fundamental throughout his fiction but especially in *Tzili,* and the opposite tendency of his work to resist such primitivism, see Yigal Schwartz, *Aharon Appelfeld: From Individual Lament to Tribal Eternity,* trans. Jeffrey M. Green (Hanover, N.H.: Brandeis University Press, 2001), 112–28. Bridget in *The Immortal Bartfuss* is a similar character who raises comparable issues. In *Bartfuss,* the mantra that circulates (which is also not uncommon in Appelfeld's fiction) is "Life isn't everything. There's a limit to humiliation" (11); "Life is valuable, but there's a limit to disgrace" (21). Bridget, who is presented as mentally retarded, and to whom Bartfuss is increasingly and protectively drawn through the course of the narrative, raises the question about whether Bartfuss's obviously true moral wisdom isn't missing something just as important as the ethical injunction it voices.

12. Lionel Trilling, "Wordsworth and the Rabbis," *The Opposing Self: Nine Essays in Criticism* (New York: Viking Press, 1969; orig. pub. 1950), 150.

13. Naomi B. Sokoloff, *Imagining The Child in Modern Jewish Fiction* (Baltimore: Johns Hopkins University Press, 1992), 132; Alan Mintz, *ḥurban,* 219. In this context, see also Rochelle Furstenberg, "The Shirt and the Stripes," *Hebrew Studies* 9 (1983): 79–83.

14. Matt Ridley, *Genome: The Autobiography of a Species in 23 Chapters* (London: Fourth Estate, 1999), 101–106.

15. Harold Bloom, *Kabbalah and Criticism* (New York: Seabury Press, 1975), 39–40.

16. Primo Levi seems to realize the same thing about the *shema*ᶜ in *Survival in Auschwitz,* originally published as *If This Is a Man,* which begins with a poem evocative of the longer form of the *shema*ᶜ. My thanks to Alvin Rosenfeld for making me see the similarity.

17. Todorov, *Facing the Extreme,* 43. In this same context, see Lawrence Langer, who critiques what he calls "preempting the Holocaust," whereby he means using—and thereby abusing—its grim details to fortify prior commitments to ideals of moral reality, community responsibility, or religious belief, so as to permit us to retain faith in such values in a post-Holocaust world: "although I find this strategy both misleading and presumptuous," he goes on, "I have no corrective vision of my own to provide, other than the opinion that the Holocaust experience challenged the redemptive value of all moral, community and religious systems of belief"—*Preempting the Holocaust* (New Haven, Conn.: Yale University Press, 1998).

18. Emmanuel Levinas, "Kierkegaard: Existence and Ethics," in *Proper Names,* trans. Michael B. Smith (Stanford, Calif.: Stanford University Press, 1996), 74.

19. Bloom, *Kabbalah and Criticism,* 80.

6. Imagination, Memory, and the Storied Life

1. Aharon Appelfeld, *Beyond Despair: Three Lectures and a Conversation with Philip Roth* (New York: Fromm International Publishing Company, 1994), 68–69.

2. As mentioned in the Introduction, in her recently published *Poetry After Auschwitz: Remembering What One Never Knew,* Susan Gubar reads Anne Michaels's *Fugitive Pieces,* and, indeed the entire tradition of Holocaust poetry as a "retort" to Adorno's dictum (Bloomington: Indiana University Press, 2003), 242.

3. Wolfgang Iser, *The Fictive and the Imaginary: Charting Literary Anthropology* (Baltimore: Johns Hopkins University Press, 1993), 3, 297.

4. Quoted by James Young, *Writing and Rewriting the Holocaust: Narrative and the Consequences of Interpretation* (Bloomington: Indiana University Press, 1988), 17.

5. Emmanuel Levinas, "A Propos of 'Kierkegaard vivant,'" *Proper Names,* trans. Michael B. Smith (Stanford, Calif.: Stanford University Press, 1996), 77.

Works by Appelfeld Cited in Text

Note: Titles have been listed according to their English titles, with the Hebrew originals cited in the same note; or, in the case of texts that have not yet been translated, texts appear alphabetically by the Hebrew title.

The Age of Wonders, trans. Dalya Bilu (Boston: David R. Godine, 1981); Hebrew: *Tor hapelaʾot* (Tel Aviv: Hakibbutz Hameuchad, 1978).

Badenheim 1939, trans. Dalya Bilu (Boston: David R. Godine, 1980); *Badenheim ʿir nofesh* [lit: *Badenheim, Resort City*] in *shanim veshaʿot* [*Years and Hours*] (Tel Aviv: Kibbutz Hameuched, 1978) [Hebrew], which contains as well the novella *1946. Badenheim ʿir nofesh* is subsequently reprinted as a separate volume (Tel Aviv: Kibbutz Hameuched, 1979). References to the Hebrew text are to this separate volume.

The Healer, trans. Jeffrey M. Green (London: Quartet Encounters, 1992); Hebrew: *Beʿet uveʿona aḥat* [*At One and the Same Time*] (Jerusalem and Tel Aviv: Keter and Hakibbutz Hameuchad, 1985).

The Immortal Bartfuss, trans. Jeffrey Green (New York: Weidenfeld & Nicolson, 1988); Hebrew: *Bartfuss ben almavet* [*The Immortal Bartfuss*] in *Hakutonet vehapassim* [*The Shirt and the Stripes*] (Tel Aviv: Hakibbutz Hemeuchad, 1983).

The Iron Tracks, trans. Jeffrey Green (New York: Schocken Books, 1998; Hebrew: *Mesilat barzel* [*The Rail Way*] (Jerusalem: Maxwell-Macmillan-Keter, 1992).

Kol asher ahavti [*All That I Have Loved*] (Jerusalem: Keter, 1999) [Hebrew], translations my own.

Laylah veʿod laylah [*Night After Night*] (Jerusalem: Keter, 2001) [Hebrew].

Masaʿ el haḥoref [*A Journey into Winter*] (Jerusalem: Keter, 2000) [Hebrew]; translations my own.

Michreh haqeraḥ [*Ice Mine*] (Jerusalem: Keter, 1997) [Hebrew]; translations my own.

Pitʾom ahavah [*Love, All of a Sudden*] (Jerusalem: Keter, 2003) [Hebrew].

Sippur ḥayyim [*Life Story*] (Jerusalem: Keter, 1999) [Hebrew]; hereafter referred to as *The Story of a Life;* translations my own.

Tzili: The Story of a Life, trans. Dalya Bilu (New York: Grove Press, 1983); Hebrew: *Hakutonet vehapassim* [lit. *The Shirt and the Stripes*] (Tel Aviv: Hakibbutz Hemeuchad, 1983).

Index

Page numbers in bold indicate extensive analytical discussion.

EMILY MILLER BUDICK holds the Ann and Joseph Adelman Chair in American Studies at the Hebrew University of Jerusalem, Israel. She is author of *Emily Dickinson and the Life of Language: A Study in Symbolic Poetics; Fiction and Historical Consciousness: The American Romance Tradition; Engendering Romance: Women Writers and the Hawthorne Tradition, 1850–1990; Nineteenth-Century American Romance: Genre and the Democratic Construction of Culture;* and *Blacks and Jews in Literary Conversation.* She is also editor of *Modern Hebrew Fiction* by Gershon Shaked (Indiana University Press, 2000) and *Ideology and Jewish Identity in Israeli and American Literature.*